CW00957704

Trading to Win

Introduction

"Trading to win" defines a goal-oriented approach designed to help traders maximize their performance in a unique way—by tapping personal resources they might never know they had, by developing a rational strategy for trading, by learning new psychological skills, and by letting go of unproductive, even maladaptive, behavior patterns.

This approach puts a special emphasis on learning to get rid of past memories and erroneous notions around which people have organized their lives. This book shows you how to commit to a future goal by *surrendering* to it, and simultaneously relinquishing all thoughts of gain, achievement, or attachment. Sounds paradoxical, you say? It is. That's the point.

This system encourages you to trust a higher power that assists you in realizing the power within yourself. Periodically it helps you refocus on your goal, realigning yourself with your objectives. Then, you use your objectives as a filter through which to make distinctions in the present moment.

The world of trading is one of high stakes and high-risk activity. The goal is, ostensibly, financial gain. Give up that goal, and you gain the freedom to genuinely listen to the sounds of the marketplace and to be able to read the movement of stock prices in a way that enables you to increase your probability of success.

For master traders, the monetary result is secondary to the gratification that comes from being able to make the right market call. They get their primary satisfaction from having an idea about a stock and implementing this idea in a profitable trade. Master traders trust their information, sense the direction of the marketplace, and assess many other variables before finally executing a lucrative trade.

This requires an enormous ability to abandon pride and to maintain equanimity in the face of loss or excessive profit. The master trader knows—and you can learn—that neither despair nor euphoria should cloud one's judgment. As you improve, the market becomes even more challenging, requiring you to commit to bigger numbers or more complex dimensions of the game. If you are willing, this can lead you to give up more of your old habits and to become more at one with the universe.

I have watched this occur in real-life traders. For the past six years I have met weekly with a group of professional traders to explore the psychological and emotional dimensions of their trading and to find ways of maximizing their performance. The *Trading to Win* principles discussed in this book evolved from these seminars and have since been tested and developed in several other trading settings. I am deeply indebted to Steve Cohen for making this opportunity possible and for paving the way to a greater appreciation of these broader issues to the traders in his and other firms.

(Because of the proprietary nature of many of the issues considered in this book, I have not identified any specific traders by name. All personality profiles represent composites of the various traders and, although there are female traders, the masculine persona has been used throughout for realism in this currently male-dominated field.)

Reading the market's direction and the directions of specific stocks is essential to trading success. It is like the childhood game of musical chairs. In that game, you have to time your move so that you do not jump for a chair before the music has stopped; you also don't want to linger too long after the music stops so that there are no seats left. This is the trader's dilemma as well. The more skilled you are, the more patience you have, the longer you can stay in as the stock rises or falls before you act. You stay in longer, and therefore maximize your profits. However, you do not stay in so long that, by trying to trade the "tops," you end up being stuck on the downturn and caught holding declining stock in hope that it will turn around. The same goes for being able to minimize your losses. Rather than hoping and praying and rationalizing your hesitation by convincing yourself that the stock will eventually turn around, you cut your losses instead.

The *Trading to Win* program spotlights a set of philosophical and behavioral principles that can help you to implement proactive trading strategies. This approach involves commitment, concentration, recovery, and preparation for the next day. It enables you to trust your true self.

This approach is not for the fainthearted. It puts much emphasis on proactive trading strategies designed to produce exponential results. It encourages you to do counterintuitive things—such as admitting uncertainty, fear, and lack of knowledge and asking for help; sharing information; and facing vulnerability. All of this means letting go of ego and arrogance, which blurs your focus on the marketplace. It compels you to learn to communicate directly and clearly with others, whether they be staff, associates, or floor brokers.

Trading to win obliges you to review each day's trades, so you can see how you may have veered from your commitment, what dropped out of your trading, and what commitment you must add to get the desired result. You might need to raise the number of shares traded so they are consistent with your level of commitment. You might have to abandon energy-draining behavior—impulsiveness, chest beating, whining, and scalping (selling too soon to book a quick profit and missing the larger upward movement of a stock). You'll need to understand how to get out fast when stocks are dropping. You'll have to shed counterproductive habits, such as taking personal calls during trading times or racing home after the bell instead of reviewing the day with other traders and coaches.

In addition, you must learn the appropriate role of money. In trading, it's not so much to be rich or secure. It is a way of keeping score. It is a way of defining the framework of events so that you can determine what actions are needed in the present. Paradoxically, the greater the amount of money, the more you must renounce your focus on it.

While this program has been developed for professional traders, its principles have value for the ordinary trader as well. Sound trading applies to everyone, including the advanced trader who must regularly return to basics. Since it concentrates on a goal, yet makes you detach your ego from it, it has relevance not only to investing, but to life as well. I define "winning" as maximizing your own potential, as seeing the world realistically, and as living life like the miracle it is. After all, trading is a metaphor for the perilous yet exhilarating nature of living on the edge.

What's the Concept, Doc?

The objective of this book is to try to get at the underlying thought process behind trades. What are you are really thinking? What's motivating you? Is it consistent with your style? Does it make sense for you? Or are you governed at a given moment by emotion, by panic, or by whatever is going on in the Street? The ultimate objective is to be much more capable of reading the tape and reading the changes in the market in terms of what is occurring based on what you understand about it. You'll hear colleagues discuss in these pages things that they don't normally like to talk about, such as weakness or getting away from one's game plan.

Trading, like sports, involves a high degree of uncertainty and unpredictability. This means playing in unfamiliar territory. Many books explore basic trading and basic psychological concepts such as relaxation, but don't link psychology and trading behavior. My aim is to develop the thought processes essential for trading in the realm of uncertainty. Whether you are hammered by fear or animated by euphoria, both can throw you off your game.

It is important to understand why you may lose after you win big, or why you may sometimes feel that you don't deserve to win, or feel guilty about it, or have an attitude about money that colors your trading. To be a super-trader, you must learn not to forget your discipline and not to forget to respect the market. How do you surrender and yet keep your consciousness and your alertness so you can move in and out?

Trading is a very high-pressure game. It triggers a lot of defensiveness that on the surface looks very rational and reasonable. I hope that this book raises your level of awareness of certain critical processes so that you can begin to use them in your work.

What Do I Mean by a Strategy?

Once you set a specific goal for the year, you must ask how you are going to meet it. How many trades at what size would you have to make in order to make your number? What should your team look like? What general rules must you establish in terms of holding on, doubling up, or getting out of positions?

If you reply with a shrug, "Well, I want to do as well as I can," you are less likely to get there. To reach your target, you'll have to elevate your game to a level where you say, "Okay, this is what I'm going to do."

Why have rules? Because some moves, which you can find in your own database, consistently work. Forget the standard litany of rationalizations. You can always blame Alan Greenspan, or the market, or the fact that it's February. But regardless of different styles, certain principles remain immutable. If a stock goes down and you own it, you're losing money. "I'm going to make it a long-term trade," you say? You still lost money today. "It's a six-month trade" or "a three-month trade"? Maybe. But today you were hoping and wishing; you read something in *Barron's*, but it doesn't happen. You may keep thinking that you can make up for the loss, but, in fact, you would make much more if your losses were less.

Once you stop having too great a tolerance for a high level of loss, you can start raising your monthly profit and loss (P&L) significantly.

Some traders, even substantial ones, stay in positions even if they're dropping, because they are "macho" and can "tolerate pain." The stock will eventually come back, they tell themselves. But you are not a wimp if you get out of a losing position.

One trader I know had to learn to get out at three points. Next he learned to get out at one and a half, and he made more money. Now he has to take the next big step: learning that it's okay to run away from a losing stock. So if he's making four thousand dollars and he starts cutting his losses, he can make five or six thousand.

Losses are always hidden in your P&L. It looks like you're making some money, even though if you look closely you lost a lot of money, and that costs slippage and opportunity as well. Start looking at how much people are *not* making because they're scalping on the way up. Let's say a trader scalps—sells for a quick profit—and makes $5 million. Maybe if he didn't scalp, he could make $10 million. The issue is tracking where the stocks go after you get out.

What if you're ahead at the end of a day, and you say, "The hell with it, I did well. Why should I look?"

Hindsight, you argue, is twenty-twenty. You're right. But I think you can learn from your past experiences. It's like athletes reviewing recent game films to see what they are doing, so as to improve the way they win. Granted, the best thing would be to be right there at the time. I'm merely trying to make you aware of your thoughts, in order to give you a chance to change your thinking.

Go ahead: Resist this idea. Argue that when you're in the middle of a loss, you're thinking about how to limit it, or how to get some back. Argue that you're as good as your next trade, not that you're as good as your last trade. If your past behavior has been successful, you ought to repeat it. If it's not successful, you won't repeat it.

This all sounds fine, but these rationales ignore a basic characteristic of human beings—we tend to remain at the same level and repeat the past. Only if we are aware of the sources of our behavior will we be in a position to change it.

Keep on resisting. Argue that people usually progress to the next level of trading, and that either they're going to make it and continue to grow or they're not going to make it. Assert that they will grow from experience by taking some losses but being right a lot of the time, and that there are no hard-and-fast rules because if there were you probably could have retired a long time ago. Point to the hotshots at your firm who have had a tremendous run in the past fifteen years and have consistently done better on a year-to-year basis.

I believe that most people are not inclined to look inward, but prefer to live in the land of denial and rationalization. And I take the position that learning the fundamentals of trading success requires much more self-examination. I believe that the more consciousness you bring to this process, the more successful you will be.

The Unique Value of This Book

The special value of this book is that it can teach you to recognize the psychodynamic underpinnings of your work (your subconscious perceptions and how they influence your trading), how to change your perceptions, and, finally, what self-observation techniques you can use to redesign your responses.

Stay with me for a bit, and you'll learn to observe yourself. You'll detect the moment you make the wrong decision. You'll discover how to stop yourself when you know you are gambling or relying on hope. You'll learn to rely on your own ability to read the tape and understand the significance of known market indicators and the knowledge about specific companies. You'll learn to perceive your stress and learn to trust your insight, intuition, and decisions, while relying less on others. You will learn to take stock, review the basics, clean up your positions, and reduce them so you concentrate on getting the right kind of information to make sound judgments.

This book will teach you how to let go of losers and overcome your reluctance to admit that you have made a mistake. This applies to buying high and selling low. It applies to adding to positions that are not profitable or are losing money, averaging up on short sales that are rising, and averaging down on longs that are dropping. In doing this you will be able to control your efforts to retrieve what you have lost. You'll learn not to fight the trend of the market by buying a stock when it's down, tricking yourself into thinking it's a bargain.

It also applies to cashing in winners too soon—scalping. You might think you want to avoid looking bad, and you don't trust your instincts. You might want to get a quick profit to look good. Instead you'll learn trust, patience, and your ability to get out later on.

You'll learn to trade in terms of the amount of money you have, and in terms of the kinds of percentages of profits you want to produce. You'll discover how to balance your expanded objectives against your available assets. As a by-product, you'll ascertain careful money management, so you preserve capital for when you need it—winning opportunities.

How could a professional trader run into the same stumbling blocks as the amateur weekend trader? Well, he (or she) may know more stocks, instruments, and subtleties of the marketplace, and may certainly play bigger and faster and with larger profits and losses. However, trading bigger and succeeding in bigger ways does not necessarily mean that one has mastered the bad habits all people seem to bring with them from childhood. The professional trader, perhaps even more than the cautious part-time trader, is constantly being exposed to the wide fluctuations of an increasingly volatile market, made more so by the marriage of computer technology and mathematics.

So the need to learn patience, discipline, review, preparation, recovery, and risk taking with good money management applies even more to the professional. That's why this book is for the pro and part-timer alike: The issues are the same for each.

Maximum Trading

1. Recognize your repetitive patterns of trading. Be aware of your life principles and preconceptions and how much they may be behind your trading decisions. At the very least, these principles provide a frame of reference from which emerge your marketing decisions.
2. Let go of the defenses of denial and rationalization that minimize mistakes. Begin to recognize the value of reviewing the previous day's trading. This can help you discern patterns of trading that may reflect an underlying perspective which, though reassuring, demonstrates that you aren't trading to win.
3. Read the tape, and follow it rather than your ego, needs, life principles, and notions about what you deserve or don't deserve. Notice how long-standing beliefs about yourself and the world come into play in the middle of action. Notice how they trigger old attitudes, resistance, and automatic responses—such that you are in the grip of what others are doing.
4. Develop purpose to your trading—commit to playing to win. Play at a committed level of responsibility in terms of producing specific results, doing what it takes to reach objectives, developing self-mastery, and following trading and money management rules.

PART ONE

Psyching Yourself for a Winning Career

Chapter One

Becoming a
Master Trader

"**A**nalog Devices is thirty-five. You see this ADI, Nicky? You got any left? It hasn't seen thirty-five since ten o'clock this morning! You gonna buy it?"

"*Westinghouse!* How many times did you ring on Westinghouse?"

"It's like a tortoise—slow and steady."

"Nope. Do nothing."

"That's an all-time high."

"Fedex at three-eighths—why not just buy twenty or twenty-five thousand?"

"What's going on?"

"Some increased action activities. It's been hopping for the past four or five days. I've been up anywhere between ten and twenty every single day!"

"Listen, Alan, Alan—nineteen-nine on that. Protect me at one, bid three-quarters for ten, and seal the rest in."

"Hey, Bob, Westinghouse—you bought the hundred at a quarter."

"Hewlett—Aetna—Global—Micron. . . ."

It's 3:45 on a Monday afternoon. You're standing at your desk, sleeves rolled to your elbows, jacket slung on the back of your chair.

You adjust your telephone headset as you watch the numbers flash across your computer screens and listen to the orders flying back and forth across the room.

How do you feel? Confident or nervous? Tense or just attentive? Eager to make your final moves of the day, or worried about whether they'll be the right ones?

What are you thinking about? Are you reliving this morning's trades, or wondering what might turn up on the tape in the next few minutes? Mulling over the latest research reports you read during the weekend or looking forward to the Knicks game or movie tonight? Are you mentally reviewing your daily goals or simply hoping for a couple of last-minute moves that will make today's profit and loss (P&L) better than Friday's?

Now imagine you're the trader who works a few desks away from you. Pretend you're inside that trader's head, glancing over at you. How would you describe the person he or she sees? As Lucky Louie, who happens to be on a hot streak lately? As Loser Laurie, who is always trying to rebound from bad decisions that often reduce profit percentages to single digits? As Sad-Sack Sam, whose losses are likely to push him out of the business before long? As Cautious Kelly, a trader who dislikes losses so invariably sells too quickly? As just another Knicks fan or movie buff in the room? Or as a consistent, even-tempered winner whose market acumen is becoming legendary in the company?

If you see the winner, congratulations. You probably don't need my advice. If you see one of the others, this book is for you.

"Trading to win" isn't just a catchy phrase. The most successful traders are out to beat the market, not to avoid losing. While they may have bad days, they keep striving to gain mastery over the trading process. You can do it as well, but it takes a paradigm shift, one that takes into account your capacity as a human being to alter your interpretation of events.

Here's how it works.

Steps to Mastery

Most of us are governed by habits and self-limiting beliefs learned early in life. If we are weekend athletes, we don't think we can become

Olympians. If we are traders, we don't think of ourselves as masters. Thus we never do as well as we are able to. These patterns are compounded by the uncertainty and unstable nature of the marketplace, which tends to foster anxiety and the development of automatic behavior. Such patterns also may lead traders to risk more to stay in a losing trade than to put more money in a winning trade. In extreme instances, gambling and superstitious behavior may be manifested. The master trader trades from a perspective of rationality, knowledge, and skill—not from an emotional or defensive perspective, not in order to feel "complete" or "excited." To succeed at trading you have to be willing to do things contrary to human nature. You need to hold on to or get bigger in winning trades and get out of losing trades faster.

A major purpose of this book is to explore these patterns, so you can expand your consciousness, encompassing the factors that affect your trading and helping you maximize your capacity to trade. Thus, you'll learn how to ride through anxiety by developing creative strategies independent of your automatic beliefs and response patterns.

To become an Olympian in the trading business—in other words, to become a master trader—means to harness the power of consciousness. You can then change your thoughts, set new objectives and strategies designed for realizing them, and become an observer of your own thinking. You can master all the internal obstacles that arise when you start moving to new levels of performance. By inventing new perspectives, the master trader begins to see the market from new angles, transcending the limits of biology and early life conditioning that limit one's horizons. The master trader can then redesign and reinvent oneself while taking full responsibility for his or her approach to trading.

The "Vision Thing"

As a trader, you start along this new path by choosing a specific financial objective or "vision." Some people made fun of President Bush for mentioning the "vision thing," but for a trader, a future vision is a way for ordering information and defining experience so as to trade in terms of specific results.

The next step is to commit to the vision. How? Promise the result, which means devise a strategy consistent with the result and begin trading in terms of it. Trading in terms of commitment should be distinguished from trying to reach the goal to gain fulfillment. The distinction is to use your future objective as a lens or template for making trading decisions in the present, rather than as a target to reach.

Becoming a master requires you to recognize that you *do* have the capacity to become an Olympian, to keep creating your life moment to moment without being restricted by notions acquired early in life. Mastery evolves as you let go of false beliefs about yourself and the markets. Mastery allows you to uncover your hidden potential and the hidden potential of the market, and begin to take action in line with your stated objectives.

Mastery means to trade independently of assumptions you have about yourself and all of the fixed ideas you have about what is possible. Making decisions based on your willingness to commit to a future vision, you begin to act in the next moment untrammeled by old, erroneous illusions. Trading this way is not a onetime event; it is a continuous process that must be constantly practiced.

As you do this you will begin to see that trading offers a succession of moments in which you can choose how to behave. Once you block out automatic beliefs, once you enter the next moment without regard for what you or others think and feel, you tap into a new dimension of power within yourself. You are more present with regard to the events of your trading. You are *in* the moment.

This may be uncomfortable at first. You are, no doubt, accustomed to functioning in habitual ways and even may define yourself in terms of certain repetitive reactions. Initially, letting go of these habits may trigger panic, anxiety, and fear of losing control. But gradually this process will evolve into an increased capacity to tune into yourself and the market during a trade as you learn to trade through the lens of your consciously chosen objective.

The issue is not so much a question of working on yourself. Instead, it's changing the way in which you relate to trading events, a method that lets you take action via specific tasks or incremental steps that fit your financial objective.

What happens is that you trade out of your consciously chosen vision rather than in terms of self-limiting concepts of yourself learned early in life. By taking on new challenges and acknowledging your potential as it begins to surface, you begin to move towards mastery.

It might be hard to believe, but mastery is effortless. You trade in terms of your vision by taking incremental steps consistent with it. You do this with a serenity and focused attention that enables you to maintain your concentration on the task before you, while keeping free of distracting concerns. Focusing on the steps leading to specific results gives you a sense of control over your actions, and liberates, rather than drains, your energy and attention.

The master trader manages entry points and downside first before trying to shoot for the maximum results. You play in terms of your goals and consciously avoid blowing up. You recognize how you can become frustrated by trading or doing too much. You continually track yourself and focus on getting your basic score.

The master trader identifies his or her own inclinations, whether they are to become too relaxed and complacent after successful trades or to be too inclined to hold onto losers to balance successes. You learn to get out of losers so as to reposition yourself to get back in if the market reverses upward. You are also aware of any inclination to get comfortable with profit and to be fearful of losing, which might lead you to play smaller after succeeding.

The master trader puts much emphasis on controlling losses. When you keep losses to a minimum by concentrating on ways of reducing losses, you increase the chances of adhering to your strategies and hitting your target numbers. This is important to do, not merely to provide sufficient capital to continue to trade, but also because the psychological effects of losing can hurt your motivation to win. Losses can prompt gambling behavior or self-destructive trading, where the trader throws caution to the winds and keeps looking to recover all the losses in a few high-risk bets. Losses stay longer in memory than do the satisfactory feelings associated with winning, and play a bigger part in influencing traders to act defensively, to cover up, to compensate. Few people do things to compensate for successes.

Because of the pain of loss, people are willing to take greater risks to reduce that pain and to avert it than they are willing to do to maximize their profitability. They are less motivated by profitability and success than by aversion to loss, and therefore they are more likely to take high-risk bets when they are at risk of losing.

This can be converted into a strategy for the successful trader who has found a plateau and is reluctant to get bigger, finding comfort in not being exposed to greater risk. Such a trader needs to find motivation by associating massive pain with failure to grow, to utilize all one's resources, and to properly navigate the realm of opportunity, and needs to see the opportunities being missed, rather than to focus smugly on victories.

Sustaining Momentum

As a trader makes more and more money, the added profits tend to count for less than the value of preserving the money obtained earlier. The preservation of capital becomes more important than the increments to be made from putting more at risk.

Some of this is explained by Bernoulli's principle of utility, which says that utility or value resulting from an increase in wealth is inversely proportional to the quantity of goods previously possessed. Therefore, as traders succeed, they are less inclined to want to risk themselves to make more. The only way around this is to keep concentrating on repeating good behavior, and to stick with their trading strategy. That's the essence of mastery rather than mere goal setting.

Mastery encompasses the ability to sustain momentum. It is not uncommon for traders to blow up just as they are reaching their financial targets. How come imminent success raises anxiety levels? Because success represents entering the realm of the unknown.

Success actually can stimulate fears about failing and about the impossibility of success. These increased anxiety levels may result in self-destructive behavior and a succession of losing trades that bring the trader back to the starting point.

Uncomfortable with success, a trader named Dave began to conjure up images of failure whenever he started to succeed at new levels. He became convinced that his past successes were due to luck. His inability to accept the euphoria of success set in motion a self-fulfilling prophecy. Before long, believing that he had done something wrong, he would make some frantic gesture to "save himself." More often than not, the gesture would wipe out his profits for the month.

What can be done to sustain a series of successful trades or successful weeks or months of trading? What can you do to perform at a level

Becoming a Master Trader   **17**

commensurate with your natural abilities? Let's look at strategies that worked for Dave, and have proven especially effective in helping other traders.

First, become aware of the sequence of events associated with success. To overcome his inclination to self-destruct, Dave needed to learn to separate the events of the marketplace from his own physical and emotional responses and his interpretation of those responses as reflective of an impending catastrophe. He then needed to see how the trading decisions he typically made as a result of these interpretations were often based on long-standing systems of beliefs totally unrelated to the requirements of successful trading in a particular market.

The second strategy for Dave was to choose what he had, to observe and accept his anxiety without trying to change it. For example, he was encouraged to notice that he had mixed feelings about succeeding and making money and to understand that was okay. If, like Dave, you try too hard to break through a repetitive pattern, you build up tension and eventually reverse gears. You wind up producing the very result of which you are afraid.

Accepting what you have means accepting your demons. In Dave's case, it meant that he had trouble accepting success. To rid himself of that demon, he needed to concentrate on playing the game quite independently of his idea of what success meant. He needed to notice the beliefs that kept him locked in the past. And then he needed to let go of them gently, recognizing that too much effort would pull them to the forefront of his consciousness and produce the result he didn't want.

A third strategy for Dave was to learn to maintain a free flow of energy. He had to get familiar with his feelings and bodily sensations of anxiety, especially as he got closer to reaching his objectives. He also learned to visualize his goals and then play beyond them while he was experiencing anxiety.

Once a trader like Dave has learned to trade proactively, he or she must make sure that successes do not influence motivation and lead to a decline in positive focus. In the normal course of events, traders basically trade in terms of regressing toward the mean, so that after a certain amount of success their performance fades.

When you are completely engaged in trading, you are totally absorbed. You don't focus on yourself or on what people think about you. You feel fine, relaxed, and are enjoying the experience. The more skillful you become in doing this, the more you can bring all of your abilities into play.

When you trade from commitment—and do what you said you would do—you generate an extraordinary amount of energy. You begin to see opportunities in the market that you couldn't see earlier. You do not need to struggle. All you need to do is to show up and participate in the context of the new trading target. Trading in terms of an expanded target means having the courage to look for what is missing in your trading strategy. This becomes the source of the breakthrough you can produce.

When you are totally committed to all the steps necessary to produce the desired result, you are likely to experience the exhilaration of "the zone," where everything flows effortlessly.

Surrender: A Key to Mastery

"Trading to win" means surrendering to the moment without trying to control it. It means to let go of fixed preconceptions about what you must do, and to liberate your self-conscious sense of self and self-protective thoughts, which color the way you experience life and the market. When you can do this, you are in the here and now of your trading, and can bring your maximum potential to bear on the tasks before you.

In effect, you develop mastery by giving up fixed notions about the way the market is, your self-absorption, and various defensive behaviors that cover up your sense of being special. When you can clear your thoughts of these egotistical concerns, you start to see the market as it is, not as a reference point for your own existence. This allows you to begin to see the extraordinary possibilities before you.

"Trading to win" even means giving up thoughts about *winning itself* and any concern whatsoever with the result.

It means acting and then moving on to the next moment, without struggling to redo your last trade. If you don't reach your target, you look closely for what else needs to be done in your next trade and in the future, but you consciously avoid judging yourself.

When you do find yourself functioning more effectively than before, you can take note of it, but don't get lost in euphoria. Instead, move on to the next trade—there is nothing to think about. There is only the chance to be alive and to trade in the moment before you.

Being in the Now

Trading in the realm of mastery, beyond the constraints of your fearful thoughts, you may experience the feeling of intense involvement in the present moment. Your perception of the market will seem unfamiliar. You may feel "strange and empty" or think that "something is wrong."

Don't be surprised by this. It's nothing more than the recurring intrusion of your own automatic thinking, which is still keeping you from being totally engaged in the present. When this happens, you can see how much you are trapped by the belief that "this isn't it," or that trading success only begins in the future. A basic assumption of this approach is that you are already there.

This is it. There is no place else to get to, and there is not some other way of being in the world of trading. This very moment of trading is your life, and the task for you is to start trading each day in all its preciousness, savoring each moment as an opportunity for expressing yourself and for realizing your objectives.

Mastery, as I am using this term, is equivalent to the Buddhist concept of nirvana, a psychological state of mind where there is no fear or desire, only the chance to exist. This attitude makes it possible to be in the world and to trade without reacting to sorrow and pain, but by recognizing pain and anxiety as an aspect of trading. In this acceptance of anxiety, pain, or risk taking, you develop the capacity to transcend those feelings.

You accept the notion that you are responsible for producing all the results you have realized, and that nothing happened without good reason. Your task is simply to deal with whatever you have created.

In effect, you learn to choose what you have. If you are uncomfortable, notice it. Own the feelings. Don't suppress them or try to get rid of them. Simply become aware of how much belongs to an old interpretation that something was wrong with you because you were uncomfortable. In fact, all you need to do is notice your discomfort and let it pass. If you can do this, you'll be on the way to grasping that there is nothing wrong with you, and you don't have to get rid of these feelings or mask them. In fact, trading to win starts with the assumption that you are already okay. Pursuing a goal is about challenging yourself, tapping your potential. It is not about feeling better or correcting for a deficiency.

According to Joseph Campbell, the late authority on mythology, the more challenging a situation is, the greater the stature of the person who can assimilate it. "The demon that you can swallow gives you its power, and the greater life's pain, the greater life's reply." This applies to trading—the more discomfort you experience, the more effective you will be as a trader.

The more you can accept the results of your trading until now, even if subconsciously, and the more you can find the source in yourself, the more you will be able to find the essential levels of your trading. You will be even more empowered to take responsibility for choosing the course of your subsequent trading.

This idea is expressed in the Hindu idea of karma, which underscores the fact that your life, and, in this context, your trading, is the result of your actions and those of no one else. You chose to trade in a certain way. There is nothing good or bad about it.

When events occur that seem to be beyond your control, choose them, and become more involved in taking responsibility for how they are handled. Be guided by your vision and not by your concern for appearances, your own compulsive drive for success, your pride, or your irrational fears of catastrophe.

By emptying yourself of ego and fear, you make room to use your untapped potential to trade in terms of a larger objective, independent of the concerns of others. Mastery focuses around the process of change, and becoming what you are capable of becoming. That means entering the realm of the unknown.

This state of being is at the core of your real self. It is beyond concept and thought. It is reached by acknowledging and then by letting go of your concerns for ego.

The more you face the facts by acknowledging feelings and misperceptions, the more you can begin to modify the way you experience reality. However, you've got to keep experiencing trading events objectively, identifying your emotional reactions, and how your old, out-moded principles distort reality.

You've got to forget both your perfectionism and your need to put on a good appearance. I know this sounds tough, but you've got to go beyond where you would otherwise stop, and embrace the unpredictability of the future. In order to achieve mastery, in other words, you must learn to trade in a new way. In this way you keep inventing the pathway as you move along toward the realization of your expanding vision.

Indeed, when you accept the fact that you are at risk when you trade, you enter the state of "no mind" sought after by all mystical activities. This state of "no mind" is the ultimate ground of being. Zen adepts call it "beginner's mind." It is a mental state of emptiness or stillness from which all is created. In this state your mind dissolves, and you are left at the center of your being—beyond fear, beyond judgment, and beyond desire.

Speaking the Truth

To speak the truth means to examine the basic assumptions that govern the way you see the market and then to let go of them, as well as your self-protective cover-up, so that you can trade without fear. You also need to let go of your need to manage everything.

"Trading to win" does not simply mean risk taking in the sense of a willingness to throw the dice and rely on Lady Luck. Instead, it's a willingness to live in terms of a future financial goal, without any certainty about how you are going to realize that goal, yet seeking the resources within yourself.

To live in the creative gap between your vision and where you are, you must step outside the self-doubts and fear of uncertainty. Trading to win forces you to act beyond what you already know, before all the facts are in, and before you have checked everything out with the experts.

To trade this way requires the development of mastery, the ability to live in the gap between where you are and where you are committed to being. It's about bringing reality into line with your consciously designed vision, rather than with beliefs that once guided your actions.

It's about moving beyond the past to pursue a trading strategy based on a vision of abundance.

If there is a gap between where you are and where you have chosen to be, you will experience the creative tension that comes with living in the gap. This disparity in turn will be reconciled either by giving up your goal and accepting the limited view of reality, or by changing present reality to conform to your goal. Choosing this change is the essence of mastery.

When you trade in the world of the gap, you trade in terms of the strategic steps you must take consistent with the result. You take action without certainty but with certain risk parameters—without accommodation to preconceived notions about what is possible.

Acknowledging Breakdowns

Are you ready to live in the gap? Can you stomach the discomfort between the present reality and your future goal, and can you keep inquiring about what needs to be done to realize the goal?

The master traders use the creative tension of the gap to ask powerful questions about what else can be done. They look for opportunities to act. They acknowledge defeats.

Failure is evidence of the gap between reality and the vision. It tells you what strategies aren't working, and what more needs to be done. To acknowledge failures, you've got to be ready to compare your results against what you have promised to produce. Otherwise, how can you assess what is needed to realize your commitment?

When you fail or veer from your game plan, be prepared to concede that you have been defeated, temporarily. You swung at a ball and missed. But that's only one strike, not an entire at bat. After you miss that ball, realign yourself with your objectives. Ask yourself, what's the next pitch going to be? Declaring the truth about where you are and recommitting to your vision let you see where to direct your energy, and activate new energy for solutions.

Most of us don't want to face breakdowns because we believe they reflect something negative about ourselves. It is as if that one strike was a strikeout, and proved that you're an inadequate hitter. This is why you may prefer to put your energy into appearing as if you are doing well, rather than into the actual task of realizing your objectives.

The master traders face the fact when their results aren't consistent with their objectives and consider what needs to be done to bring about the results. Avoiding this process or covering up the breakdown keeps you self-protected, preserves your self-image, and prevents you from using all of your potential and resources to produce extraordinary results.

Look more closely; the reality of the tape is reflective of itself. It's not a reflection of you. If things don't work out there is no reason to feel guilty and withdraw. The tape is a measure of where you stand in relation to your goals. When you live from your vision, you accept breakdown and failure as a measure of reality—as the starting point from which to create, not as a stopping point or as a sign of failure.

When there is a breakdown or withdrawal from creative action directed by the vision, you had better face the fact that you may not have done all that was possible. You may be too quick to rationalize why things aren't the way you want them to be, rather than looking to see what new strategy you need. You may be too quick to blame circumstances or other people for the fact that things haven't worked out. Or you may be inclined to retreat, withdraw, or withhold all patterns designed to lessen the pain of failure, but which actually keep you resigned to defeat.

Admitting breakdowns helps you to leap over obstacles, by doing away with the effort to protect your sense of self-importance. Do this, and you discover a power within you that you never realized was there. Telling the truth about breakdowns, failures, mistakes, snafus, weaknesses, communication snags, the failure to produce what you promised to produce, and the failure to stay committed to your goal will help free you from the constraints of the past and your fears of recrimination, reprisal, and criticism.

Yielding to reality releases you from some early learned behavior patterns of trying to appear to be someone other than who you really are. When you can accept your vulnerability and your failures, you no longer are dominated by them. You'll set the stage for creating positive responses or new responses to the reality before you.

Breakdowns offer you an opportunity to see how much you have been living in the vicious circle of your own interpretive system. Only then can you create a breakthrough or a new interpretation of events based on reality. You begin to see failure as a neutral event, so that you can address it in a more conscious way by trying to create an objective, a solution, or a new way of dealing with the events rather than retreating into your automatic response.

When you see the world through your vision, you produce breakdowns and breakthroughs. Breakdowns immediately become opportunities for breakthroughs when you shift your stance and see what's missing in your strategy and what you need to do to take action in line with your objectives. They also help you to see everything that you are doing out of habit and out of a need to perpetuate a certain image, so that you will be empowered to begin trading in a different, more dynamic way.

Producing Breakthroughs

Breakthroughs refer to new ways of perceiving the world. They occur when you give yourself permission to effectively express your vision. They give you the courage to take action consistent with your commitment to your vision and not in terms of your self-protective needs or your limited notion of who you are.

Try my suggestions. See how you can experience a dramatic dissolution of anxiety and resistance and a newfound sense of flow, where everything seems to magically unfold before your eyes. Feel what it's like to do your best and not have the need to protect yourself or to conserve your energy. Grasp that sense of living life like the risk that it is, going for broke without holding back.

Breakthroughs occur when you begin to consider how to stretch yourself. A stretch may be as simple as acknowledging your responsibility for a bad trade. This may feel strange or like acting, particularly if you have never done it before, but doing so will change you by giving you the opportunity to view the world differently.

Feeling pressured by this idea? Afraid it could be a source of burnout and workaholism, particularly if you hear it as being full of effort? That's not the case. What I am talking about is not making more of an effort, but figuring out what strategy is needed in place of the one that failed. It is an approach to being grounded in the future where breakdowns can actually create breakthroughs.

Handle the breakdowns in the context of new perspectives, and you'll produce breakthroughs. Look at the event through the lens of your new creative vision, and you will begin to see things that you have not considered. Here you may want to invite the coaching of someone who has a broader perspective and can assist you to shift to more creative responses.

As you begin to behave in a new way consistent with your vision, people will start responding differently, too. "You are the dog that bites you," says Reverend Ike. All the dilemmas that we face are really the products of our own thinking and the stand that we take.

Results? What Results?

Having once established a specific objective and a strategy for realizing it, you must rid yourself of your concern about results, and your belief that you need results to prove yourself. You do not need confirmation. All you need to do is to toss the ball out in front of you and then swim towards it.

If you can let go of your expectations about results, you can stop holding back, stop playing it safe. The key is to keep acting beyond the holdback without thinking about how far you can go.

This is the very model of change. You don't become a slave to your actions, or your past results, but rather you keep expanding your trading performance. You entertain new perspectives so as to find new opportunities in front of you.

Mastery means accepting your power and your potential and permitting your trading to flow from your already existing trading style. You choose what you have, and enter into the next moment with the confidence that you can produce results consistent with your goals, knowing that things will evolve as they were intended to evolve.

Commitment to a specific objective will take you beyond the limitations of your own self-concept—provided you don't become attached to the results. If you do, you become trapped in a vicious circle in which you pursue the results to sustain your image and not as an expression of a larger trading vision. Attachment to results increases your sense of being inadequate. So while you commit to the results, be alert not to become attached to them. To sustain momentum, stay focused on actions to take.

Momentum blends action and intelligence to produce specific incremental results, which ultimately become the seeds of further actions. It refers to that level of interest and involvement that allows you to stay on target without becoming overwhelmed by excessive stimuli or bored by insufficient challenge. It requires careful monitoring of both the results and the way in which you are functioning, paying attention to whether you are able to resist becoming distracted, whether you are fully engaged in the action, and whether you are bringing all your energy to the process.

To become fully engaged in your trading you must learn not only to ride out the anxiety and to float with events, but also to let go of the pull of ambition and other distractions. You may also need coaches to help you through novel situations that you never have been through before, or just to stay on the track.

The Tale of the Tape

You generate momentum by accepting the unpredictability of events, and by trusting that extraordinary results come from some unpredictable "X" factor that is set in motion by committing to a specific result. This approach lets you incorporate what you learn into your trading style, rather than retreating into automatic self-protective reactions.

To keep experiencing the novelty and freshness of the market, and to keep from being trapped by your preconceptions, it's important to keep distinguishing between the tape and your interpretations of the tape. View as neutral both the events and your inclination to impose your interpretations on them. You enter the market without expectations, surrendering to it rather than struggling with it for personal gain. Ultimately, you are able to fine-tune your responses.

Anxiety and Euphoria

As you get closer to your goal, you need to relax more, to visualize the goal, and to be able to play beyond the goal. This has to do with pacing and preparation. Learn to tolerate your position and not allow feelings of euphoria to throw you. In upcoming chapters, I'll offer you some mental techniques in centering and visual imagery to help you prepare and pace yourself.

Remember, feelings of triumph and euphoria associated with success may trigger anxiety and guilt (if you feel undeserving) or cockiness and a relaxation of discipline (which may keep you from doing what it takes to realize your ultimate ambitions).

Perhaps most important—don't try to prove your self-worth through the results of your trading. Learn to trade in a less ego-centered way. Satisfaction can come from the development and implementation of your skills and trading strategy, not just from a profit and loss statement.

At the same time, it is essential to take responsibility for your successes and failures by defining specific strategies and measuring your adherence to them. This will help you to stay focused as your trading positions change.

It's also of value to discover how to experience the euphoria of success without being distracted by thoughts of glory. Such thoughts may lead to unnecessary risk taking or the rejection of good feelings because, like Dave, you don't feel you deserve them. Similarly, if you are succeeding, don't think that you've stretched yourself too far or that you won't be able to do this again. Notice your negative thoughts and let them pass. Do not try to suppress or change your response, but consider the possibility of an alternative nonresponse pattern. Approach your trading from an entirely different viewpoint, one that's unrelated to your emotions.

Essentially, you can trade your concepts and utilize all your trading instincts and skills by setting your goals, deciding on your strategies, and then focusing on what it will take to make them happen. But first you need to let go of negative self-concepts, as well as negative ideas about making money. You need to stop being too invested in the personal significance of your financial outcome and begin to see trading strictly as an opportunity for self-expression.

Think about this: You can expand the internal space you need to succeed, not by undoing the past, but by creating a new space, or as I prefer to call it, a new vision. Consider whether you can grant yourself the right to grow. What would that take? How much are you invested in the negative image of yourself? What do you get for it? By answering these questions you can begin the process of self-examination. By learning more about how you function in the trading world and the obstacles in your path, you will begin to own your mistakes, correct them, and move closer to trading mastery.

Chapter Two

What the Best Traders Look Like

The best traders have certain characteristic, measurable trading patterns. The largest percentage of their profitability comes from a small percentage of their trades. This means success comes from a small number of very large trades, where they have developed an edge (based on such things as intermarket information, supply and demand, and the movement of other stocks) over and above their basic understanding of the fundamentals of a stock (for example, earnings and cash flow).

The best traders have a high risk-adjusted rate of return (RAROC) and Sharpe statistics. (The Sharpe ratio is a risk-adjusted measure of profitability.) They tend to do better trading low-volatility/low-beta stocks. Their profitability correlates positively with the number of shares, price per share, and amount of dollars invested. They tend to have higher average dollar gain per winning share and per trade than average dollar loss per share and per trade. Their success is also positively correlated with length of time a stock is held.

Examining some of the negative characteristics of less successful traders, on the other hand, one finds negative correlations to holding periods and dollar volume, as well as high commissions and acute clustering of profit and loss (P&L) around a handful of transactions that suggest overtrading. In other words, some traders may hold on to positions too long.

One trader with a high winning trade percentage shows a relatively flat ratio of winning trade/losing trade margins on a per-trade and per-share basis. This suggests that he might be able to increase his profitability by staying with winning positions longer.

Of course, there are differences among successful traders. Some excel at using the Instinet, trading the short side of the market, and trading in the technology and financial sectors. Others tend to perform better using brokers rather than automated trading mechanisms. One trader who thrives by focusing on biotech and pharmaceutical stocks shows lower Sharpe and RAROC statistics, which are reflective of the erratic nature of biotech stocks.

There are variations within these ideal patterns, too. Some successful traders don't hold their shares for a long time, even though they are winning trades. Others have their performances too highly correlated with market indexes in general. Still others may hold on to losers too long, as indicated by the relative equivalence of their average dollar gain per winning trade and the average dollar loss. They may even show that their average losses exceed average profits on a per-share and per-trade basis.

Psychologically, the best traders all have much in common. They possess risk taking ability, flexibility, and a capacity for conviction. They are able to trade without letting their ego get in the way. In other words, they have the ability to stay in the present and view events truthfully and, therefore, objectively. They focus on the movement of stocks, without distraction by disappointment or euphoria—either of which may interfere with the correct view of reality.

While I know extremely successful traders who do not share all of these characteristics, including a good friend of mine who is convinced he lacks a "capacity for conviction," most successful traders have a strategy for winning, and they adhere to it with persistence, creativity, and drive. And when they are winning, they don't become lax but actually play bigger, continually upgrading their game.

How You Can Become a Winning Trader

The best traders set an objective—an amount of money they want to make, a percentage gain they want to achieve in a given period, a portfolio total number they want to reach—and then try to make decisions in line with that vision. They strive to become independent and self-actualizing, and they are ready to face the consequences of their own decisions rather than rely on others.

Like them, you need to develop your own power, and to be circumspect about the power you bestow on others. Like them, you can let others contribute to your vision, but you can't depend on others to make you whole or to realize your objectives.

The most successful traders bring their vision to a focus with specific goals. You need to do the same—and to promise the result to yourself. Many traders are reluctant to do that. "How can I know what I will do until I see where the market goes today?" they ask. "I'll see where the market is headed, then take advantage of the opportunities I see." Some traders are hesitant to really win big, either because of an unconscious belief that they may not deserve that much money or because they aren't clear about the complex meaning of profits and high salaries on Wall Street.

However, when you look at the market, what you see reflects what you *think* you'll see. If you commit to a certain vision or concept of a result and keep looking for evidence of that result, you will watch the market in terms of this new set of expectations. You will thereby increase the likelihood of your expectations becoming a reality.

When thinking about your goal, imagine what it will do for you or enable you to do and how it will increase your ability. As you begin to consciously choose your own trading objectives, you will notice how much of your life has been focused on pursuing unconscious objectives conditioned in childhood. You will learn how much more satisfying things can be when you begin to actively pursue consciously chosen goals.

When it comes to trading, motivation is critical. Make sure you really want to trade. People are often drawn to the "easy" money of trading. It's easy in the sense that all it takes is money to get underway in the business. But more than money is involved. Self-understanding and self-mastery are critical. You have to be willing to put in time and effort to learn about yourself, and to do what it takes to change attitudes and behavior so as to make them consistent with your trading objectives. There's nothing easy about this "easy" money.

If you want to gamble, this isn't the right field for you, nor should you enter trading if you are unwilling to tolerate, or learn to tolerate, the emotional changes and roller-coaster effects of risk. The basics—an ability to solve problems, analyze situations, and work with numerical choices—should feel natural so that your efforts don't infringe on your performance and leave you too uptight.

You have to get used to being wrong, because you are going to be wrong most of the time. As in baseball, you may be wrong seven out of ten times. If you can't handle that, you don't belong in the business. The key issue is to minimize your imperfections and maximize your potential, to ride out errors, to keep your emotions under control, and to continually assess the variables of the market so that you begin to make optimal choices more of the time.

To do this, you have to learn to stay with the winners and focus on getting rid of losers. You can't do this without internal strength, faith, trust, and acceptance of uncertainty. Without these qualities—or the eagerness to develop them—fear is going to govern your behavior.

In the following chapters, I will help you learn how to take action and begin working toward the changes that will help you become a more successful trader.

Can You Commit?

A dictionary defines commitment as a decisive choice that involves a definite course of action. In trading, this refers to a proactive approach where you promise a result—a financial goal—and then behave at your trading desk in such a way as to bring about that result. The promise creates a discrepancy—a gap—between where you are and where you have chosen to be. That gap is the source of creative tension that, ideally, motivates you to determine what new style you need to follow in order to bring reality in line with your new objective.

Commitment in finance is not simply a matter of working harder or motivating yourself with positive affirmations. You must be enthusiastic

The Ten Cardinal Rules

1. Learn to function in a tense, unstructured, and unpredictable environment.
2. Be an independent thinker versus a conventional thinker.
3. Work out a way to handle your emotions and maintain objectivity.
4. Don't rely on hope and fear in the conventional sense.
5. Work continuously to improve yourself, giving importance to self-examination and recognizing that your personality and way of responding to events are a critical part of the game. This requires continuous coaching.
6. Modify your normal responses to certain events.
7. Be willing to face problems, understand them, and recognize that they are in some way related to your behavior.
8. Know when problems can be resolved and then apply methods to solve them. That may mean giving up some control in order to gain a different control. It may mean changes in your personality, learning self-reliance, or giving up independence and ego to become part of a trading team.
9. Understand the larger framework in which trading occurs—how the complexity of the marketplace and your personality both must be taken into account in order to develop the mastery of trading.
10. Develop the right mind-set for trading—a willingness to commit to the kinds of changes in personal habits and beliefs that will drastically alter your life. To do this requires a willingness to surrender to the forces of the game. In order to be able to play at a maximum level, you have to let go of your ego and your need to have things your way.

enough to explore all the ramifications of your trading behaviors. Trading in a committed way is a lifelong practice, and requires continuous self-examination and monitoring of your attitude and approach.

In all the best traders I've met, I see three crucial attributes. The first is a willingness to dig in, put yourself at risk, and become what you say you will become. To do this, you need to ask yourself very specific questions and commit to the answers.

As you will see in more detail in Part Two, one top trader rarely deviates from a set of ironclad rules he has set for himself. They include:

• Have a reason to trade.
• Initiate every trade with a long or with a short position.
• Consider your costs on a trade before you make it, rather than merely selling.
• Shun safe, boring stocks, and instead dig out stocks that will move.

This trader knows ahead of time that if the twelve stocks on his sheet include National Semiconductor he can sell whenever he wants to, unless he is trading enormous amounts, like 500,000 shares of stock. If he does have a huge position, he scales out 50,000 shares at a time.

But the master traders also ask themselves broader questions and know what their answers are.

These are simple questions, but they are not easy to answer in a committed way. Until you learn to tolerate the discomfort of trading at new levels, you will feel psychological pressure to lower your target and revert to familiar old ways of buying and selling. It takes awareness to resist such tension-reducing impulses as scalping quick profits or holding on to a losing position in the hope that "things will turn around." It takes just as much awareness to catch yourself when you are beginning to withdraw from your commitment because of the tension that naturally intensifies as you get closer to the fulfillment of your objectives.

The second attribute, then, is the identification of those pesky, persistent, sometimes painful beliefs, conditioned since childhood, which, without your knowledge, influence your performance. I call this set of beliefs and responses the "life principle." It governs what you think, what you perceive, and how you interpret the world. Your life principle is the largely unconscious template around which you organize your life.

> ### *Ten Commitment Questions Every Trader Should Internalize*
>
> 1. What is the amount of money you intend to make?
> 2. How long will it take you to make it?
> 3. What do you have to do to make it?
> 4. How much capital do you need?
> 5. How many shares must you purchase?
> 6. How long should you hold on to those shares to reach your objective?
> 7. When should you change your position?
> 8. When should you enlarge your position?
> 9. What must you pay attention to with regard to managing your losses?
> 10. How much more capital can you put at risk so as to increase your profitability on the upside while managing your downside risk?

Early in life, to avoid painful experiences like fear, rejection, or criticism, we each adopted a set of beliefs and responses—such as being good, not making mistakes, fitting in, taking it slow, or not taking risks. You have been living out of these patterns and perspectives ever since. Mostly, you do this automatically. (It's not just you—it's all of us!) You are not aware that these patterns, while they feel comfortable, keep the original underlying fear alive. These defenses manifest themselves in behavior patterns that become permanent aspects of your personality. They include old perceptions about impossibilities or about what you perceive to be the agonizing consequences of "pushing the envelope."

Every time you try to break out of these patterns, you experience fear and anxiety, and usually resign yourself to conforming to the life principle without taking significant risks.

Creating a New Life Principle

I hold the view that to achieve trading mastery, you must learn to live your life by interacting more directly with reality, rather than through the filter of your life principle. To do this, you have to relinquish those patterns that both create and perpetuate your underlying fears.

To gain maximum effectiveness and vitality you must learn to recognize these fixed patterns, so that you can respond to trading events in terms of what the events call for, not in terms of automatic responses that were programmed in you during childhood.

As you begin to be aware of how much your unconscious life principle rules your responses, you can begin to act more consciously in terms of your own present choices, in line with your new financial objective or vision. When you trade independently in terms of your newly designed vision, you bypass your inclination to withdraw, withhold, or retreat in order to protect yourself from imagined fears.

When you can do this, you will be able to engage in your trading career at 100 percent and not have to wait for the so-called right moment before you begin to act.

Ask yourself two questions to find out where you really stand as a trader: How much are you governed by automatic thoughts of failure or a fear of losing? Do you secretly believe that you are inadequate or unworthy of success?

Such doubts may lead you to blow your gains after a successful run or to rely too much on positive pronouncements, which may ultimately result in burnout from excessive efforts. It's important, therefore, to learn to emancipate yourself from self-doubts, from your outmoded life principle. Negative judgments are merely thoughts that have to be noticed and then allowed to dissipate, so that you can get to that Zenlike state where your mind is "empty."

You don't see yourself as a Zen-type person? Neither did a master trader I'll call Sandy, whose trading partner had to take an eight-week sick leave. Sandy had to make the research calls his partner ordinarily handled, as well as trade for both of them. The double duty forced Sandy to focus so single-mindedly that he made several million dollars more than usual for two months in a row. "I don't know what happened," Sandy said. "I don't know what was going on in the market. But I was trading out of my mind"—with extraordinary results.

You must become prepared to observe events without imposing inaccurate interpretations on data. Otherwise, when you're faced with the frustration of failure, you risk watching the goals to which you've committed erode. You feel internal pressure not to lose. As your perceptions of the market become distorted by your emotional reactions, you begin to make compromising decisions. At this point, it is important to be able to declare a breakdown. You must acknowledge this emotionally so that you can change your actions and once again bring them in line with your commitment.

Putting aside these old, negative thoughts is not a rote exercise. Nor will you master this ability simply by reading about it. What I'm suggesting is a rigorous self-examination, during which you must overcome part of the natural human instinct for self-preservation—the part that inhibits action and creativity in favor of maintaining the status quo.

We humans don't ordinarily practice these maneuvers. Life involves functioning with uncertainty, but we usually don't embrace it. You must ask yourself, "How willing am I to allow my trading success to be as good as it can be?" When you can achieve this step, you can maximize your performance and learn to ride out the creative tension of the gap or even the excitement of extraordinary trades.

The third attribute of great traders is their capacity for increasing the complexity of the task at hand and the size of the promise. This demands even more of yourself. You must be able to find ways of supporting yourself in the gap so as to trade bigger, such as calling on someone to coach you, making more research calls, and reassessing your strategies in light of changes in the marketplace.

Strategy—The Hallmark of the Super-Trader

The super-traders always formulate a strategy or set of rules that enable them to act quickly while watching the market. It's a strategy that leads them to trade or take action in line with objectives rather than in terms of old habits and beliefs about what is possible.

At a periodic trading review, Dirk, an experienced trader, brought up his strategy for staying with airline stocks. "The numbers I want are somewhere around two hundred thousand dollars a month until I get consistent. This month, it's seventy or eighty.

"I can take a huge amount of risk," he added. "In the past, I wasn't taking the right risks." To begin with, he had to get his ideas "all squared away." When he stopped doing charts on the weekend, thinking they gave him "too many ideas," he wound up losing money for two consecutive days. This made him so defensive that he feared he had "missed the whole market." He saw himself "going back and forth, following my reactions," instead of having more of an opinion.

"I have to go back to trading to make money," Dirk vowed. "If I play by these rules, I'm going to win more often. I won't make sixty-two hundred dollars, I'll make sixty-two thousand dollars, and it will be less aggravating."

Commenting on Dirk's observation, Benny, another trader, said to him, "The rules are there. All you have to do is to follow the rules. You don't have to do anything but follow the rules and it will make your life very easy. Obviously, you know how to pick stocks and you know how to trade. But if you follow the rules, there's less of a burden on you. Last month you didn't have to think that much. You were in the zone. When you're not doing well you've got to go back to fundamentals and consistently do things the same way."

Benny listed some specific rules: "Don't play takeover stocks; be patient—you can come back to them. Don't take home losers. Don't average down. Eliminate the things you do poorly. And stop rationalizing your mistakes by pointing to how well you're doing."

He summed this up by saying, "In a nutshell, do the things you do well consistently. Make the commitment, create your own lists, and live by the lists. Consider what you are willing to do so you don't lose. Can you make a list of ten things you're not going to do to save yourself money? Make it up before you get in the game."

Benny concluded: "If you are sticking to it and you're losing, then the list doesn't include all the things you need on it. The one thing that has to be on the list is to be brutally honest with yourself; you have to be honest enough not to allow yourself to screw up."

Benny's methodology helps him make choices and make sense of the volume of data that is available at any given time. He develops skill at his own personal method while also empowering colleagues to help supplement and expand his ability. He can then create research, statistical analyses of operations, and analyses of statistics so as to determine where he needs improvement. He also has a risk-management method for assessing the negative characteristics of the trade in both the in and out positions. When put together, this amounts to a set of guidelines for evaluating positions, measuring the effectiveness of trades, and improving subsequent trades.

> ### *Four Pertinent Questions to Ask Yourself*
> ### *before Going into a Trade*
>
> 1. What amount of capital am I willing to risk in a trade?
> 2. What will be my exit point?
> 3. If I lose a predetermined amount of capital, do I retreat and take a breather?
> 4. When I am losing overall, do I cut down on trading size of only the losing positions and enlarge the winners?

The master traders' strategy takes their competition into consideration but leaves plenty of room to execute their own vision. They have a positive mental image of the actions needed to make money. They may get much input from others, but ultimately they choose their own goals and targets and remain independent, trading and developing their own ideas rather than simply following the choices of others.

To be a super-trader, you'll need an edge to overcome the laws of probability and the uncertainty of the marketplace. That edge comes from information flow, the ability to correct your habits in terms of the market's characteristics, and being able to take risks, cut losses, expand your information network, ferret out ideas, and take recommendations.

To do this, you will need to develop a trading strategy that is suited to your personality and temperament. If you are naturally cautious, build elements of this personality characteristic into your strategy. If you don't like the decision-making aspect of trading, then find more mechanical or mathematical models. The point is to know yourself well enough to develop a strategy that fits your temperament so that you can push the envelope of success.

Truth, Confidence, and Creativity

In trading, telling the truth is what separates the big people from the little ones. Are you willing to face the truth about your trading? Or are you inclined to withhold the truth from yourself?

One of the most critical characteristics of a successful trader is an ability to take responsibility for results. A pro who blames others and the market, or the seasons, for outcomes cannot get to the next level. That's why you will need to admit vulnerability and identify problems in order to deal with them and reduce uncertainty. The only acceptable uncertainty in trading is the uncertainty found in the gap between what is present and what is possible, not in the realm of hope and wishes.

While super-traders own up to mistakes and do not rationalize failures as being at the mercy of market forces, they are also willing to surrender to the market, recognizing that they have no control over it. This does not mean that they trade willy-nilly. They do not fight the "elephants" and get crushed. They go with the trend of the big players, follow the momentum of stock movements, and don't short a stock at the bottom when it is certain to go up.

The positive value of committing to the truth is that it will not only optimize your trading results but transform your capacity to be more fully present to your trading experience. Facing the truth about the market and yourself will allow you to remain an independent thinker, not dependent on how other people are trading. Follow the trend of the market, influenced by huge mutual funds—the elephants—which create momentum by the size of their orders. You can thus make your own assessments and stock choices with confidence and go into the trading day with the expectation of winning more often than not.

Your belief in yourself will grow by testing your own hypotheses, facing the truth, improving your performance, and developing confidence that you can avoid losing money, develop methods for getting new ideas, and, finally, learn how to let the winners run. This set of skills will give you the confidence to trade successfully. Without them, it is easy to trade and *not* succeed.

Being Comfortable, Being Right

The market is a force bigger than any one trader. If you go against it, you will feel pain. The traders who go with the tide are more free and easy. They don't like the pain. They like themselves. They know there is no point in fighting the force of the market. They let go of their egos and admit that the market is greater than they are.

For some traders, this is difficult to do. Take Leo, who like many

> ### *Eight Questions for Truthful Traders*
>
> 1. Are you willing to face your failures without recrimination?
> 2. Do you delude yourself with notions and rationalizations that you are limited by the nature of the marketplace or the tape?
> 3. Are you willing to acknowledge your successes, or are you afraid that others will be disappointed or hurt if you tell them you have succeeded?
> 4. Do you hold back from succeeding because of some childhood notion about not deserving to win?
> 5. Do you hold back in your trading because of a reluctance to let it be as good as it can be?
> 6. Are you held back by imagined restrictions placed on you by other obligations?
> 7. How much do you distort reality because of fear of the consequences?
> 8. How willing are you to commit 100 percent to being in the game?

short sellers has a high tolerance for pain. He likes to trade against the tide. He doesn't want to admit fear and doesn't want to put a tremendous premium on cutting risks by making a trade with a higher upside potential and lower downside risk. Sometimes this happens after he has had a good month and wants to "give something back." Feeling good and having money in his pocket, he slips into a gambler's mentality and "bets it up."

The best traders, though, are patient. They can wait for the right moment—when a stock turns—and then trade to win. This is important, since the result may take twice as long as they anticipated if they're holding while a stock is rising. Yet they're not so patient that they waste opportunities, nor so anxious to take a profit that they nibble at it and lose upside opportunities. They may trade to test the market, but they don't ride it just to ride. They have the drive to stay with trades that are working, and the ability to sit tight and wait for the trade to be completed. They know they can go broke by taking small profits, since the slippage and brokerage costs are so high.

Characteristics of the Master Trader

- Has a rational approach to trading. Does not trade for egotistical reasons, to feel good, to get high, to work out long-standing psychological needs.
- Is skillful at self-mastery in the setting of high tension and stress in the marketplace. Is confident of ability to deal with reality rather than be governed by interpretation and reactivity. Builds confidence from experience and learns skills from adversity. Regularly monitors his or her performance so as to enhance it.
- Is able to see low-risk ideas. Can read reality without misinterpreting it in terms of hidden agendas or unrealistic dreams. Is able to drop low-risk ideas that don't work, without investing in failure cycle, or overreacting to own reaction.
- Has basic disciplines of hard work and concentration, and knows about extra effort. Has self-monitoring skills and capacity for visualizing future events and rehearsing them mentally. Interested in activities and in the processes involved.
- Is committed to objectives and able to modify strategy based on feedback from performance. Is able to cut losses and increase risk appropriately and not hedonistically or foolishly.
- Is able to empower others to assist him or her in realizing objectives; able to identify with others compassionately and to assist them to stretch and grow; able to rely on others and to profit from them but not dependent on their approval. Takes responsibility for success of efforts. Is humble in recognizing the necessity for the support of others.
- Is adaptable to change and able to modify course as he or she progresses.
- Sees the challenge of the trading game. Is not overly invested in money. Is able to enjoy profits but not dominated by them; able to bounce back from failure; able to recognize that losses are inherent in the process.
- Can handle success and failure without self-destructing.

Trading requires the drive to take new risks. Ideally, you minimize losses by measuring the risk/reward ratio, but you cannot trade without living with some inherent uncertainty. Losing is part of trading. The best traders don't get perturbed by losing trades, since over the long run they know they will be successful more often than not. When you are afraid of losing, you end up losing or missing opportunities because you are afraid to trade.

The best traders are able to distinguish between the right trade and the comfortable trade. In fact, they know that the right trade is often uncomfortable and have devised a strategy or set of rules that will let them override their emotional fears. Less experienced traders have a hard time distinguishing what is really happening. When they are under stress, they don't adapt to the new market but rely stubbornly on what they think they know.

To continue rising to the challenge, successful traders need to increase the money available and find new ways to maintain profitability. They try to identify new trends in the market and reassess their own personality traits in order to determine how best to trade. The great trader will view this as a magnificent adventure, a great challenge. Most of all, he or she will trade even if there is no money in it, simply because he or she loves the game.

Chapter Three

Centered Trading

In the course of my work with traders I have the good fortune every now and then to run into a gifted individual who has spent many hours learning to master the mental and emotional states that are consistent with top performance. One of the more enlightened practitioners of this approach is Tim, a thirtyish ex-football player whose specialty has been Asian markets. Tim and I have spent many hours exploring the subtleties of staying centered while trading in complex markets.

"I have spent a lot of time learning to get centered so I could concentrate on assessing very subtle intermarket inefficiencies," says Tim. "I keep reviewing reams of data and keep looking for 'very good' trades in Asian securities, anticipating how American institutions are going to perceive these stocks and then how Asian investors are going to perceive the perceptions and actions of American investors. I focus on finding discrepancies in the way in which these diverse markets perceive opportunities."

To find these subtle distinctions and then apply them means that Tim must be able to sift through tons of information to find data that fits his paradigm, narrowing the focus of his attention at the same time as he tries not to become too absorbed in believing what it is that he is seeing so he can maintain a certain degree of flexibility.

For Tim to remain disciplined and not too vulnerable to distractions, and yet relaxed and not too invested in what he decides on since
it is subject to change, is a complex set of psychological processes. Continuous effort is required for Tim to remain focused and concentrated
and yet totally relaxed. This is the centered state where he allows himself to focus on the data and does not get too invested in the success of
his choices.

"I've got to keep focusing on finding liquid situations. Asian
stocks are now illiquid and I've got to move to Europe. I've got to
narrow my focus and get rid of mediocre trades that are using up my
energy and diverting my attention. I can't concentrate on too many
things at once. In doing this I have to resist the compulsion to trade
in the comfort zone and avoid big swings in profit and loss. Trading is
seductive and I can easily get caught up in it, but I achieve less in this
type of activity than in those situations where I carefully review the
data," he says.

"When I'm detached from the whole process and can focus on what
is important I am at my best and I know what steps to take. It's almost
magical and I can do no wrong. I have total focus when I am centered
and the trading doesn't take much effort. The only danger here is that I
get too confident and run the risk of getting trapped with my opinions.
When I lose that mind-set, then I am grasping around to get involved
in a trade, and can easily latch on to nonsense."

If you believe something that is no longer relevant, you have to correct your focus and act independently of your beliefs. You may have re-
lied on your beliefs all along, but you must recognize when the game
has changed, reframe your perspective, and move into the present. This
is sometimes painful, since it means relinquishing the past and getting
ready for the next event.

Two major changes that you will need to deal with as a trader involve managing emotion and fear, and cultivating the discipline to adhere to your trading strategy. You can juggle these complex tasks by
using psychological skills that increase concentration, reduce anxiety
and tension, and decrease the impact of distracting internal and external
stimuli. One of your most critical tools is centering.

Centering teaches you to keep focusing on the essential elements
of the task before you, while distancing yourself from emotional re-

sponses and negative interpretations of stressful and unsuccessful trades.

The centered state of mind is very familiar to athletes. In football, for example, it's the unspoken connection between quarterbacks and wide receivers who communicate intuitively with each other. In basketball, it could be seen in the passing wizardry of players such as Larry Bird, Isiah Thomas, and Magic Johnson. Centered traders use a similar skill to see connections among diverse marketplace phenomena that enables them to go beyond their natural fears and create innovative trades.

Centering lessens distractions. It helps you to disregard past mistakes and to avoid worrying about future events. Centering leads to better control over the autonomic nervous system, enabling you to stretch yourself beyond conventional limits so you can be guided by your trading objectives and the tape action.

Turning Off Self-Doubt

To adjust your behavior so as to respond to events in a disciplined way in line with your trading strategy, you must learn to recognize the automatic nature of negative thinking, self-doubt, and self-criticism. By dialing in to these automatic reactions to stress, you can restrain your impulse to react emotionally in such moments, which often results in selling your longs too soon or not covering your shorts soon enough. You can also learn not to withdraw from trading altogether when your trading is not proceeding favorably. Centering lets you turn away from that fearful automatic movie in your mind, the one that projects negative images onto events.

Metaphors for Trading

It's interesting that traders often use war as a metaphor to describe their trading experience. For instance, one says, "Being in the pit is the equivalent of war because you have so many changing circumstances." Others think that's not really true. Instead, as one fellow believes, "If I blow off enough money, I won't be here." Still others define trading in terms of a "rapid exchange of information under very tumultuous circumstances, trying to process stuff where you have very little time to make a decision."

However, some super-traders eschew the use of military metaphors and images of anger and hostility in favor of Zenlike notions of tranquillity and serenity. They are centered.

The center is often a metaphor for visualizing the concentration and distribution of energy throughout the body. In Eastern systems, this has been placed at a person's center of gravity below the solar plexus. It is known as the *ki* or the *hara* in Japanese, the *tan t'tien* in Chinese, and the *chakra* in Hindi. Much of Western psychology is also governed by theories that emphasize the discovery of the center of the self through sublimation of sexuality (Freud), the realization of power (Adler), or the expression of compassion and concern for one's fellow-man (Jung).

In all of these systems, the point is to activate your creative potential by gaining control over instinctual drives and the self-critical and inhibiting intellectual functions of your mind. The capacity for being totally centered and fully present and aware of your life is *right there* within you. It is the state of mind that leads to satori, or the sudden recognition of what is going on in the world, such that you can distinguish actual reality from your interpretations and projections of it.

However, although everything that you need and everything that you seek is within you, it is masked by a psychological layer of fear and other negative emotions and memories that constitute the "shadow" or "negative self" and an outer layer of personality or "social persona." You can harness your center only by detecting how these dimensions operate in your life. The conditioning process has taught you that you are less than adequate, so you are in constant motion trying to get what you believe you need from outside yourself. To center yourself, you need to stop focusing on your image and surrender to the tao or the path before you. You can do this by learning to ride out anxiety, discomfort, resistance, concern for the opinions of others, and the need to control all events.

Once you are centered, you become totally involved in the reality of the marketplace. Able to respond directly to the tape, and not merely to your preconceived perceptions of the market, you can begin to act consistently with reality by interpreting it through a creative vision. This perspective allows you to see all market events as part and parcel of a greater, meaningful whole. You are able to trade in a neutral or objective way, seeing stock actions as they are without imparting unnecessary or excessive emotional coloring to events. You can observe that market fluctuations are not directed against you, so you don't react as their victim.

In the centered state, you focus on the task at hand, without concern for justifying yourself or making yourself right and others wrong. You allow events to flow, knowing that everything is as it was meant to be and that losing trades are learning opportunities, not a cause for self-flagellation.

In the centered state, you integrate mind and body. You sense a heightened affinity for others, a greater sense of the meaningfulness of the world and a sense of harmony with the cosmos. Going beyond egotism, you can trade in a more mature and generative way than before. The centered state of mind is at the basis of creative thinking, enabling you to disconnect your present thinking from powerful past images, and to examine trading decisions from a new, less stressful frame of reference.

In the centered state, you are able to detach yourself from material objectives and from distracting internal drives, which are obstacles to spiritual and creative freedom.

The centered state is also extremely useful in high-stress situations that require immediate action and the suspension of conventional thinking. The classic example is the mother who summons up an extraordinary amount of energy in an instant to lift a two-thousand-pound car from her child pinned beneath. In the emergency, she has been able to tap her hidden strength by suspending the conventional beliefs that ordinarily inhibit action. The crisis has activated powerful emotional centers and disrupted the normal self-critical and logical thought patterns that would discourage such incredible efforts.

Centering is a process in which you detach yourself from preconceived intellectual formulations, images of the past, and external stimuli and seek to approach the creative side of trading. By increasing sensory awareness, centering intensifies everything you experience. It facilitates relaxation and the restoration of energy and promotes the use of visual imagery techniques.

Centering the Target

Centering is dramatically demonstrated in archery. In this sport, any tension created by trying to control anxiety would be transferred directly to the bow and the arrow at the moment of release. To avoid having this tension interfere with one's aim, the skilled archer allows thoughts to pass through the mind without reacting to them. The best shots occur when the arrow is released effortlessly.

At the world-class level, the archer, the bow, and the arrow all act as one. The archer allows the fingers to unfold as the bow is released. Since the correct actions have been mentally programmed during extensive practice sessions, they now need only be allowed to function.

Being centered enables you to commit to a specific trading objective, and then control your fear of losing so you don't trade too cautiously. Fear of failure traps many traders in a narrow trading range, making them reluctant to expand their profitability. Once centered, you can follow the market trend, cut your losses, and let your profits run.

Most important, you will be able to follow your own rules and not keep trying to explain your results in terms of market vagaries.

Master of Your Destiny

A self-starter, the centered trader has an image of a stock or an ideal trading model or track to follow and has an exit strategy, too, just in case. As a centered trader, you can accept responsibility for your trading results and recognize that your greatest asset is your ability to control your own actions. If you are able to follow your experience and game plan, you are more likely to succeed in your trading. You recognize that your internal concept of the marketplace influences your interpretations and decisions, and as such you seek to maintain your centered state so that your fears and emotional reactions to market fluctuations do not significantly influence your trading.

Through a conscious process of centering (or being in the zone, which occurs spontaneously), you choose to break the endless loops of destructive trading when buying is linked to losses or selling is linked to the need to recover losses. Let's say a trader is caught shorting a rising over-the-counter stock and cannot find any buyers. One who then becomes obsessed with daily loss-and-recover maneuvers could make inadvisable trades and keep sinking. On the other hand, a centered trader can separate losing trades from trading style and thus can continue to follow his or her trading strategy, despite carrying a continuing loss.

Centering also frees you to pursue your own concepts. You are no longer afraid to trade a stock that has begun to move rather than only when it appears to have reached its limit. You do not have to be first to a trade or be certain of the outcome before placing your order. As a less emotional and reactive trader, you focus more narrowly on your trades. You are confident about your decisions and do not dwell on past errors. If you are a day trader, you are assiduous about daily marking your losses to the market (computing the value of shares in your brokerage account based on the daily closing price). You are able to expand as you succeed, and in high-momentum bull markets as compared to choppier markets or correction periods (such as occurred, for example, in June and July of 1996) you are able to extend your time horizons, maximizing the profitability of your trades. You do not shut down or become unable to act if you lose, and are willing to cut your losses rather than sticking with them solely to avoid admitting you made a mistake.

Techniques for Centering

Centering is a process that you can do anytime, anywhere—before you go to sleep at night, en route to work, or even at your desk. You can enter a centered state through meditative exercises that shut out the world, by focusing on specific goals, or by means of increased observation of present activity. Whichever technique you use, you begin by focusing on a single activity or objective and simultaneously withdrawing your attention from the external world. By turning your perceptual system to inward rather than outward events, you reach that receptive state of mind that is generally described as being "clear," "still," "free," "empty," or "euphoric." By focusing intensely on a visual image or by meditating, you arrive at the alpha state, where the slowed electrical rhythms in the visual centers of the brain reflect decreased visual attention to the external environment.

Those slow alpha brain wave patterns are associated with a slowing of time and the capacity to perceive minute and precise details. In effect, the slower the brain wave pattern, the more information can be processed and the more accurately you can respond to trading events *as they are*, rather than in emotional terms.

As you learn to achieve the centered state, you'll notice a reduction in tension. You'll find yourself able to increase the amount of information you receive and process. You'll be able to tap into knowledge already residing in your memory, knowledge that might have been less accessible to you when you were too consciously striving to bring about specific results.

A Centering Exercise

The key element in all forms of centering is actively blocking out all thoughts except the object you are focusing on and/or the process of focusing itself. The following relaxation technique is relatively easy to do. By changing the posture of your body, by getting relaxed, you begin to change your thinking. In the calm, meditative state, you can think about things in a totally different way. Progressive relaxation exercises help you be more serene as you go through life, in addition to helping you access your center. Practice this technique on a daily basis when you're faced with fear or anger or any kind of unpleasant emotion, and it will be easier for you to transcend the emotional reactions of the stress response. It's a kind of self-hypnosis.

The following exercise, which is best done away from the workplace, demonstrates the power of the mind over the body. It releases knotted muscles; banishes feelings of fear, anxiety, jealousy, anger, envy, and physical pain; and even cures headaches, replacing them with pleasant feelings of deep, satisfying calm.

First, tighten and then relax the muscles in various parts of your body in order to experience the difference between tension and relaxation. When you tighten different areas of your body, do this to the point of real tension, not pain.

Pick a quiet, comfortable place and sit with both feet on the floor, hands resting gently on your thighs. With your eyes closed, focus your attention on your breathing. As you breathe in, try to feel the air moving in through your nose and then into your lungs. While you do this, focus on your chest wall and your belly expanding as you breathe in. Then breathe out through your mouth and note the passage of air. Pay attention to the breathing process, noting how the exchange of air and the expansion of your chest and belly occur without any effort on your part. The air moves smoothly into your lungs and out, almost by itself.

Let your breathing become even more calm and smooth. Notice how your body feels. Also notice how calm you can become while focusing on your breathing and forgetting other concerns. In this calm state of mind, you can easily shift your focus to other parts of your body and to the environment as well.

Continue to breathe deeply with your eyes closed. Put your arms gently on your thighs and make a fist with your right hand, pressing your fingers against your palm. Tighten the muscles in your wrist and forearm until you feel moderate tension. Take a deep breath and hold it for a moment. Breathe out and let your muscles go limp as the tension drains from your fingers, wrist, and forearm. Feel the relief of relaxation. Note how this differs from tension. Tell yourself, "My right hand and arm feel relaxed and calm." Keeping your eyes closed, sense your left hand and arm and notice that they feel different from your right hand and arm. Take a deep breath in and out, repeating with the left hand and arm what you did with your right.

Clench your right and left hands into fists, and tighten the muscles in your wrists and forearms until you feel moderate tension in the whole area. Take a deep breath, hold it for a moment, and then, as you breathe out, let your muscles go limp. Feel the relief of releasing the tension. Then focus on your face and head. Close your eyes tightly, and stretch your forehead muscles up as far as you can. Pull the corners of your mouth back until you feel the tension everywhere in your face. Experience that sensation of tension. Now, breathing out, let all these muscles go completely limp and say to yourself, "My face and forehead feel relaxed and calm." Notice how different this feels from tension. Enjoy the sensation. Keep your eyes gently closed each time you breathe out. Feel your hands, eyes, and forehead become more deeply relaxed.

Keeping your mouth closed, tighten your neck muscles by moving your chin towards your chest and tightly forward until you feel real tension around the base of your neck. Stretch and hold those muscles. Now breathe out and allow these muscles to go limp. Return your head to a comfortable position. Say to yourself, "My neck feels relaxed and calm." Sense the flowing relief and notice how different it is from tension. Let all remaining tension flow out of your neck, hands, arms, face, and head. Now focus on your shoulders. Move them forward and up, and hold. Gently breathe out and let your shoulders go limp. Say to yourself, "My shoulders feel calm and relaxed." Notice how different this is from tension. Repeat this process of tightening and relaxing with your chest, abdomen, and thigh muscles, as well as legs and ankles. This exercise takes twenty to thirty minutes. With practice you can reach a relaxed state in five minutes.

Other Centering Techniques

The centered state can also be produced by praying, reading a story, humming, or through movements of the body in dance or physical exercise. All these activities temporarily bypass intellectual activity and block the input of external stimuli.

Another centering technique is to consciously shift the focus and rhythm of ordinary habitual actions to increase consciousness and produce a state of centeredness. Shifting to new ways of doing things returns automatic defenses to full awareness, which in turn will increase your capacity to become absorbed in the here and now and enable you to observe your own automatic and negative thoughts and the feelings associated with them. You can learn to focus your mental machinery in new directions, enabling yourself to be in touch with your center.

Centering is an invaluable skill for successful trading, the way it is for any activity that requires dedication, concentration, and practice. Like so many other activities, successful trading cannot be achieved with an absentminded, offhand attitude. You must commit to the management of your emotions, and centering helps you make that commitment.

Chapter Four

Visual Imagery—
Rehearsing Your Moves

On the frigid plateau of Tibet, certain holy men for centuries have practiced an occult art known as *tummo* or the art of inner fire. It is another route toward centering. Their art involves intense and prolonged meditation, breathing exercises, and the creation in the mind of a visual image of fire. When a Tibetan religious master is doing *tummo*, many travelers have attested that he is able—by summoning up this purely mental, visual heat—to withstand the devastating cold of the Himalayan mountain passes dressed in nothing more than a simple cotton robe and sandals.

To demonstrate the force of the inner fire, some masters even have their disciples lay dripping wet cloths on their naked backs. Many previously skeptical Western observers have reported seeing holy men dry dozens of these wet clothes with the "imaginary" inner heat of their own bodies.

The lessons of *tummo* are clear. Experience is governed especially by those thoughts that occur in association with strong visual images. Since you can choose the images you think about, you can make your trading more meaningful by selecting a specific trading objective for yourself and infusing your thoughts with powerful, concrete images of this objective. In this way, you can overcome the restrictions of habit and thought that now limit you, and you can even change your trading success. For example, new images can help banish thoughts such as "I'm on a losing streak" or "I can't seem to get on track," or other negative thoughts that color your market perceptions and sap your energy, confidence, and capacity to trade profitably. Visualizing your chosen objective in a concrete, positive form is perhaps the most astute move you need to make on the road to fully realizing your potential.

The power of visualization results from stopping intrusive intellectual functions, coupled with intensifying your intuitive responses in performance. Redefining a situation by seeing it in a new light, even before it happens, will help you to halt vicious circles, and will open you up to act simply and directly, at your own best level. Visualization, in other words, allows you to prepare yourself so that when the time for action comes, you are always ready.

Exercises in visual imagery help you program desirable images, while eliminating negative ones. They can help you overcome pain, learn relaxation techniques, increase endurance, and reduce your fears about your trading performance. Visualization facilitates the concentration, boosts the courage to overcome inhibitions, and makes it possible to achieve trading goals way beyond your own conventional limits.

Using visual imagery techniques, you can choose specific financial targets and then develop specific trading strategies consistent with your goals, plotting your movements mentally for the actual activities that enable you to hit your target.

When I review trading events with traders, I ask them to consider where they entered a trade, the movement of the stock after the trade, the price action, the bid and asked movements on the stock, any other events they observed, when they decided to exit a trade, and what was going on in the stock at the time. They are asked what they were thinking about at the time of exiting the trade, their reasons for making the trade, their reasons for not getting bigger or selling only a portion of the stock, and so forth. In the context of this review it becomes possible to consider a variety of alternative responses to the same basic information, so traders can consider what factors were operating at the time that compelled them to take the action they took, and so they can learn the various options that may have been available from a trading perspective.

What did they see about the stock movement and the price that suggested things were flattening out, taking off, or any of a number of other patterns that may have ensued? How did their emotional response and their characteristic way of responding to events influence their judgment and their decisions? What else could they have done? All this discussion begins to help traders to expand their frame of reference for trading and to begin to consider a number of distinctions that can expand their trading, giving them many more options than before. With practice, traders can begin to anticipate movements of stocks and can see how these visually imagined scenarios influence their willingness to stay longer in a stock.

You can build morale, activate energy, and magnify alertness by creating new strategic plans through visualization. In addition, you can even keep ordinary arousal from turning into panic. You stay focused on the strategies rather than on yourself or on any fears about your performance.

Practice Makes Proactive Trading

The mental image you have of an event influences your performance in that event. Thus, you can enhance your trading performance by modifying your recurring and negative mental images of your performance to fit a positive, desired outcome. That way, gradually over time, your performance can be adjusted to correlate with an ideal inner image of trading success.

This process can be compared to ice skaters' practice of new routines again and again in their mind before doing them on ice. Skaters must not only analyze their mistakes but must visually see themselves performing the routine correctly. By rehearsing this in the mind's eye, a skater is imbedding an image of success. Embedding this image enables the skater to overcome memories of falling and eventually perform the routine perfectly.

Such visual imagery practice will enable you to modify the most crucial variable in trading that you control: yourself. A proactive image of successful trading, based on your own assessment of what works best for you, will provide you with a new template for assessing stocks and market activity. Such a proactive image will enable you to see opportunities that were unseen when you were trading to remain in the comfort zone. This image lets you ride out fear and anxiety about shifting stocks and go beyond your concerns about winning and losing so that you can focus on what needs to be done. Visualizing proactive images also empowers you to keep taking on new challenges, such as buying stocks or futures you don't trade normally or taking your limits higher, or getting your supervisor's approval.

It is useful to determine where you plan to exit a stock so that you can concentrate on the movement of the stock and not on your own internal responses to the tape action.

The seminars that I hold weekly give traders a chance to mentally rehearse a variety of new behavioral patterns that they may bring to their trading. They can discuss possibilities, verbally commit to trading targets, practice new communication patterns, express thoughts that are ordinarily uncomfortable, or even get comfortable talking about emotional patterns and responses that are normally taboo. By expressing themselves, they expand their emotional and behavioral repertoire and therefore enhance their trading potential.

Discussing new behaviors gives these traders a forum in which to mentally visualize and plan new approaches to the market and to interaction with others. The seminar also opens an avenue for discussing new methods of trading, learning about exit numbers, monitoring plans, and finding out how to ensure implementation of results.

Selecting the Image

If you relax and close your eyes, you will notice that thoughts and images arise continually and naturally in your mind, but—and this is the most important thing to remember about visualization—note that you can focus on only one thought or image at a time. This is true regardless of whether the thoughts or images are "real," since when you visualize, you cannot distinguish between the reality of your experience and random thoughts. In fact, you focus on real and imaginary imagery in the same way and with equal intensity. This is important to know because visualization can only help you if you accept the mental (and therefore the potentially physical) reality of what you see in your mind.

The central point here is that you can shift your attention from one image to another and ultimately select the image on which to focus. You are not at the mercy of your mind: You can choose what you want your mind to observe. When you select an image, it becomes more distinct than all others, and conflicting images tend to fade into the background.

Masters of yoga have demonstrated this for centuries, and some Indian fakirs have taken the knowledge so far that they can endure astonishing physical pain, simply because they don't choose to focus on the nails that are piercing their skin or the coals that are covering their feet.

Nattering Nabobs of Negativism

Visualization doesn't mean that as soon as you "get the picture right" in your mind, you will immediately produce the result. But it does mean that generally, over time, your trading decisions and actions can be adjusted to correlate with your new financial objective.

Your mind continually scans large quantities of information. Then, it selects a very small portion of that information on which to focus. There are layers and layers of mental images that influence your every activity, and learning how to select among them is a major step in learning how to control not only your thinking processes but your behavior as well. If you wish, you can become very active in this scanning and selecting process, and can actually choose consciously images and thoughts that will enable you to trade more freely, going beyond self-protective instincts that keep you from trading the way you would like.

The more you can learn to control the focusing process, the more you will become centered on the present moment, and the better you will be able to participate in trading events each day.

In the words of an olden dervish saying, "When it is time for stillness, stillness; in the time of companionship, companionship; at the place of effort, effort. In the time and place of anything, anything." Understanding this maxim makes it easier for you to accept your own best efforts—and more likely that those efforts will mirror your "pre-played" image of what they should be.

As you pay attention to your thoughts, notice how so-called good and bad thoughts are mixed together and how, in a sense, you cannot say there is such a thing as negative thinking. As you begin, be aware of the fact that these thoughts are randomly generated and you have little to do with them. You seem to be thinking these thoughts, yet when you begin to focus on them you see that they are being spontaneously generated and represent the activity of the neural structures of the brain coupled with programmed thoughts embedded in your memory by the variety of experiences in your life. Beyond these random, continuous thoughts, there are other thoughts that you could bring to the surface; but you cannot get to them until you understand the automatic nature of these thoughts, which come from the conditioned life principle discussed in Chapter 2. It takes time to be able to differentiate these thoughts from the ones that you generate from your true inner self.

Once you have practiced becoming aware of your thoughts, you can begin to nudge your thinking to objectives of your choice. How do you do this? By standing outside your automatic, judgmental thoughts that keep you locked in the past. Since your own thoughts lurk behind these random repetitive ones, you gradually get in touch with them as you gain control over the thinking mechanism.

The Past Colors the Present

Becoming aware of your automatic thoughts is the first step in learning how to separate the unconscious past programming from creative thoughts generated by focusing on the reality outside yourself. Observing your thoughts from this perspective, you can begin to see how your interpretations, based on your past life principle, color the way you perceive and react to events. You'll discover that present events are not so stressful, but your memory of past experiences—and the interpretations they lead to—can create the emotional upset of stressful trading events, which can dominate your trading. You keep creating situations based on these interpretations and trade from them rather than trading in the here and now.

Jim is a case in point. Raised by professional musicians, he always has been plagued by fear of failure. He has approached his trading with great ambivalence, both wanting to succeed, but fearful of not living up to his parents' high standards. He has mixed feelings about winning and has had a great deal of difficulty being able to sustain a winning streak for more than several months at a time. All his trading thoughts are colored by emotionally laden notions of guilt and shame about performing at less than the best he can.

A compulsive short seller, Jim is rarely able to find anything positive in the market. He's afraid that the market is about to turn, yet he can't play banks long.

"The researchers are saying that the banks are the cheapest they've ever been," he noted in one seminar not long ago. "I listen to the negative side of the story and I say, 'Okay, that makes sense.' I never see the positive side—I don't believe that they're doing what they're doing. I've been saying that for four years."

Jim continued, "I'm afraid that as soon as I play anything long it'll turn on me. As a result, my upside, where all the profitability is, is negligible. In buying stocks—whether banks or techs or drugs—the price always seems to change adversely against me."

When Jim buys stocks and they trade down half or three-quarters of a dollar against him, he doesn't reassess and hang in there. Conversely, when the market is going up, "I always think it's too late to buy anything."

Jim has to look for a reason to do something. If he thinks the banks are cheap and he wants to be long, that's enough information to hang his hat on. But he sets up criteria that are so impossible that he's missing opportunities much of the time. He thinks his reasons must be as good as the analysts'. He cannot see the forest for the trees.

"When stocks are way up I feel like I'm missing the whole thing and I get in on the last chair. When the price starts changing—whether it's moving up or down—I just drop it and go on looking for something else. I don't stay with that thought," he said. When he does see a potential trade, he hesitates. Then he gets angry that he's hesitated—figuring the price is going up too much—and pulls back. Somehow he convinces himself not to play. He loses great opportunities.

Mitch, a former pro baseball player who, at 27, is already making several million dollars a year, sees the same behavior in his associate, Jake.

"I'll tell Jake we're long this stock because four days from now the company'll report earnings—they're going to be really good and we want to be there," Mitch said. "Even when the situation is good, Jake gets frightened if the stock moves down half a point. He'll want to sell. A half point doesn't mean anything. It's just noise. It's one guy banging bids. We're there for a reason. Who cares if it goes down another point? We want to make four points on this trade."

Whether you act in ways similar to Jim or Jake or you don't, simply being aware of the structure of your thoughts will give you a much greater capacity to actively participate in present trades. You will be developing a capacity to differentiate between impressions that color your experience of the marketplace and what is actually before you.

A major step in visualization is recognizing habitual, negative thoughts and self-characterizations most likely to surface when faced with a difficult trading decision. A mental image of "getting into the market late" or being "last to arrive at a party" can keep you from buying a potentially advancing stock after others have already acted. You may be reluctant to be a follower and choose to stay out of transactions you may have been preparing for because others have acted before you. While the caution resulting from these images may be rationalized as being analytical or consistent with the principles of capital preservation, it may also keep you out of profitable trades.

Excessive concern for your image as a successful trader may lead you to focus too much on your profit and loss for the day. This may in turn push you to sell too soon to make a quick profit or lead you to avoid marking your daily trades to the market so that you can hold on to an overnight profit. A related image of not losing or not being the last to trade may reinforce an inhibited style and hold you back from trading more aggressively. The image of winning or succeeding at all costs may keep you focused on outcome rather than the opportunity in front of you. Needing certainty and control may prevent you from entering into the real investing world of uncertainty, where the object is to go with the flow rather than to try to control things you cannot control.

Awareness of your own repetitive thinking helps you participate nondefensively in the here and now. The same awareness helps you create a new way of relating to the trading opportunities before you. When you do this, you're more in touch with your immediate experience.

When you trade with a newly created financial target, rather than from the past, you may undergo an altered state of consciousness. This state of mind, which is often achieved in the course of exciting and concentrated work, is, of course, subject to shifts on a continuum from boredom (when the activity is dull and routine and requires less concentration and attention) to anxiety (if the task is too complex and time is limited).

But the new financial target will give you a new perspective for your trading. Additionally, you can visualize your account as a portfolio in which you can maintain positions for several days, if it's a good story. Or you can sell some, leaving a small position on while you keep your eye on it and, when it starts to get better again, get your whole position back.

You can add to your visual image of your portfolio with fundamental research, with the economics of the situation, and with the talk on the Street, and let that event play out. Don't simply sell because there's a two-point loss. According to one technology trader: "Trust your research, create an opinion, and let those opinions play out, especially in volatile tech things."

This sector is fundamentally driven, this trader says, not because of a chart, but because "a new product is coming out" or there is some other development. "Take some heat and don't get out because the S&P 500 and the index is getting whacked and you're down a little bit," says the technology trader. "Hold positions a little bit longer and think fundamentally. Do a reality check at a point and a half or two points, and evaluate as objectively as you possibly can."

Visualization Exercises

Here are some step-by-step methods of stimulating new visual images:

Breath Control

Close your eyes gently and breathe slowly and evenly, neither forcing nor holding back the natural flow of air. Your body knows how to breathe in a regular, easy fashion, and the only trick to practicing relaxed breathing is to listen to your body's own messages. Once your breathing is relaxed and regular, focus on some pleasant place you have visited or visualized (it need not be a "real" place), and imagine you are there, taking in all its sights, smells, sounds, and feelings. By visualizing this scene on a daily basis, for short periods of time, you can learn to develop the capacity and skill to enter this relaxed state precisely at moments of intense stress—thereby calming the body's physiological stress reaction.

The natural, unforced observation of your own breathing is a standard technique for relaxation in numerous exercise systems, from the Indian schools of yoga to the various Oriental martial arts. If the mind is likened to a movie projector depicting pleasant or unpleasant images in your consciousness, then breath control is a way of oiling the gears of that projector and of making it easier for you to stop the film when and where you wish.

Shifting Mental Images

Learning to shift the mental images in your mind, once you are calm, also helps you to listen and to observe all that is going on, both internally and externally. The closer you can get to a condition of restful alertness, the more effectively you can act—in a specific performance or just in the routines of your daily life. Please note: Relaxation, as much as it conjures up an image of restfulness, actually makes you more, rather than less, alert.

Close your eyes. Focus on your external environment—sounds of passing cars, birds, the radiator, or the air conditioner. Now shift back and focus on your own physical sensations—the warm and tingling feeling in your toes provides effective internal focus—or the blood passing through your feet, legs, and thighs.

Now shift back and forth three times, focusing first on external impressions and then on internal sensations, but calmly. Don't force it, or you'll set yourself up for producing tension, the opposite of relaxation.

When you are relaxed, you are sufficiently comfortable to perceive accurately what is going on around you so as to enjoy what you are doing. In this calm atmosphere, you can appraise both the situation and your performance, and can establish a more realistic, natural strategy for coping with fear, pain, and negative feelings.

Imagery and Trading

After learning to maintain a condition of restful alertness, a second step in visualization is to select or design positive mental images that facilitate proactive trading, and help you consciously face your fears. Selecting positive images reactivates dormant sources of confidence, and confirms the necessity to trade past your habitual stopping points.

To start on your road to success, develop a list of affirmations that support your trading to win program and allow you to go for the gold without hesitation or guilt. Develop concrete images of what successful trading is like, based on past successes:

- What does it look like?
- How does it feel?
- What were you able to do that was beyond the ordinary?

Think of your past successes. (If you have not had such experiences, make them up in your imagination.) What was your most successful trading day ever? Your most successful single trade? What happened? How does it make you feel? Keep feeling this way as your imagination summons up mental images that correspond to your trading strategy. Visualize the outcome you wish to achieve. What does trading success look like to you? Is there a dollar amount, or an amount of capital you wish to trade, or any other tangible parameter you can translate into a visual image?

Hang on to those feelings of success as you visualize future success. Dwell on those feelings, and they'll help you recognize opportunities in front of you.

You can develop sophisticated trading images by staying with those emotions associated with successful past experiences, and then thinking through the details of new trades, along with chart analysis and a macro picture of the economy.

Ideally, your visual trading image should include entry and exit points, and initial positions larger than you usually take on particular stocks. Additionally, you can prepare to enter positions earlier rather than later, and visualize yourself staying longer in a position.

In that same calm atmosphere, you can also review more complicated real or imaginary trades, by way of establishing the most desirable mental grooves that you'll need. Visual images of chart patterns can be particularly valuable in helping you extend your time horizons and raise the stakes in your practice trades.

What the visual imagery does is let you rehearse the way you intend to trade. When you visually practice a proactive trading approach but do not carry it out in your actual trading, you can review your trades and correct mentally for what was missing. Then keep practicing the correct moves, so that your ability to do them in the actual trading world becomes more real for you.

Power of Positive Imagery

Positive images help you adhere to your trading strategy in the face of the stress of day-by-day trading. Most successful traders I know pay close attention to going past their psychological stopping points. Over time, they have learned to face their anxiety and keep trading their strategy rather than retreat to their comfort zone. They have learned to interpret their fear as excitement and as a signal for action and to believe that opportunities abound on the other side of the anxiety. Further, they have also learned that breakdowns or errors or bad trades don't reflect on their ability or self-assessment but are actually the stepping-stones to breakthroughs and extraordinary results. Rather than retreating from uncertainty, they view a loss as an opportunity.

You See What You Expect

Within this general trading framework, think about how your characteristic way of playing is hampering you because it's reducing your flexibility. Conjuring up a mental image of what you expect to produce may help you consider what elements could be *added* to your actual trading style. For instance, you may visualize what you want to produce so that you can consciously stay longer in bull markets, or increase your level of risk, or get others to help you get out of bad stocks if you are frozen with inertia and a misplaced pride. Talk to more people, get more ideas, play a little longer, and get in there a little bit after the stock has moved, if there's still room. You may be able to learn to buy more of a rising stock and to keep raising the stop points as you go, and learn to sell if it starts down.

The more you learn to choose your own visual images, the better able you will be to participate in the trading opportunities of the day.

Now you're ready to trade beyond your habitual trading levels. Now you can develop more proactive result-oriented images.

Each step, each visual image, guides you to others. Now you can be aware of initiatives that you can take, and procedures you can learn. In that way, you can keep yourself more engaged in trading action without being dominated by the need to remain in the same trading comfort zone you have traded in for years.

Chapter Five

Concentration—
The Key to Preparation
and Recovery

The best traders make a conscious effort to get themselves into the game. At one weekly meeting in November 1997 when the markets were particularly quiet, a lot of the younger traders were complaining that there were no good ideas available and not much to do given the flat nature of the tape. Sandy, the master trader, took each one of them on, emphasizing how he always was trying to increase his edge by finding ways of getting more involved in the game.

It is not something that is given to you. According to Sandy: "You have to keep mining for the good ideas. Create the ideas. If you don't get involved in a stock today, maybe it will open up tomorrow. If so, set yourself up for tomorrow. If you miss an opportunity, remember trading is a continuous process. You can get involved tomorrow. You have got to make the effort! There is always something going on. You have to be willing to stay until 5:30, to make the extra phone calls, to do the work. It will pay off in greater satisfaction and greater success.

"Be more proactive," Sandy urged his traders. "Whenever people say there is nothing going on, I tell them I create my great trades when there is nothing going on. Talk to a few people, look at the calendars, see what is going on. There is always something more you can do. Trade your ideas. Don't wait until everyone sees the same situation."

Sandy continued, "If you feel burned out and don't know how to remotivate yourself every day, make it interesting. When you are too small relative to your ability, you take yourself out of the game. If you are really out there you would be more motivated. When you are in the game, you are not preoccupied with fears, volatility, blaming the month. I notice when I have thoughts of boredom or being burned out I'll ask people to get me in the game. I know I am not in the game because I am not thinking clearly—I don't care, I get lazy, I have the same uncreative thoughts.

"It's hard to stay that motivated. Ask for support. Get out of yourself. Get in the flow. Do things to motivate yourself. My attitude is that while I am sitting there I will try to do something intelligent. I have a lot of people around me to bounce ideas off of. Walk around the room. Talk to somebody.

"The game itself creates great trades. It's a stream of consciousness. I like talking to people—out of that comes a good thought. Pick up the phone and call someone. Call an analyst. Get the creative juices going. That gets you out of fatigue. Get past those thoughts. This is a great, interesting game. There is a lot to do. If you are bored you're not in the game. You can't be bored in the game if you are in this game," Sandy concluded.

Athletes and Concentration

The techniques of relaxation, centering, and visual imagery are time-tested avenues that you can use to bypass the all-too-familiar preoccupation with past failures, and to reacquaint you with the positive paths associated with past successes. As I've mentioned in previous chapters, great athletes in various sports are the poster children for these methods. They know how to quiet the mind of self-doubts and focus nonjudgmentally on the next moment.

Imagine, for instance, trading as if you were a world-class tennis player. Hall of Famers such as Jimmy Connors and Chris Evert paid special attention to their movements in preparation for a point. Between points, almost all tennis pros shift their racquet to their nonplaying hand and walk back from the net, consciously adopting a confident posture associated with a positive mental image so as to create a winning mind. You can do the same before each trade.

A trader named Jess has made the connection between tennis preparation and trading preparation by rehearsing a certain stroke. "I used to go home and I'd look at my forehand, my backswing, my backhand in the mirror five hundred times. I'd repeat certain rules for myself such as, 'Step into the ball.' 'Keep your eye on the ball.' 'Keep the elbow tucked in.' 'Throw in preparation, and get it back as soon as possible.' I've been playing tennis for fifteen years and I still do that mental preparation," Jess says.

Why bother with these staples of sports psychology? Because for you, not just for Pete Sampras, tighter muscles lead to tension and slowed reflexes. That, in turn, diminishes your ability to visually track and assess the activity of rapidly moving stocks. Shortness of breath may reduce endurance, hamper concentration, and trigger panic attacks. With relaxation and deep breathing exercises, you can master these anxious responses, and then enter into a calm, meditative state in which to access past positive memories in order to enter your zone. These affirming memories recreate your sense of purpose and help build a positive set of expectations that will increase your ability to take calculated risks in following your trading strategy, just as Sampras takes risks when aiming for a winning shot.

Entering into a meditative state of consciousness reduces anxiety and tension and decreases the impact of distracting internal and external stimuli. Centering helps you to distance yourself from the sequence of emotional responses and negative interpretations of stressful and unsuccessful trades that spur panic, denial, rationalization, and avoidance, all of which perpetuate the likelihood of failure.

Concentrated Action

At the heart of both playing tennis and trading on a world-class level is concentration—the ability to stand back from your emotional responses and to focus on only what is before you.

Concentrated action means seeing clearly the next steps to take toward your goals without being thrown by your own nerves, self-doubts, or fears. Concentrated action enables you to keep going under stress, to hang in beyond pressure-cooker situations without reacting to your own responses. It means maintaining a state of calm in the midst of chaos, refusing to become frozen in your efforts to control such situations, refusing to be overwhelmed by them.

When you concentrate, you focus on the intricacies of the activity and therefore can perceive more accurately what is going on around you so that you can establish a more realistic strategy for producing effective results. Focused on the details, you find that it becomes easier to deal with discomfort, pain, and other negative feelings. You are also less likely to be concerned with the meaning of the results and less likely to get caught up with trying too hard to avoid failure.

Concentration enables you to face reality without shrinking from it.

Improving Concentration

To continue the tennis analogy, Chris Evert probably was born with the laserlike powers of concentration for which she was famous. While you may have been born with little capacity to concentrate, you can improve your concentration by learning to control a number of factors associated with concentration. Obviously, having a calm mind and body facilitates concentration.

The best concentration results from allowing events to occur, without focusing too much on results. Ideally, you should focus only on what you can do, not on the results. In fact, too much concern for the results can stifle concentration and reduce your perseverance in the face of obstacles. Focusing on the immediate present rather than past images is also useful. This can be translated pragmatically into focusing on one mental image at a time, as described in the previous chapter.

Focusing on specific tasks during the trading day can help you to minimize the distracting effects of intrusive thoughts and external stimuli, much as focusing on a mantra provides a symbolic sound for concentrating energy in yoga.

In the focused state of mind, the reduced input of stimuli from the external world allows your sense of time to expand, and magnifies the current market activity. As a result of this fine-tuning of the nervous system, you may be able to separate critical information from "noise," so as to be able to make connections between events more accurately and rapidly. You may be able to make decisions more readily, without fatigue or distraction.

On the other side, excessive efforts to concentrate can lead you to focus too much on a single trade, so that you lose awareness of the larger context. You can avoid this by learning to shift back and forth from the specific item to general background or context in which you are acting. In this way you will not become so absorbed by the specific that you become distracted and lose touch with the realities around you.

Additionally, you can practice shifting your concentration from a narrow to a wider focus—for example, from focusing on this word to focusing on the room you are sitting in and then back from a wider to a narrow focus. This will teach you to sustain concentration on a single narrow set of objects or activities for an extended period of time and help you to stop shifting unconsciously from one object to another. It is also useful to practice shifting back and forth from internal thoughts and sensations to external sensations and events. The more you do this the more you will recognize your own best concentration skills.

Another aspect to improving concentration is to minimize boredom, which often sets in as the quality of performance improves and becomes automatic such that concentration drifts off. Over time, you begin to tune out stimuli until you stop responding to them. The problem is that you could tune out critical stimuli and start making errors. However, shifts in concentration can prevent this from happening, so that you can continue to respond just as strongly to external stimuli after you have been at a task as you could at the beginning. You can do this by increasing the challenge or by raising the level of your financial objective.

You'll discover that you can improve your concentration by *not* putting in extra effort, by *not* pushing to control the result. You can still become acutely aware of your successes and failures, and to the extent that you monitor your progress, you empower your performance. This mind-set lets you factor in results as you progress, and act accordingly—not by way of effort and manipulation but by way of being conscious of the process. Continual monitoring of your trading is like keeping your hand on the rudder and not going to sleep.

Consider how much time you spend fully engaged and fully awake in your trading. How much time is spent digging deep inside to find new ways of dealing with new issues? How much effort goes into avoidance, comfort, escape, and not facing the issues at hand?

How much work do you put into trying to control the result? Are you in the same boat as the trader who told me: "I'm afraid if I give one hundred percent I won't have anything left. So when I give one hundred percent I soon retreat in fear, especially if I don't produce results."

The fact is, when you are totally focused on your trading, when you *are* giving 100 percent, you don't have control, and you don't know how things will turn out. You just commit to your financial objective and relate to the events that occur in the context you have created. If you feel out of control, you keep going. One hundred percent is not about what you feel or even the results. It's about 100 percent engagement or absorption. It is about total involvement of our heart and soul.

Total, 100 percent concentration is also about taking responsibility. When the momentum seems to be flagging and you are starting to lose interest, look carefully at how much you are really engaged. One hundred percent produces exhilaration. Less than that produces a concern for winning or losing, which then becomes a symbolic victory, and a hollow one, rather than a real encounter with success.

Consider to what extent you are not fully engaged in your trading. Are you playing it safely or self-destructively? If you are successful, you may be covering up the fact that you have not given your all to the action. Success creates the appearance of commitment and the appearance of competency. Do you avoid losing because it doesn't look good and marks you as vulnerable?

When you are really winning, you are fully engaged and can go with the flow, accepting success and failure as two sides of the same coin. In effect, while concentration leads to results, inertia and past patterns keep rearing their ugly heads, so that it is necessary to keep recommitting to your goal.

Concentration and Momentum

Sometimes concentration creates a terrifying momentum. You feel a sense of being out of control, of being unpredictable, of being immersed in a totally new experience. This means trading in the moment or the present without any sense of what is likely to happen, since this moment has never occurred before.

To sustain such a momentum, you have to keep creating the context in which it is possible to do what is necessary to tap your potential. This means creating the structure of support to ensure that all the steps taken will be designed to produce the results consistent with the goal.

When concentration falters, keep going in terms of what you said you would do, rather than being governed by your feelings or your thoughts. When people do really well, they often stop doing what helped them to do well, and start being too creative and too flexible— they let go of their discipline.

A young trader I'll call Sean, for example, takes a contrarian position whenever he is successful. The success goes to his head and makes him more confident than is useful. He starts thinking he is invincible. He becomes explosive, which generates a thought process that allows him to make judgments that are contrary to his game plan. "When I am emotional, I'm likely to get hurt. My gut is telling me I am too extended."

Sean, who was an all-American soccer player, is beginning to recognize those moments when he is out of his zone. In one case, he says, he made a pact with himself at the beginning of the month that he would not lose $10,000. Then one day he found himself losing and his commitment got sidetracked. All of a sudden he was down $10,000 and then $5000 more. He then told himself, "I better make back some money. Let's try to pair things up and make some money to get back my losses." So he put up another trade—"and I'm down another four grand. Now I have to make back nineteen grand." He tells himself, "Let's wait. Let's be patient." But it doesn't work. "All of a sudden I am down another four thousand dollars. I've got to make twenty-three thousand dollars. Then I say, 'It's not worth it today. Stop.' Then I really screw up. I let my downside escalate. Sometimes I'm confident that I can make it back. Other times I know it will be disastrous, and I'd better do something else."

Sean should recognize that he doesn't have a high-confidence trade and does not just want to roll the dice. Sometimes the market isn't giving it to him, or he isn't digging deep enough to find the high-probability trade. Instead of trying to prove how big he can get, he should ease up on the trading unless there is a really high-percentage choice where he can reduce the risk of losing more money.

The successful trader is able to get past the euphoria or despair of the last trade and concentrate on the present. After a series of successful trades you can allow yourself to feel good, but also remain aware of any tendency to become so relaxed that you stop following your routines of preparation and strategic planning.

Unless you identify your emotional responses and how they color your trading, the patterns will continue. If you're like Sean, you are going to be cocky the rest of your life, and you have to identify that piece of yourself and see how it interferes with your trading. The trading game requires that you trade your strategy, not your emotions.

Concentration and Losses

When recovering a sense of strength after a loss, you must remember that every loss is a potential learning experience. There is a tendency to focus on the loss rather than on the new opportunities that loss provides. The key to making the most of a loss is in reframing each issue in a positive light. Ask yourself, what new directions do you see from the loss? How can you turn a loss into a gain? Instead of beating yourself, consider whether you can start buying the stock that you shorted and lost, or whether it is time to go into a new sector. It may be time to shift to a new angle, new direction, or new stocks.

The main thing is to stay focused on your objective of trading to win and to not get caught up in a "poor me" spirit of defeat. Keep considering what was missing, what caused the loss, what more you can do, and what you can do next. There are always new directions to take.

Why Concentration Is Key

Do I seem to be concentrating too much on the idea of concentration? That's because I believe it's the key to preparing for greatness, the difference between being a master and just remaining in the same old trading rut. Develop your concentration, and you'll soon acknowledge that your own actions and your decision to persist despite adversity are the critical variables in your business. When things are not going well, it is the result of insufficient concentration. As you concentrate, you'll channel your potential and take responsibility for what happens in your trading career no matter how much it appears to be due to something or someone else. The more you can do this, the more alive, powerful, and in charge of your trades you will feel.

When you concentrate on the tasks before you, you can maintain the delicate balance between compulsiveness and fearfulness on the one side and spontaneity and assertiveness on the other. You can monitor your efforts so as to reduce tension and potential errors generated as you approach each goal. This focused, "less is more" approach becomes especially critical when you have failed to accomplish something in the past and are fearful of being able to perform in the present. Tense and intent on succeeding, you can easily press too hard to compensate for your past failure.

Trying to do something is different from doing it. *Trying* implies effort and struggle, while *doing* implies believing in the possibility and accomplishing the result almost unconsciously. In effect, by doing "less" rather than "more" you are able to flow gently into the activity, reducing the errors that come from excessive efforts.

Concentration favors efforts that are tempered and gentle, slow and easy. Effortless movement in fluid drive is the key. Concentration permits you to get more impact with less effort, to tone down, try less hard, and accept things as they are. It helps you to look at objects before you with "soft eyes" (that is, allowing the thoughts or objects to come to you rather than making an active effort to focus on them).

Allowing Events to Unfold

If you can let go of the past, your dependence on others, and your need for maintaining a certain public identity, and can live in the world in terms of focused attention on the tasks in front of you without expectations, the world will become a place where all kinds of things can happen, where your life can become exciting and full of joy. As you grasp the idea of concentration, you participate in your trades as exciting and interesting experiences. You live your life as the adventure it is, not in a "what if" or "if only" mode. Thanks to concentrated action, you don't control your life but rather allow it to unfold, knowing that it was designed to work; you need only set your life on a course of your own choosing and then focus attention on making small shifts and adjustments in the tasks before you so as to keep your life on course.

It is very much the way you guide an airplane or steer a car. To turn in a small plane you need only concentrate your thoughts on turning in a certain direction and you will gradually shift the control wheel to that side. Similarly in a car, you are always making slight adjustments with the steering wheel—even when no drastic or rapid movements to steer around a curve or to make a left turn are required. Trusting your instincts, you are able to become one with the activity. You make small adjustments instinctively but spend little time thinking about how you look, or what the outcome will be. The same applies to trading fully in the realm of concentrated action. You take your mind along for the ride but you allow yourself to be with the experience. You become fully engaged in the moment, trading at the maximum level.

Where Do You Start?

Concentrate on what you can do today. How can you improve your immediate actions, your relations with others? What do you have to let go of to improve the quality of your trades? What grievances, opinions, attitudes, entitlements, grudges, expectations, and the like do you have to let go of, so your life and your trades can just be?

In other words, focus on the means rather than the end. If you focus on your efforts, the results will take care of themselves.

Concentration and Fear

The effort involved in keeping your defenses up can also keep you from concentrating. Fearing failure, you may focus too much attention on results. Fear of failure will increase the chance of error by setting in motion a self-fulfilling prophecy where your expectation of failure leads to failure. This occurs either by reinforcing an inclination to quit before reaching your objective or by leading you to interpret cues as indicative of failure so that you grow tense. A concern with failure also may occur if the challenge you have set for yourself exceeds your capabilities.

Since dropping your defenses about failure can trigger considerable anxiety, you need to learn how to do this while remaining centered. You can do this by accepting your own anxiety and not trying to cover it up. In learning to flow with feelings, you can differentiate anxiety and negative feelings from your basic self.

Admitting to fear is often an effective tool for reducing it. Reducing the effort expended to hide fear effectively eliminates it. By concentrating on how specific feelings feel, how long they last, and what thoughts are associated with them, and taking responsibility for them, you can dissipate the fear and anxiety that come from trying to suppress feelings. Concentration, even on those things that cause fear, has a strong effect on reducing ambivalence, indecision, and weakened efforts. It can be a great stress buster.

What Happens When You Lose Concentration

When you are distracted by tension, confusion, anxiety, self-consciousness, or boredom, it's natural to focus on trying to eliminate them. Unfortunately, when you do, you can lose your concentration and get off the track of the task at hand.

Faltering in your commitment to your vision, and slipping into negative thinking, self-justification, or denial can cause lapses in concentration. These lapses may manifest themselves as a failure to follow your plan, an unwillingness to trust or empower others, a lack of concentration on the details that need to be taken care of to make sure the trade takes place, and a failure to sustain responsibility for making the trade happen. When there is a lapse in concentration, with a resulting failure to produce specific results, there is a tendency to deny it.

If things have been moving along well and suddenly you start to slip, it may be that you have become bored with your trades, have stopped engaging in them, or have stopped enrolling others in them. Additionally, you may have failed to keep alive the intensity of involvement of others, or you may have moved toward dominating rather than enrolling others.

Do you enlist others in your trading, and then withdraw? Or do you own a project and ensure that it stays on target even when you have delegated important functions to others? Lapses in concentration occur when you stop creating and begin to rest on your laurels.

When this happens, you can bolster your concentration by recommitting to your vision. Here it is useful to consider what else is possible, rather than function with what you accept as immutable truths, which box you in. Be willing to recommit to your goals and be willing to discuss what is necessary to make things happen. Don't blame others for your failures. When things aren't going well, don't give up or resign yourself to failure. Don't invalidate yourself or others. Instead, look to see what you are doing or omitting to do. Concentrate on what was missing in your trade and try to establish a procedure that will make it work better. Be willing to admit what has changed, what is missing, and what will be done to correct this. Take responsibility for what has happened in a fully committed way. Lapses in concentration or a reduction in momentum are part of the investing business, and you shouldn't dwell on them. They don't mean that there is something wrong with you. It simply means that you have not handled some of the specific issues. There is no value in focusing on how wrong you are, or how wrong others are. All you need to do is to notice what's missing and begin to move along in high momentum again.

When you have lost your concentration and are in some kind of breakdown, it is useful to see what is stopping you.

The Psychology of Losing after Winning

Have you ever wondered why winning days are often followed by plateaus and losing streaks? The answer often is lost concentration. It is easier to make money and lose it than to make money and hold on to it.

The psychology of losing after winning is well demonstrated by Sean, the former all-American. "I will lose if I have a really big day," he admits. "When I eventually get closer to winning, and am getting ready to fill my reserve and think I'm on the right road, and I start to make money, I begin to get sloppy and self-destructive, and stop concentrating.

"Last month was the first month that I made money almost every

> ### *Eight Questions to Ask When You Lose Concentration*
>
> 1. What are the recurring issues that keep you from moving forward in your trading?
> 2. What are you afraid of?
> 3. What is the life principle that gets in the way of action?
> 4. What is it that you think might happen that keeps you from staying on track?
> 5. How does your personal history hold you back in your efforts to trade successfully?
> 6. How do your recurrent self-doubts limit possibility?
> 7. When you lose money on a trade, do you consider whether you failed to formulate your plans to ensure that the trade was successful?
> 8. Are you willing to commit to your goal as though there are no alternatives?

day," he continues. "It was my best month ever. Then all of a sudden I had this trading idea that I thought was going to work. I got bigger, into a size larger than I was used to trading, and the market reversed. I was long, and while I was on a conference call, I watched everything reverse, and it wasn't going according to my game plan, and I wasn't reacting quickly enough.

"Part of the problem, I guess, was I wasn't in motion," he admits. "What gets me out of motion is that I think I know too much about the situation where, in actuality, what I might know doesn't matter. Instead of allowing the price to dictate what I am going to do, I say I know the story. But when what I expect doesn't happen, I should take action instead of rationalizing the movement of the price against me. If it isn't doing what it is supposed to be doing, I should get out."

But instead of acting, Sean let his concentration lapse. "People were getting hit hard. I figured they were just overselling this group and that it would go back up in relation to the market," he says. The fact is, he knows better. "If everyone else is selling, I have to be selling also. Whenever I don't do what everyone else is doing, I get into trouble."

Other traders have to figure a way of not getting caught in the last hour of the trading day when they are short a lot of futures, especially if they tend to move very fast. By the end of the day, you are mentally and physically tired, and you may be psychologically worn out from a difficult day or a losing day. You may feel as though you have been through the wars, and yet as close as you are to the end of the day, you need to be ready to regroup for the last hour when things will be even faster, when computerized trading programs are instituted and push the market every which way, when the resolutions of many of the day's trades occur and others are lining themselves up for the next day. It is a highly intense time period, perhaps even more intense than the beginning of the day, since there will be little time afterward to make corrections for the decisions you make.

It is imperative therefore to keep your concentration up at the end of the day and remember to stay focused on the critical issues before you. Besides the resolution of the day's trades, you may want to position yourself for the next day. What's tomorrow going to be like? Are there any catalytic events expected in your trading group? Are there any significant government numbers to expect? Any mergers? Earnings reports? Pay attention to all these things and pay special attention to the stocks you are trading, since this is the time of day when you are physiologically most likely to want to retreat from concentrating and are getting ready to wind up the day, or are starting to react emotionally to the results of the day, or are starting to distance yourself from the day or prepare mentally for the return home or the evening's events.

It's important to be very conscious during the last hour if you are very short and the chart looks a certain way. If Micron reached a high of $37\frac{1}{8}$ and now it's $36\frac{5}{8}$ coming off the high, maybe you are not sure about it running up again, so you need to examine your thinking. Why did you miss it? If it was a technical reason why you missed it, you might not have been able to get it because of the way it traded, which forced you into a different mode of operation that made you uncomfortable. You have to examine what you are not good at. How can you extend the time you hold on to a position?

For some traders, losses after big gains come from feeling they don't deserve to win and must give back to redress the unfair balance. Others, like Sean, feel too good or euphoric, and their discipline and control over losses goes out the window. A trader starts to think he or she has some magical prowess, that Lady Luck is shining, and then gets careless. A loss of concentration stops this trader from remembering that the market is fickle, treacherous, and seductive.

How do you raise your level of expectations so that it is consistent with your new level of performance? What did you do to make that happen, and what can you reproduce? You had a great idea, played it right, and hit. It worked. You have to find good new ideas, execute them, bypass fear, and accept how good you are—or you can revert to losing money.

What must you do to reach each new target? Examine the situation. Concentrate on it, consider what to do to reach it, and then monitor your steps. Once you see the repeated behavior that keeps you in the correct zone and the steps that move you forward, you will feel internally pressured to take the necessary action in terms of the new targets you have selected. In all of this, it is important to be aware of any inclination you might have to pull back and become overcautious after a run of successful trading.

This was the point I tried to emphasize to Lenny, a young trader at a large trading company who had begun to generate sizable profits, but still had not been rewarded with an increase in salary over and above the base salary he was given when he first came on board. "I'm not going to try to make any more money and put myself at risk, especially when I'm not going to be able to earn any more money if I increase my results," he boldly asserted when encouraged to expand. "Why should I work hard when I am not getting financially rewarded?"

I won't get into the mechanics of income on Wall Street, which differs from company to company, but suffice it to say, he was reassured by the head of the trading desk that he would soon get a larger payout and one where he could anticipate making more money as his trading earnings went up. Aside from that issue, the reason to keep trading to win, rather than trading to stay in place, is that you will soon find yourself losing if you approach trading from that latter viewpoint. You have to keep stretching yourself in order to stay current with the market.

Another trader facing the same issue, Seth, made close to $250,000 three days before the end of the month of July. "I don't want to risk losing anything," he noted, "since this is my greatest month." But, the danger in reverting to trading at smaller multiples than he was now doing would be that he would lose confidence in the bigger game, and would find that he was still trading cautiously when the next month began. So he was better off sticking to sizable positions to make sure that his discipline was in place and that he wasn't putting himself at greater risk.

A special problem is sometimes seen in experienced traders who no longer find trading to be a source of pleasure, excitement, or interest. This is the case with Jack, a hedge fund manager who has lost his motivation. He has reached his stopping point and is no longer motivated to trade proactively. His first task is to acknowledge the facts and recognize that he is trading automatically and not proactively or in terms of an objective. Only then can he recommit to becoming master of his destiny so as to overcome his demoralization. He must set up a challenging but doable goal and develop a strategy consistent with it.

Part of this effort involves facing his unconscious investment in the peculiar comfort of maintaining the status quo and not putting himself at risk. The psychological value of holding on to his winnings and resting on his laurels is greater than the value of risking them on the next bet in the future. Thus it is that there is a conservatism built into successful trading that sets in motion the inertia and negative direction that often occurs after traders like Jack succeed.

Commitment is the kind of psychological step that is required to help a trader like Jack overcome his inertia toward doing what has utility value (that is, his staying in the cautious position). Commitment enables him to concentrate on his discipline and override emotional responses and/or defensive responses to his emotional responses; avoidance of trading in order to avoid anxiety leads to paralysis. This is what Jack needs to do and concentration is one of the skills that will help him to overcome the tendency toward inertia and self-protectiveness.

Commitment also means to stay focused and not be swayed by the crowd movement that occurs at the extremes of the trading cycle. The master trader is able to take contrary positions. Although psychologically difficult to do, being able to do this allows the trader to be positioned contrary to where the crowd is being positioned when the trading cycles move toward the extreme. In this way, the contrarian is able to move first.

One spur to an experienced trader like Jack is the fear of becoming just another face in the crowd if he gives in to the inertia. This is an intolerable idea and motivates the experienced trader to be willing to take the risks associated with the contrarian position of leading the pack into new directions.

Concentration and Recovery

Recovery from a succession of losses involves a series of steps designed to access the mind-set of successful trading. Successful trading is made up of many small day-to-day decisions. The objective, of course, is to get better at trading and to get better at adapting to the constant changes in market conditions. What works today won't necessarily work tomorrow. The best traders have learned how to keep adjusting to the constant flux and know that because the game is continually changing, they will never get it exactly right. What's important is to keep trading and moving. By doing so you will get a feel for the market so that when something comes along that can explode, you will be in a trading mode. Trade even when the profits are small to keep your hand in it and achieve a better level of skill.

One step in the recovery phase is to practice relaxation and focused attention each day. Relaxation and visualization exercises, as described in earlier chapters, can help your mind to let go of self-doubt and enhance your ability to focus on the next moment.

For you, as a trader, the key to recovery is to observe events and your own reactions to events so that you can concentrate on your trading strategy. With practice, you will begin to see the value of letting go of negative images and fears.

After a series of losing trades, it is beneficial to take a break from your trading, get centered, and spend time remembering and recreating the images and feelings associated with past successful trades. These affirming memories tap into internal sources of confidence and help you to reestablish your sense of purpose. In so doing, you will develop endurance and a positive set of expectations that will increase your ability to take calculated risks and follow your trading strategy. In effect, you will move from a reactive to a proactive state of mind.

Recovery also entails envisioning a strategy consistent with your objectives and learning to implement it. Be specific. For example, decide on the number of shares you need to trade in order to realize your objectives and the specific parameters you wish to measure in order to track your performance.

One useful measure you can utilize is the Sharpe ratio. According to Gilbert, a risk manager at a major firm: "The Sharpe ratio is useful for measuring your efficiency in terms of your ability to generate a certain return relative to the amount of risk you are willing to take. With experience in controlling your downside risk, for example, you may be able over time to trade bigger while maintaining the same degree of risk. Using this kind of productivity/risk measure, you should be able to determine whether you are taking appropriate risks with your capital, without being so risk-averse as to miss significant opportunities for profitable trading."

Stages of Recovery

Recovery between trades may be divided into time-limited stages. The first is a stage of relaxation, which occurs after one series of trades ends and before a new series begins and which lasts between one to twenty seconds. In this stage, you clear your mind and enter a relaxed meditative state.

Next comes the stage of preparation. In this stage, you begin generating strategic ideas to pursue in trading. This stage is followed by one that involves visualizing specific targets such as entry and exit points. The next stage involves surrendering to the immediate action. Here, you stop thinking about how you are doing and start executing the process.

Via these stages, you slip into a positive frame of mind. You prepare and plan your strategy and at the moment of execution, you relax, let your thoughts go and execute by focusing on the actions to take. Regardless of whether you succeed, you review your performance and determine what you need to do in order to succeed in the next trade.

Using Creativity in Recovery

Creativity flourishes where work is approached as play. Even in the process of recovery, there is always a need to take action. This is even more important than meditation. Get more focused on specific actions to take. One way to help you do this is to exercise. Physical exercise helps you to get in touch with the outside world and away from focusing too much on inner thoughts and opinions.

Trading is both a right and a left brain activity that requires openness, vulnerability, and the use of unconscious processes. Therefore, an exercise such as bike riding, where you are constantly pumping the pedals rhythmically and repetitively, may help you tap into your creative centers better than obsessing about a needed solution. The rhythm of exercise gets you in touch with the artistic, creative right brain and away from the obsessive left brain, which may be overworked and overanxious.

Exercise also may help you get back into the present, the here and now. It puts you in the right frame of mind for trading, where you can go with the flow and not be so conscious of what it is that you are doing. Then you can trade intuitively and independently of your conscious thoughts.

Walking, swinging a racquet, running, or climbing stairs may help provide you with visual images of serenity and a sense of your own harmony in relation to the universe. A good workout can help you experience a sense of freedom and centering. These activities can give you a sense of accomplishment and awareness of your own ability. You can celebrate life in these moments and learn to celebrate the excitement of trading more than the thrill of making money.

Because exercise can help you become more focused, more energized, and better able to respond to external events on the computer screen, it may be wise to trade immediately following a morning exercise routine. It doesn't have to be complicated. Walking to work, for instance, may allow you to begin thinking in a nonlinear way. The variety of sensory input that you experience while walking also can awaken your inner right brain and creativity.

If you pay attention, you can become aware of the times when trades seem to happen serendipitously—when things fall together without any apparent reason. This will happen most when you are open and centered. Your heightened receptivity increases your capacity to integrate more complex pieces of information and to respond spontaneously to signals coming from the tape, the room, and your own internal creative centers.

A Conscious Approach

This conscious approach to recovery and preparing for the next trade or trading day is all about accessing the right state of mind. It's about focusing on the present. It is also about learning to accept strengths and weaknesses. When you give up playing mainly not to lose and wasting energy, you will bring more of yourself to bear in your trades. Accepting your strengths and weaknesses will enable you to ask the hard questions and do what must be done to succeed.

PART TWO

Putting Psychology into Practice

Chapter Six

100 Percent Commitment—
Promising the Result
and Expanding the Risk

Promises, Not Guarantees

Commitment implies a willingness to promise a result when there is no guarantee of the outcome. Simply making the promise—taking that risk—taps enormous energy that fuels the realization of your financial goals.

Emerson wrote of some dimension of yourself that flows without friction. When you commit, you are showing the courage to state what you stand for and to become what you are capable of becoming.

Commitment is an example of what Joe Greenstein, a circus strongman in the early years of this century, believed was necessary to overcome what he called "impossibility thinking." He believed in a Life Force that we all have but fail to activate because we think "impossibility thoughts" from the time we're born. We are constantly thinking, "I can't do that. I'll hurt myself." According to Greenstein, the little voice in us—that instinct for self-preservation—does not give us an accurate picture of our capabilities. We all have mental and physical abilities beyond our own estimation, but to realize them the mind must be deconditioned from "impossibility thinking." Only after overcoming the instinct for self-preservation can you really achieve success. Greenstein believed you could do almost anything if you applied your mind and body to the task with enough diligence.

Nothing could more vividly illustrate the importance of believing in a favorable outcome than the large number of people who have been able to run sub-four-minute miles since Roger Bannister broke the "magic" four-minute mile barrier on May 6, 1954. Until that time, the four-minute mile, according to Bannister, had become "rather like an Everest—a barrier that seemed to defy all attempts to break it—an awesome reminder that man's striving might be in vain." Once the obstacle had been conquered by Bannister, the event itself suddenly became relatively easy. By the end of 1978, 274 runners had broken the "magic, impenetrable" barrier.

What you commit to—the financial objective you wish to reach—is the promise. The promise produces a discrepancy between where you are and what you promise to reach. And it's this gap that is the source of creative tension. When managed correctly, the tension is not so great as to overwhelm you, but is strong enough to stimulate you to uncover new paths to the expanded results you have promised. Commitment to a specific objective is the most critical dimension of trading to win since it provides more of the focus and energy than any other single factor. But, it is not easily grasped. Talking to a fairly successful trader at one of our weekly meetings, Sandy the super-trader underscored the meaning of commitment: "It may take you three years to really understand it, for the light to go on. This game has nothing to do with being a superstar for a day—which may have more to do with luck," he pointed out. It has to do with overcoming the reluctance to play 100 percent, even when you think you are committing.

Sandy continued: "You don't want to commit, because you're not willing to put yourself on the line to do it. You're willing to make a few calls and sort the information. You really don't know what to do, and then when the stock you've picked starts to move you're not there. You missed it, and all you hear is, 'What I could have done but I didn't do it.' The bottom line is: You get what you get. Maybe you need to be in your stock for the two-and-a-half- or three-point move. Maybe you need to take your work, whatever it is, and the people you're talking to and then conform it with the price action and let it run.

"You can't get too caught up in the market and the bonds and the S&Ps and forget the reason that you're in the stock," said Sandy. "You know that you are wasting time with the bonds and the S&Ps but you don't have the discipline to say, 'I'm not doing it anymore.' You're wrapped up in talking about why you're losing and other nonsense as opposed to making money. What does trading two S&Ps have to do with you putting together a good year? Nothing. It's an ego trip. It's a way of saying, 'Oh, I got it right.' Meanwhile, you could buy ten thousand shares of Citicorp, make two dollars, and get yourself to the same place. Now, if you want to trade forty or fifty S&Ps, that's something different. Now you stand to make thirty grand on a trade. Then maybe it's worth your time."

Commitment as I use the term means promising the result without any evidence or certainty of how you are going to realize it. It means putting yourself in a situation where there are no alternatives other than to create the result you have promised.

Commitment is a proactive approach in which you promise to produce a specific financial result in a specific time frame—for example, one year—and then conform your daily trading to that result. In redesigning your trading strategy toward that end, the goal is not so much something to be reached as it is a template for making powerful decisions. How does this work?

At the heart of proactive trading is making a conscious commitment to a financial objective *greater* than what you are accustomed to achieving, and then doing what it takes to realize the objective. This means putting yourself in that mental set where you decide in advance to find that combination of factors—based on what you've been doing, based on the calls, based on whatever work you're engaged in—that is consistent with your goal. You've got to decide in advance that this is going to be a $10,000 or $20,000 day; having decided that, you're going to have to trade in such a way as to make that a reality. Instead of waiting to see what the market gives you, you've got to go out and make the world give you what you've decided. It's the way to go to the next big level.

Too many people promise to "do the best that they can," without realizing that "the best you can" is limited by your concept of best. I'm suggesting that you decide on a number that's a real stretch and then trade in terms of that number. The number you choose is only limited by your imagination. Instead of waiting to get the conviction, you start to play at the level that you've chosen and get the conviction afterward.

Consider what you need to do to be able to perform at that level. If you want to make $1 million in a certain number of days, figure out what you have to do each day to get to the million. Maybe you need to start with a larger position or stay in a little longer, or you need to get more information so you can be more confident about the shares that you're trading. To get to this size, you have to do the work that allows you to feel comfortable. You don't want to feel comfortable first and then move on. It doesn't work that way. You get to the next level by playing at the level before you have the conviction. You've got to do the work so that you have increased your level of conviction. If you really have the conviction, and you're really at the zone, then you get even bigger. Success is those times when you're consistently playing at a level that forces you to do things that you don't ordinarily do.

Make the call, even if it's uncomfortable. That's where the growth comes from. It's like exercising. You'll do an activity until it's uncomfortable, then you'll stop; but if you have a trainer he'll make you do two more and that's where the muscle growth comes in. But if you're by yourself, you'll put a stop on it. Sometimes you enter the zone by chance. It happens from time to time, but you can accentuate it by setting up a more challenging target. It's the extra calls and a bigger objective that make it more interesting. You're dealing with the unknown all the time, and to bring any order out of that is very difficult.

Otherwise you're waiting for it to happen as opposed to making it happen. You can make it happen as big as you want to if you start setting a bigger goal and then figuring out what you have to do to realize it. The standard way we all function is to do what we know and produce the familiar result because that's comfortable, but to commit to something beyond that is scary as hell. We're all trained to cut down on the pain by doing what's reasonable. That's the most secure place to be, but it's not necessarily the best place to be. The comfortable number, whatever it is, is not tapping your potential or stretching you.

In trading there's a tendency to hold back, to avoid being hurt or disappointed.

"A perfect example of stretching is what we did today with Cardinal Health," one trader told me during a discussion on the subject. "We called five times and finally got the information we needed that allowed me not to just buy the other fifteen thousand shares, which I was just about to do, but an extra ten thousand shares in our favor."

I suggested that this trader get on conference calls around earnings time, instead of relying on others. Having research or background information about a stock gives you a little more confidence about knowing what to do and knowing the meaning of the tape action. It helps you assess the quality of the calls you are making. It may help you to know why a stock is moving and add additional perspective to your decision. The information you get is not absolute knowledge, but it may give you a feel for the market. This will help you to read uncertainty in the unknown a little bit better.

The more you know and understand the quality of the information, the more intelligently you can trade. It reduces the risks. It's how you maximize your performance in this very unpredictable, uncertain kind of game. At every opportunity consider what else you can do.

The trader said, "I could have called other analysts."

I agreed. If you make just one or two more calls you extend your network and increase the value of your information. It's thinking outside of the box. Every small profit builds confidence.

"Of course, time is a constraining factor," another trader declared. "We're doing a lot of things at the same time and there may not be enough people on the desk to be able to handle making another call at that particular time. The bottom line is, I think, that certainly we can do more to be better informed.

"How we go about doing this," the trader continued, "is something we probably should set up a system for—putting different people in charge of being on top of different groups, even if they're not experts. Like Maryann is trying to be an expert in the drugs sector. She should probably be in charge of HMOs and hospital companies, too. So, if something comes up in those, she knows which analyst to call. She can get on the phone and she'll understand what the question's going to be. And Tom and Jeff and I should probably have a couple of groups."

All of this means saying good-bye to comfort and safety, good-bye to self-doubts. It's up to you to align your choices of price, volatility, and size of positions with parameters that can meet or exceed your new goal.

Your new financial goal provides meaning and purpose to your daily trading, a direction to pursue. In addition, it provides a meta-concept for your trading, so that trades do not occur willy-nilly but are understandable in terms of a larger perspective. A financial target links ostensibly unrelated trades together in a meaningful whole and gives you a larger frame of reference, letting you make order out of the chaos of the market, letting you relax into trades without trying to control them. You're headed for a higher level of psychological integration, what yogis consider to be "enlightenment."

Since you can focus on only a limited amount of data at any given time, your new financial goal will help you to refine your focus, concentrating on finite bits of information. Now you can be more present in the moment-by-moment experience of your trades. The goal determines what you permit yourself to think, feel and remember about the events of the marketplace. It becomes the guiding principle of your trading.

Selecting a Goal

A goal helps you ratchet up the challenge to bring more of your resources into play. Your task is to get out of your own way and motivate yourself to shoot as high as you can.

How do you know where to set the target? One way is to consider the amount of capital you are running. Ask yourself, "How much can I grow it?" Then figure out how much to trade each day consistent with the target.

Here's how Sandy aims at his target:

"I work backward. Let's say I've got so much capital and need to make X dollars to realize my usual percentage of return. I ask myself, 'What do I have to do to get there?' There's no way I can make my target in this firm trading KLAC. But I could do it with Wal-Mart or Ford or GM or EMC Corporation, or Silicon Graphics when it's right. I also can't afford to step in front of the big mutual funds every time, because if I'm wrong I'm going to be giving up my whole month. I lost 1.7

million dollars in three days' trading by being ahead of them. What's worse about it is that I take everybody else over that cliff with me. So now I have a responsibility to stay in the present and trade, because that's what everybody else is depending on. I may want to do other things, but I choose not to, because I know to get to a goal I've got to do it this way. And that's the way all traders should think."

You may be fearful that jacking up your target will force you to play the game in a different league. Of course it will, but that's the challenge. That's what will get you fired up in the morning. You can move into situations where you can be big, as well as into more liquid situations. This approach forces you to focus on your strength to produce new results. You can't venture off and do arbitrary stuff. The more you stay on your game, the better off you will be—you trade better because you are concentrating.

You don't have to start a new game, only improve the game you have always been playing. There is a fine line between developing additional skills and going off on a tangent. Don't get swayed into doing other things. Instead of just getting bigger and hiring more specialists to deal with other activities, the best way to improve is to do more of what you do best. If you are the head of a desk, or own your own trading firm, you can teach these principles to the traders who trade for you. You can help them get bigger, trading in your account. You can pay people to forget their own risk, and show them how to get involved in a bigger way in all their positions that warrant it. You may want to give each person who works for you a different sector to work on. When you add people, add those who are willing to trade the firm's profit and loss (P&L) and are willing to be team players. I'll talk more about teamwork in Chapter 9.

Observing Your Inner Thoughts

What do you say to yourself when you are going to trade? Do you think of trading to win versus trading not to lose?

"I am going to concentrate on not losing," says a trader named Sid. But then, he loses because the mind doesn't seem to correct for the negative characterization. It focuses on what he is concentrating on, in this case, losing, which is not the same as trading to win. It is better to set up a positive self-fulfilling prophecy.

Thoughts such as this have a significant impact on your performance, so it is a good idea to pay attention to them. If your thoughts are negative, you need to modify them in positive terms, to find ways of getting more excited about your trading. Don't think, "What if I lose money?" "What if I have a bad day?" Think: "How can I get bigger?" "How can I have a good day?" If you are down a bit, try to get smaller. Pay attention to your internal conversation. Think whether you are as aggressive as you should be. Are you gambling? Find a good idea you can believe in so you can say to yourself, "I have a good idea."

When you get aggressive about a good call that is confirmed by the market, you will feel on top of the day. These are the best moments of trading, and will give you confidence to keep pressing.

If you are tired and unsure, you are more inclined to make bad trades. Be patient. Work the count like great baseball hitters—Wade Boggs, or Tony Gwynn—do when they're at bat. Wait until you see the opportunity you have been preparing for. Being patient is especially important on a day when the market opens down and you start off in the hole. Don't let your early-morning loss color your judgment. Rather than quit and go home, wait for your pitch. If you see a good trade, don't delay in taking a decent position. Of course, there's no guarantee a move is going to work, but trade at a reasonable level. Don't fold or buy only a little when you know instinctively that the probability is good. Play the probability.

The most critical thing is to be able to make minute-to-minute decisions without hesitating. For example, Dale is a trader who routinely hesitates to buy a stock at the very moment he recognizes its potential. Invariably, he discovers that fifty percent of the advancing positions in these stocks have already taken place by the time he is ready to act. This delay in action is followed by public self-flagellation in which he draws attention to his failures. If he is to grow and take on bigger challenges, he needs to shun this self-defeating habit, which he holds on to because it lets him "be right" about "being wrong."

A new trader named Bob was inclined to hesitate and often found himself chasing after stocks as they went up in price. He, too, needed to learn that the time to act was when he first thought of buying the stock.

You have to learn to move when you are in a position. If you think the market is turning against you, get out. Once you make that decision to get out, don't wait until you're absolutely certain whether you're wrong or right. Don't get stuck waiting for more confirmation, or you'll invariably be behind the move. Keep making decisions all the time.

Choosing a Trading Method

Pick a trading method that works for you. You may want to play only certain sectors, like airline or bank or high-tech stocks. You may want to rely on several methods or several sources of information. To do this, you should try different methods and combinations until you find the method or combination of methods that meets your own needs. "Everyone who is successful has a very definitive style," says one super-trader, "but not a style carved in stone; it's got to be adaptive."

Talking to a group of new traders at a weekly seminar, Ric, head trader at a small trading house, had this general recommendation for developing a trading strategy: "What's the environment? Is the Dow up or down? What stocks are going up or down? What are the names and where are you today? Follow a list of fifty stocks. Can you find two or three names that fit the direction of the market? Which stocks are acting well? If you are bullish and have a big bid in a stock, focus on it if it is going up. Keep cycling through your list over and over again until something moves you and you buy five thousand shares. If you are bearish and think it is going down, look for shorts. When you finish the list, go back to the top of the list."

Ric continued, "If you start with fifty stocks every week, by Tuesday or Wednesday you will find something. Do your chart work and investi-gate these stocks. Keep cycling through the list. Is the stock up or in a down day? Stay with it for a day. Follow the stocks. On big up days you can see something and can pick the direction. Look for bids in your names. If you like the bids and like the actions—S&Ps are going up and somebody took the offer—why wait? Buy a little. If you are hot, buy five thousand. If you are cold, buy two thousand. Keep rotating names. Go through the cycle every fifteen minutes."

The trading method you have selected in the past might have been based more on your need for reassurance than on the value of its methodology. Whether you rely on technical analysis, fundamentals, or mechanical computer models will in large part be reflective of your life principle. Do you believe that history is likely to repeat itself, that a stock will follow certain patterns from the past? If so, you may be inclined to rely on a technical analysis.

If you are more flexible and freewheeling you may prefer a fundamental approach. This is especially true if you are the kind of person who relies on auditory learning and you like to get your information from others. You may get valuable information by talking to researchers and learning to assess the different opinions you hear in order to come to your own conclusions.

Keep in mind that the trading method is only a tool. How effective it is depends on you and, in large part, on your belief in the method, which should give you the confidence to trade intelligently.

Once you have a method and money management technique, you are faced with the day-to-day vagaries of the market, your own emotional reactions, and other challenges inherent in the trading process. This is the most crucial part of the game. This is what separates ordinary traders from the masters.

Creating a Structure of Fulfillment

Ideally, your goal helps you determine the strategy you need to take to realize it. Then you keep doing what is necessary to build the strategy. When your trading flows effortlessly from your strategy, you have found the path of least resistance. You don't need to keep struggling to realize your goal. You trade in terms of what is necessary to fulfill your commitments. You keep looking to see what is missing and remain comfortably involved in the process without getting anxious or interpreting errors as reflecting on yourself. You keep reviewing your trades without emotion, and keep correcting them in line with your goals. You remain totally focused on the task before you and use failures as feedback to bring you back to your center.

When you have committed to a goal, when you are doing what's necessary to express it, you'll find remarkable reserves of endurance and perseverance within yourself. You get beyond "good" and "bad," and you start seeing the marketplace as it is. You're on track to create your results from nothing but your commitment to a goal.

Each day provides the opportunity to commit. Problems and conflicts reveal themselves as occasions for growth and self-actualization, and you actually begin to welcome them.

Once you have determined the goal, your task is to determine what you need to do to trade consistently with the goal. It is not essential to think about the goal once you have established it and the steps for realizing it. You define your strategy in terms of the goal but you do not get obsessed with the goal. At the end of the day or the end of the week or month, you look back and check your results against your objective. You see whether you realized your objective and if you did what you were doing that was working, and if you didn't what you need to add to ensure that you do reach your goal. You want to see whether you were following your strategy or whether it dropped out for whatever reason so that you didn't reach your number.

I discussed this perspective with Max, a fairly successful trader who seemed to plateau every month at the same $300,000 figure.

From a review of previous performances, it was apparent that when he felt good he got too confident, and his strategy went to pot. He stopped doing those things that work for him. He let his discipline slide, and he become too complacent. Quicker than the blink of an eye, he was off the track. Now he had to build in a strategy that would not drop out. It was a game on top of a game, because he had to keep doing all the things that worked, and had to be on guard against things that didn't work. The game consisted of trying to raise his level of consciousness about all the thoughts he was having that were interfering with seeing the market or were coloring his view of the tape in the wake of his success.

Taking note of his tendency to stop trading when he reached $300,000, Max commented: "I have to recognize this point and decide I'm not going to get out of my good positions and take the profit. I'm going to hang in there. I've got to hold positions longer. If a stock is acting okay, I'm not going to sell it."

As an example, he mentioned his thoughts about Chase. "All day today I didn't make any sales in Chase, but I wanted to sell the thing twelve times. I'm holding on, holding on, holding on. The market was coming but I was holding on. I've been fighting my urge to sell all day long."

In fact, he actually bought more. "I'm trying to view it in the present as opposed to viewing it as 'I've got a profit.' "

Max's shifts underscore the value of a goal. As you raise the goal, you have to consider what parameters to change in terms of such things as the size of the trade and the time you stay in a winning trade before you take your profit. As the target gets higher, the strategy changes to be consistent with it. You keep trying to learn what is essential to learn to be able to play at that more advanced level.

Committing to Specifics

Committing to a specific goal means leaving behind a lot of old habits, such as "trading not to lose" or trading by following the crowd. It also means sidestepping your concerns about fluctuations of the marketplace.

Jason is reluctant. "How can I know what I will do until I see where the market goes today? Then I'll take advantage of the opportunity."

It is difficult for Jason and other traders to understand that if you commit to a certain vision and keep looking for evidence of that result, you don't have to press. You can keep looking in terms of this new set of expectations and increase the likelihood of your vision becoming reality. It won't happen if your thought is, "I'll see what will happen." Then you will simply see what happens rather than deciding in advance that you will see X amount of transactions.

Dirk, too, says this is hard to do. Older than many of the traders he works with, Dirk tends to overintellectualize, and often speaks from a platform of experience when referring to how things were during previous bull markets. He interprets commitment as pressing and believes that there is a very narrow difference between being at the cutting edge and pressing. He, therefore, gets nervous when he thinks about his avoidance patterns and his unwillingness to commit. Obviously, commitment is tougher to do than simply correcting bad habits and letting the numbers grow bigger.

Trading by objective does not mean playing big simply to play big. Rather, the trading objective enables the trader to stretch, to decide consciously on a course of action, rather than passively wait for market trends to govern decisions.

Are You Ready to Commit?

- How willing are you to commit 100 percent to being in the game? Are you held back by imagined restrictions placed on you by other obligations?
- Do you hold back in your trading because of a reluctance to let it be as good as it can be?
- Do you hold back from succeeding because of some childhood notions about not deserving success?
- Are you afraid that others will be disappointed or hurt if you tell them of your successes?
- How much do you distort reality because of fear of the consequences?
- Are you willing to face your failures without recrimination?
- Do you delude yourself with notions and rationalizations that you are limited by the nature of the marketplace or the tape?

The committed trader doesn't allow emotions to limit trading. This trader recognizes when habitual patterns come into play, especially in a negative market, but refuses to be influenced by them, as long as the original data supporting decisions remain tenable.

The committed trader is willing to embrace uncertainty in the process of expanding horizons. Because of this ability, the trader is able to make remarkable things happen.

You can tell whether you are genuinely involved by looking carefully at the way you are trading so as to see what factors are influencing you.

Rungs on the Ladder of Commitment

To be a committed trader, you must remember past trades, good and bad, and be careful to differentiate between what happened and what you believe happened. You must mark your day's results to the market so that you can see what you *did* and differentiate that from what you *felt*. What's the point? In the future you want to be governed by the facts and their relationship to what you did. In this way, each day you can correct your experiences so that your memories are clear, and you move forward with sharper perceptions about the market.

In essence, commitment requires three major stages:

The first is a willingness to dig in and put yourself at risk. It involves learning to function with uncertainty, without knowing how events will unfold, even though this is not the ordinary way in which we function.

The second stage is to recognize and then put aside all the negative thoughts about the consequences of raising your sights or of stretching the envelope. To do this you must learn to overcome the instinct for self-preservation, which favors the status quo. There's a tendency among traders is to play it too safe.

Billy is a case in point. Explaining one trade involving Eli Lilly and Company, Billy says, "Today I was long Lilly. I made one point on twenty-five thousand shares. Kept twenty-five thousand shares. Then it went up another two points. I made a decision not to sell it, and it went down two points without doing anything. I had figured on a big profit. In retrospect, it was a mistake not to sell it. Even if I bought it back, I would have made fifty thousand dollars."

Billy's trading reflects a reluctance to be flat (even) in a situation, and a concern about not making a mistake. Billy didn't buy enough initially, and kept a position so as not to miss the high. When you trade this way, you stay in a neutral zone. You are not reacting fast enough. Billy's negative thoughts about the past hurt the ability to profit in the present.

If you are at all like Billy, you may experience an erosion of goals and a resurgence of an internal pressure "not to lose" in the face of frustration or failure. When your perceptions of the market are distorted by your emotional reactivity and your decision making is compromised, it's a good idea to declare a "breakdown" and acknowledge the effect of your emotions.

How do you overcome such inhibitions? By bringing into play the third stage of commitment, which is to increase the complexity of the task and the size of the challenge that you make. This forces you to bring more of yourself into your work, to pursue your own trading vision consciously and actively. The positive value of raising the stakes will be reflected not only in optimizing your trading results but in transforming the rest of your life.

For instance, a belief in your own insufficiency may lead you to start

Thirteen Ways to Increase Commitment

1. Use all your talents.
2. Cut out distractions.
3. Eliminate the tendency to trade more instruments or sectors than you can follow.
4. Choose good fundamental names over poor names.
5. Stop hesitating and holding back.
6. Be willing to ask for help when you are stymied.
7. Identify your usual constraints and beliefs, and go beyond them.
8. Learn to go beyond your usual style. If you are an event trader and need an earnings report or some catalytic news event to trade, increase your communications. Make more research calls when there are changes. Call other analysts who deal with your sectors.
9. Find out more details about the sequence of events leading to decreased stock prices.
10. Get to work earlier.
11. Write down the most important things.
12. Write down your day's target.
13. Develop a checklist of tough questions to ask regarding moves to make on particular trades, especially when you are stopped or don't know what to do next.

relying on others who you think have power. In fact, to become independent and self-actualizing you need to develop your own power and be circumspect about how much power you endow in others. Let them contribute what they can, but don't rely on them to make you whole or to realize your vision. Ultimately, it is your ability and your effort that are critical to your success.

Sometimes traders give up their self-reliance as they get bigger. The task for them is to stop tuning into ambiguous signals from the boss and concentrate on trading their own style. They may need to get an assistant to clean up their bad trades, so they can go to the next thought without spending time on getting out of losing trades. If you want an assistant, go get one. Bite the bullet. Stop second-guessing yourself by waiting for approval.

The key question is to decide what your game is, how to get better at it, and how to take advantage of the capital available. Don't keep expecting the boss or someone else to do it for you.

Once you become independent, your boss is certain to notice you are moving forward. But you need to make those moves on your own. There will always be more capital for you to use.

Commitment, therefore, is not so much hard work as it is promising yourself to realize an uncertain goal and then doing what it takes to reach that goal—which often means giving up old habits and beliefs. It also means a willingness to allow yourself to be uncomfortable when you are in unknown territory. It may help to keep a diary. Record your feelings so as to see the relationship between your emotional responses and your performance. You'll neutralize anxiety by writing about your discomfort, facing it, and discovering how transient it is. Keep asking yourself: What else can I do to raise my level of commitment to 100 percent?

Living in the Gap

By putting an emphasis on commitment, you empower yourself. You realize that your goal is not about building your image or getting approval, which you may search for when you feel envy, jealousy, or boredom. Rather, it is about focusing on doing what is consistent with your goal.

Let me emphasize that living in the gap is not so much about achieving the results as it is about living in terms of the goal, rather than becoming attached to it. Results are simply a measure of your commitment, telling you how you are doing and what is missing. If you don't produce a result, look to see what is missing from your strategy and trading actions. Don't become attached to your results, either exulting in having reached them or feeling inadequate for not reaching them.

Ask yourself constantly, "Am I willing to do what I said I would do?" Repeated review of this question over time will help you to get more engaged in your trading and less handcuffed by fears and outmoded habits. Focusing on the present in the face of failure and uncertainty is an inherent part of living in the gap.

When you act in terms of your commitment, you step to the edge of the abyss, all the while devising a strategy in line with your vision. Old self-doubts and distractions compete with that vision.

For example, Austin realized that trading in futures was a distraction for him. They gave him a small sense of winning, but in the meantime he was not trading the stocks in which he had major positions. Once he stopped trading futures, he doubled his profits on his basket of stocks.

The gap between where you are and where you want to be can be a source of creation or a source of problems, depending on how you deal with it. You can deny the gap, or you can recognize it as an opportunity for growth. You can respond to it habitually, or you can use it as a source of mastery.

The power of living in the gap comes from your willingness to admit to your problems. Once you acknowledge them, you can begin to enlarge your trading successfully. One trader we know sits at his desk and pouts about being ignored. He is invested in a long-term self-concept of being abandoned and left behind. The repeated reactivation of this familiar demon keeps him from investing his energies into trading. To trade in terms of his abilities and his conscious desire to succeed, he must recognize and give up his self-concept of being abandoned. This will help him let go of his built-in negative expectations of himself, which reinforce his impulse to keep taking certain but limited profits.

You can't get away from telling the truth to yourself. If you really want to produce a specific result you should acknowledge it, and then develop a strategy consistent with the result.

Once you realize that you don't know what your limits are, you are better prepared to live in the gap. In fact, it is the size of the discrepancy you can tolerate that determines the amount of energy you can generate so as to shift your life into a miraculous realm.

Overcoming Fear

The greatest resistance I run into when working with traders concerns fear—the avoidance of the tension that is created when a trader is asked to commit to specific financial objectives. Most traders prefer pursuing vague goals such as "doing the best possible." Like most people, traders are reluctant to commit themselves to an uncertain future without a guarantee that they will be able to produce the result. They may not see for a while, if ever, that promising the future will raise their level of performance.

This process does not simply mean working harder or pumping yourself up with positive affirmations (which more often than not cause burnout and frustration). Instead, it involves a willingness to explore all the ramifications of your trading. To do this, you must ask tough, specific questions.

You will experience discomfort when you begin trading at new levels. Until you learn how to tolerate it, you may experience internal psychological pressure to lower your trading target and to revert to old and familiar ways. Before you know it, you are "trading not to lose" instead of "trading to win."

How do you learn such tolerance? Start by observing how your thoughts and behavior patterns keep you locked into a particular trading plateau. Only then can you develop new behavior to go beyond that comfort zone.

Jed, for example, had been consistently successful in making a steady daily profit for more than a year, and with prodding from his manager committed to an increase in position size. After several months of unsuccessful trading, close analysis revealed that he was trying to scale into a longer position a little bit at a time and was paying more each time, perhaps even contributing to the rising price. "If you are confident about the stocks, buy more to start with. That's how to play bigger," his manager said. "Trust your judgment."

It takes a firm decision and considerable practice in self-awareness to resist impulses to reduce tension, whether by taking positions that are too small, as Jed did; by scalping quick profits; or by holding on to a losing position in the hope that things will turn around. It takes a strong resolve to circumvent the natural pull toward avoidance and withdrawal, which gets especially intense as you get closer to reaching your objectives.

Most of your distress comes from covering up your feelings and thoughts, not from the actual event. When you are trading, if you are fearful, feel the fear. If there is sadness below the fear, notice that as

Ten Tough Questions to Ask Yourself about Your Goal

1. What is the amount I intend to make?
2. By when will I make it?
3. What do I have to do that I am not doing now in order to produce this result?
4. What beliefs and habits of trading do I have to relinquish to stay with the goal?
5. How much capital do I need?
6. How many shares must I purchase, and how long should I hold them?
7. When should I enlarge my position?
8. What must I pay attention to with regard to managing my losses?
9. How much more capital can I put at risk so as to increase my profitability on the upside while managing my downside risk?
10. What else can I do to increase confidence in my trading selection?

well. Allow yourself to be fully alive to whatever you are feeling in the moment before you. Allow your financial goal to create a context of challenge, which will lead you to become more engaged in the now.

Living in the Present

To be in the now is to be present to the world with the knowledge that you have everything you need to realize your vision. You allow time for things to develop without pushing for closure. You accept the uncertainty of reality, and do not see it as a reflection of your own inadequacy or incompetence. You stop focusing on the future and recognize that there is only the moment before you in which to act.

Your goal is both a compass and magnet, but it is not an end in itself, nor is it the be-all and end-all. It is useful in helping you to become as fully engaged in your trading as possible, but its realization will not fulfill you.

Shifting Strategies

With a new and expanded vision of yourself, you will be able to ask difficult questions of yourself and take difficult positions to transform your trading approach.

Proactive strategies usually require a conscious shift from habit. Phil, dominated by memories of "crashing and burning," was afraid to use larger amounts of his trading capital to buy and hold volatile stocks. Slowed by chronic fears of disaster, he had to learn that his manifestations of anxiety were identical to those of excitement. When he began to trade proactively, he consciously put himself at greater risk by buying larger orders of higher-priced stocks than he had ever bought previously, so as to play commensurately with his strategic objectives. He also began to use significantly more of his available capital. With the help of others who were willing to help him realize his objectives, he significantly changed his style of trading from one dominated by fear and past memories to one based largely on the perspective of his trading objective, and has, thus, increased his monthly profits. In time he has learned to interpret the discomfort of anxiety as a clue to the fact that he is entering the zone of creative trading and that his successes could be correlated with his willingness to track in this zone.

In effect, traders must learn to notice the impact of their unconscious fears and expectations on their trading behavior and take more responsibility for their actions, using their discomfort to empower them in terms of conscious choices based on their stated goals. This allows you to see that the result is only a reflection of your strategy, and not a reflection of yourself. In this way, you only need to focus on determining your capital amount, the stocks' volatility, and your position sizes, in line with your strategy, to begin to realize your financial objectives.

This may mean raising both your exit and stop-loss points and buying more of a rising stock if the fundamentals are unchanged rather than following your inclination to take a profit. It may also mean letting go of losing stocks rather than holding on to them. Studies of risk-taking behavior have consistently shown that most people tend to avoid risks when seeking gain but accept risks to avoid losses. This explains why people are more inclined to hold on to losing positions that in reality they should discard.

Here's how Jed handles such a situation. "I check out my losers when I know there's no upside to them, when a stock doesn't reach the point where I think it should go. Hoping becomes a distraction, and I find that if something becomes a distraction it's like rolling the dice—I don't have an edge. I have to kick the whole day out. Granted it may go up, but it's just one of these up-in-the-air situations."

To succeed, the trader must separate comfort needs from trading reality in order to act rationally. This proactive approach enables a trader to drop a preoccupation with losses amid a negative spiral. If there are no willing buyers or if there is a rush of sellers, the committed trader can begin to look for new opportunities without spending time fruitlessly in an attempt to get his or her money back.

Choosing What You Have

A vital aspect of trading in the gap is to "choose what you have." I use this phrase to mean noticing—even embracing—certain judgments and interpretations you make about yourself and your circumstances that foster feelings of inadequacy and incompleteness. Embrace them as aspects of yourself—and then let them go. (As Jed noted in the prior example, hoping was simply a distraction.) These feelings are generated the moment you look to be elsewhere or to get somewhere else to feel all right. So if you can choose what you have, right in front of you, many of these feelings will naturally dissipate.

Choosing what you have means finding the resources within yourself to make your life work. To look elsewhere for the answer out of the erroneous notion that your sense of self will come from someplace outside yourself is to split yourself psychologically.

By choosing what you have, you can reduce the pain, struggle, and waste of energy that comes from looking for something you do not have and ignoring the strength that you *do* have. By accepting yourself and focusing on the moment before you, listening without judgment, taking risks, and letting go of superstitions, you are able to move beyond the psychological comfort zone to a more creative zone.

For instance, Jed knew he had "turned a little bit of the corner" one Friday, when he had his biggest day ever—$50,000. "I definitely did gain some confidence because I knew I could do it. I proved it." Now, he adds, "I'm more patient. I've been staying with the good things longer. I've been selling the bad things that aren't working."

To be fully present in the moment before you, you must choose what is, rather than trying to change things to fit what you think is the right answer. Waiting for the right answer before you act is a trap. You may think you are doing something when you are deciding on the right way to go or the right path to follow, when in fact you actually are mired in your thinking. The issue is to choose or not to choose, not choose the right answer.

The more you do this, the more you'll get into the zone. The more you're in the zone, the more you discover that life is not something to be grasped or gained or to be realized through achievement but is something to be lived fully in the present. You can only live in the next moment. Ideally when you enter fully into the next moment through the perspective of your vision, you uncover your potential for courage and creativity. Choosing what is does not require effort but only a willingness to go past your fearful thoughts and preconceptions and to bring as much of yourself into play as possible in the moments before you.

The same principle of "choosing what you have," rather than denying it or trying to change it, applies to unpleasant emotions. Instead of struggling to contain or escape your feelings, you can learn to experience them and thereby master them, instead of using up your energy hiding them. When you own up to these uncomfortable feelings, you reduce the internal split or psychological separation that you create by trying to deny your feelings, and you become more alive in the present moment of your life.

It doesn't matter whether you think you should or shouldn't be angry, jealous, guilty, frightened. Notice your feelings. Accept them. When you struggle to separate your emotions from yourself, you may project your own fears onto the world—and the world begins to look frightening and unpredictable. If you can accept your fears as part of yourself, your fears of the world will pass. I'll have more to say about feelings of fear in Part Three.

What Commitment Means in Different Market Cycles

Commitment to a goal demands patience, since the result may take twice as long as you anticipated. It also means paying attention to negative results—breakdowns—as well as other indicators that suggest you should examine what you need to do to correct your course of action.

In a bull market, the committed trader is willing to increase risk by extending time horizons—by being late to buy, and by not selling so soon—and is also willing to buy more stocks that are volatile. And the trader continues to ask what is still missing from his or her strategy. A chartist, for example, should be willing to make more calls to get fundamentalist confirmation of tape activity.

In a stock market that's starting to reverse itself and is becoming choppy, the committed trader may want to get out in a shorter time frame and take profits. In choppy markets, you have to sell stocks when they are up and buy them when they are down.

In rising markets, when interest rates are stable or going lower, you buy more stocks when the interest rate is moving down. An example is the high-momentum type market that occurred in the first half of 1996 when fund managers were buying what was going up, thereby creating momentum.

With high interest rates you look for inflation and lower corporate profits and a falling market.

In a bear market, you're en route to becoming a committed trader by learning to feel the discomfort of betting against the trend. Bearish traders also must learn to ride out countertrend rallies by continually adjusting their stops upward. In addition, the experienced bear traders must learn to protect themselves from losing too much by covering short positions when they are wrong or buying into the rally rather than holding on.

The Value of Proactive Trading

As a proactive trader, you won't be governed by your own cautious responses to trading dilemmas or market downturns. You can continually assess whether you are utilizing an appropriate amount of your capital or whether you need to trade larger for more volatile positions. In the process, you grow more confident, and you're able to embrace the inherent paradox of excitement and discomfort associated with risk taking.

The trading room contains the Holy Grail, and each trader must search to find the components of it. It's right in the room, but most traders don't see it, because it's very hard to see. It's invisible. It's intangible. It's between the lines. It's a very subtle thing, but it's out there—and those who are 100 percent committed are able to discover it.

Chapter Seven

Basic Trading Principles

A market exists as long as there are a buyer and a seller who put a different value on a particular item and are willing to negotiate a price that satisfies both of them. Traders buy and sell stocks and other financial instruments in order to benefit from fluctuations in prices. The process maintains a fluid market.

The price of a stock is determined by the interaction between buyers and sellers who together create a market. The fluctuations in expectations about these prices are subject to myriad variables and have strong emotional effects on buyers and sellers, which contribute to the fluctuating nature of the markets. If prices are expected to rise, there is a natural increase in the sense of greed in the participants. If there is an expectation of prices dropping, emotions of panic are triggered. Between these two extremes varying combinations of these emotional responses influence events. Various factors influence beliefs about the stocks, which in turn influence stocks' behavior in the future. It is because of the uncertainty of this behavior, and the interaction of the variables, that there is a market at all.

The skillful trader learns to read these variables while analyzing the market. The problem inherent in analyzing the market is that the markets are always changing and past events can at best give you only some indication of future events. Past events are not correlated with future events and do not predict them.

While there are numerous methods for analyzing the market, you are well advised to pick the one that is most compatible with your approach to stocks. If you are inclined to focus on price action, you will most likely want to do technical analysis. If you prefer to focus on information about the goods themselves, you ought to rely on fundamental analysis.

Trading, too, is the result of many variables, not simply the trading method you have selected. It takes many ingredients to make a successful trader. How you handle the seesawing effects of the marketplace and the emotions they provoke often turns out to be a more significant factor in your trading success than the trading method you have chosen. You may have used a good method and selected a good stock that trends upward, but suddenly it gaps down on the opening of the next day. You begin to panic and experience anxiety and the fear of losing. You hold on hoping against hope that it rallies. It does rally, and you experience an uplifting of spirits and a surge of confidence. But then it drops again, and you are plunged into a crisis mode, until finally, at the day's end, you are exhausted and uncertain as to whether you want to continue. Meanwhile, you have been focused on this stock all day long, and it has taken your attention away from many other opportunities.

Although it cannot be separated from your mastery of the basic elements of trading, ultimately how you think, feel, and manage your feelings is critical to your trading success. Emotions can throw off your trading by influencing your ability to function in a high-risk situation. Fear can paralyze you into inaction or it can lead you to act impulsively so as to get rid of the fearful thoughts and feelings. Fear colors your objectivity and ability to consider all aspects of a question and to maintain that degree of internal calm that will enable you to stay with your discipline.

Greed is another emotion to master. Afraid of being late to the party, or being left out, Jim would often jump into a position impulsively, trying not to lose an opportunity. He would pay more for a stock and then proceed into self-flagellation. Gad would compulsively pursue high-flying stocks over $100 because of anxiousness for a quick profit and the chance for a home run. Over time, Gad became addicted to the quick fix or a big win to be bailed out of previous losses.

You can't outwit the market. It is bigger than you are and less predictable than you would like it to be, even when you think you are trading rationally with a mathematical system. No computer model, no market theory can take into account all the subtleties of the marketplace. Besides, the psychology of the marketplace does not necessarily follow mathematical logic. Sometimes, factors that give you an edge might happen in an instant before they can be evaluated by your computer. That's why a day trader has certain advantages.

I should also note that advances in technology have made possible the rapid dissemination of information to market players throughout the world. This adds a new element of speed and momentum, which intensifies the changes. You must be able to adapt to this speed if you are going to be successful.

While economists think the market follows certain laws in determining the fair price of a stock, in actual fact there is only uncertainty. According to Drew, a mathematician turned systems analyst, "Most traders have no reliable information, but believe they are randomly rewarded for their efforts." This "selection bias" suggests that the market is almost a crapshoot, and that success doesn't always mean that you know what you are doing.

"The quality of information is exploitable, and gives you an edge," continues Drew, an individualist with a long beard who wears baggy pants with suspenders, and who is able to casually reduce complex themes into simple terms. "But this differs from trader to trader, and firm to firm. It takes experience to assimilate information that can improve your trading. You don't have to understand your trading to do well. The market's random pattern lets everyone win at least some of the time."

As a trader, your role is to function in this uncertain environment and to adapt on a daily basis to the market's fickle nature. To become a really good trader, you can't rely on early successes; such reliance instills false confidence. You need to learn how to trade. You need to be able to assess your trades, and know why you have won and what you must continually do under changing circumstances to win consistently.

While you can't control marketplace variables, you can detect trends if you look and listen for repetitive patterns. You can learn to read the market, rather than control it. You can learn to go with the flow, or go against it when you have information about certain stocks that helps you anticipate stock market moves.

You can't win all the time. However, mathematically, if your expectation of your reward is greater than your loss, you will win most of the time. To find trades that are more profitable than risky takes effort and discipline, two things that are vital to making your trading strategy a success.

You have to develop counterintuitive abilities that allow you to maintain your balance despite the roller-coaster moments in a volatile system. Your intellectual ability won't help you here, nor will money management methodology. Past performance is not always related to present performance. The best you can do is develop a probability model. Then, you've got to discipline yourself to follow that model, rather than follow your gut instincts.

The capricious, random character of the market can provoke stress and other emotional responses. Sure, stress is a natural reaction—but it can be deleterious to your performance, and it must be conquered. I'll talk more about how to deal with stress and anxiety during the workday in Chapter 11.

Even more than dealing with stress, you must be capable of accepting responsibility for your moves during the trading day. You need to be patient and enthusiastic, while remaining emotionally detached from your trades. Unfortunately, most traders, even professionals, even floor specialists, lack training in managing their responses to the challenges. I'll deal more with this, too, in Chapter 13.

The very uncertainty of the market is one aspect that makes it so appealing to super-traders. Magic, for a super-trader, occurs when he or she overcomes the uncertainty and figures out what is happening before it happens. It is when the trader can sense a change in direction, and unlock the puzzle before the pieces have come together. That's what every trader shoots for—that kind of perfect day!

But what about the tough days? When the market starts to move against you, you need to be able to move out, take your losses, and adjust your positions. You perform best when you keep the good trades and shuffle the bad ones. But many traders only look at their winners, and forget their losers. In order to succeed, you must concentrate on the losers and limit your losses. All day long, on the perfect days and the lousy ones, you're taking risks, reaching into the unknown.

Studying Risk-Taking Behavior

The market is a natural laboratory for studying risk-taking behavior and the ways people handle the unknown.

All traders try to reduce their risk by understanding patterns in individual companies, and the marketplace in general. Super-traders, however, do this and more. They monitor their own perspectives based on their own past experiences and their own stress response systems. The master trader puts great importance on managing risk and keeping losses under control. Once this is mastered, the chances of increasing profitability increase exponentially.

It's natural to cling to your original belief in a stock. Remember, however, that you are a proactive trader, not a passive investor. You can buy and sell. On the best trading days, you have the most amount of motion possible.

To deal with risk, you need to comprehend basic trading tenets, as well as possess a set of psychological or mental skills. Among other things, when you are assessing the market, try to determine if the activity is real. Are the leaders participating in the market? The computer screen will not tell you who is trading, but you can follow the flow. If the market is down 40, and they (the market, the mythical forces behind the market) are taking NASDAQ stocks, it may not be the right time for you to sell stocks.

You can assess reality by watching the buying and selling of others. Suppose there are bonds and blocks trading up. Depending on how close you can get to the action on the floor, you can see whether there are buyers and sellers. The same names will show up on the floor. You'll see sectors moving in unison.

While stocks turn around after much buying when all the buyers are out, this doesn't matter to traders. The market may go down 500 points, but there are rallies all through the day in which you can trade. And throughout the day, the risks continue. You must adapt your reactions to them.

Thirty-One Basic Risk Management Guidelines

1. Consider the risk of a trade when you enter it.
2. Evaluate the potential profitability of the trade.
3. Determine entry and exit points based on your approach to the market. If you are a technical trader you look for factors such as support levels, violation of which would trigger a sale. If you are a fundamentalist you look for factors such as reversals in the interest in the stock.
4. Establish an exit point based on the amount of profitability you want from the trade, using a number or a percent of total value of the trade.
5. Establish a set of rules about closing down your trading for the day once you reach a certain amount of loss.
6. Stay with your established discipline.
7. In highly volatile markets, be extra cautious in managing your positions, especially short positions.
8. If you are short and you see the market going down and your stock is not coming in, start buying back the stock instead of waiting for the market to continue coming in. Overcome your tendency to keep from covering your shorts because you think the market is going to fall apart.
9. Don't fight the tape all day long. Don't keep looking for shorts when the tape is trending up throughout the day.
10. Look at each position on its own merits. Don't justify being in one stock by being ahead in another stock. Keep figuring your risk/reward ratio on each position and on each new increment you take in stock.
11. Be satisfied with your positions if they are stretch positions. Don't always be looking to hit a home run.
12. Stay with things longer and try to get bigger, rather than trade in and out. Get bigger in your winners and kick out the ones that aren't working.
13. Try to diversify. Traders lose the most money when they are loaded up on one side of the market and making a big bet the next day. Diversity doesn't mean to hedge but to have a diversity of ideas.

14. Keep moving. Don't get wedded to your choices. Keep reviewing and renewing your choices.

15. If you're a compulsive gambler, you need to focus on a reasonable target and stop copying the big guys by swinging for the fences. If you make five thousand dollars a day consistently, you will make over a million dollars a year.

16. Devise rules you can live by and stick to them.

17. When your Achilles' heel is exposed, admit your vulnerability. Recognize that you can't do it all yourself. When you reach your target, notice any tendency to keep trying to squeeze more profit from your trades.

18. Keep asking yourself questions about alternative strategies or reasons why stocks are moving in particular directions.

19. When stocks are closing against you, get out. You can always get back in.

20. Measure your risk/reward ratio. Compare your risk to the profit potential in a particular trade. If your trade is going well, stay with it.

21. When you add to a position consider how much risk and reward you are adding. If you are doing well, perhaps that's all you can expect for today's trade. Don't stretch your luck.

22. If you get bigger and stay longer you increase your risk in a high-volatility market.

23. When you buy a group, you increase your profitability and you reduce your risk through diversification. Increase the number of positions you take and you increase your chance for profitability.

24. Keep looking at what compels you to trade in a certain way. Is it rational from a trading viewpoint or is it merely a reflection of your personality and style?

25. If you take too many positions to cover yourself, you lose the maximum punch.

26. Remember that traders lose the most money when they load up on one side and make a bigger bet the next day.

27. Diversity is good.

28. Trade more quickly.

> ### *Thirty-One Basic Risk Management Guidelines (Continued)*
>
> **29.** To be successful, keep moving. Don't get too attached to a stock.
>
> **30.** If you are a compulsive trader who frequently blows up, control your risk by lowering your targets and being more aware of your risks. Stop swinging for the fences. When you are about to do something stupid, ask for help. Go back to making a steady $5000 to $10,000 a day and you will soon be successful.
>
> **31.** Have good reasons to buy a stock. Is it at the low end of the range? Has it been upgraded by an investment house? Is the valuation of the group going up?

Keeping the Faith

"Stay with the winners and get rid of the losers" is a basic tenet. It sounds easy enough to follow, but you need internal strength to do this. You can't do it without having faith in your decisions. If you don't build your confidence, you'll let the pain govern you. Some guys blow up (lose big). Conrad, a whiz kid who attended New York's Stuyvesant High School for super-smart youngsters, and who retains a touch of the big city's wise guy attitude, refused to cover his shorts when the market went against him. He was still operating out of some grandiose notion of himself based on the past. Conversely, when he was winning he could not control his euphoria and often started shooting for the fences. He began experiencing wide swings of profits and losses until he finally lost all of his profits.

Traders like Conrad who don't go with the trend often lose money. They bounce up and down. They think they can outsmart the market. For them trading is an intellectual game. It's stimulating, but it's not profitable. They are making it five times as hard for themselves—like hiking up the side of a mountain instead of taking the paved road.

Brent, an old tape trader I know, had to stop trading against the trend in order to be more profitable. Since he was getting into trouble on short stops, it was recommended that he never sell a stock that was up and that he should short stocks that weren't going up. That way he would make money on the long side, and not lose so much on the short side. In effect, he was encouraged to eliminate the short side in order to become profitable consistently. Six months later, after repeated sessions and two forced withdrawals, Brent began to demonstrate a string of consistently successful weeks of trading.

"What are you doing now that's different?" I asked him at our weekly seminar.

"I'm limiting my risks," he replied. "I'm not exposing myself to a forty-thousand-dollar loss. I know I can come in every day and make between ten and twenty thousand dollars trading. But I didn't think that was okay in the past, because everybody else was making a hundred thousand every day. I was the wrong way on the market most of the time, my timing was off, and I was shooting to make fifty grand in each position when I didn't have the cushion if I was wrong. I feel better now making ten to twenty grand and sleeping at night. It's easier to be long if I'm short a couple of stocks. I feel more comfortable if it's balanced.

"The great temptation is to try to be smart and short into a rally figuring it's going to turn around and drop. It's hard to go in the direction of the market. I could go with the flow if I didn't have the fear of what could happen if the market ever went down. I wish I didn't have that fear."

Brent continued, "I've been here for four years. I guess I have been afraid that the market's going to turn because I saw it turn once in the past. I also feel uncomfortable when the success is so easy. The correct way is to buy strong stocks and sell weak stocks, and that's what works, and to buy low and sell high."

That's why you have to mark to the market (track your position as a win or loss against the actual value of the stock at the end of the day so you know whether you lost or gained profitability—the true measure of your performance), and know your profit or admit your loss. This keeps you in the present moment.

How do you minimize your imperfections and maximize your potential? How do you ride out your errors and keep your emotions under control and keep assessing reality in order to make optimal choices more of the time than not? To begin with, as I mentioned before, be proactive. Have a reason to trade. Take time to research your stocks and to devise a strategy.

The Psychology of Profit Taking

Trading to win is not a perfect game. To be a risk taker, you have to be able to face the truth and know the odds, even if you've been wrong. You don't have to be right every time. Telling the truth is what separates the big guys from the little guys.

Traders may be unwilling to postpone their profit taking in order to make a larger profit. They may be unwilling to ride out successful trades. They prefer a sure trade to a fairly safe gamble for a bigger profit. Sometimes these same traders are reluctant to take a small loss and get out of a losing position, or to make a high-risk gamble that a falling stock will reverse direction.

It's better to sell and take a profit than to hold on to a stock because you believe it can't go down. Here, you need to learn that you can always buy back into a stock you have sold. It doesn't matter what you did earlier in the day. If it is going down, it doesn't matter where you got in. You should get out, and instead find what's going up or sell short.

There is also value in staying in a position if the fundamentals still hold. As Ric, the 40-year-old head trader, explains: "You have to have a purpose. I buy a lot of things on fundamentals, and if all the fundamentals are still there, if the business is supposed to be sound, and the management knows what they're doing and each quarter they meet their numbers, then if nobody else in the whole world recognizes what the stock is worth, I still think it's worth it. It's not costing me a loss if it never trades."

Trading strategies vary with the longer-range objectives of the trader. Most portfolio managers don't dare step up and sell when they have to perform against the Standard & Poor's 500 Index (S&P). All they're concerned about is matching the S&P. For example, let's say today you saw a melt in the high-cap stocks, people indexing more, buying S&Ps, putting the excess money in T-bills, the excess money that they would normally have put into stocks. But portfolio managers aren't going to get out of the market. They can't. If they underperform, they lose their jobs. Chasing the index now won't enhance your performance against the S&P. It will just match you to it from this point on. The only way to catch up is to buy the dips.

Psyching Out the Losers

The losing trader cannot tolerate the stress of a changing market. While focused on disaster, it is difficult to process useful information and to trade wisely. Stress also reduces the ability to make decisions. As the trader loses, anxiety intensifies, producing behavior that may multiply losses. The losing trader increasingly relies on others because of anxiety and cannot make independent decisions.

Another response to loss is to repeat oneself, to make more of the same efforts rather than to step back and reassess. The losing trader keeps trading the same stocks in the same way. Reliance on memories of past trading experiences and remaining stuck in an old trading style keep one from seeing what is happening today. A trader may put too much energy into trying to protect a losing position, hoping that it will turn around, rather than saving energy by getting out of the trade. The unwillingness to face the truth and readjust to the new requirements of today's market is a good example of the psychological defenses of denial and rationalization that lock the losing trader into repeating yesterday's errors with yesterday's strategy.

Micky, a new trader, described quite vividly this phenomenon:

"I had a bad day. I was on the long side of Sara Lee. While it was happening, I was in a vicious circle. Being down overnight produced an urge to get it back. When that happens I do irrational things thinking the stock will go back up, not selling it, hoping it won't lose more. Then the stock goes further down and I'll twist myself thinking the stock will go to zero, and then I will try to sell it—selling it right in the hole, taking it right back to the place I originally bought it at. I am whipsawed. Then I lose that chance. Just wrong, a very uncomfortable, confusing, lost feeling.

"On Friday the market was trying to break. I was down three to four thousand. I sold three different stocks—three thousand shares of each. Market whipped back up. I bought them at the market, covering them all up half a dollar. Fifteen hundred, fifteen hundred, fifteen hundred—that was another forty-five hundred. Then I was completely exhausted, wiped out; at 3:30 I was done."

At first glance it appears that Mickey was acting rationally. The stock opened against him. He got out. He traded three stocks when he thought the market was breaking and it was wrong and he got out. But for Mickey, "I was wrong; given the volatility of the market I didn't have to be as big as I was. My goal is two thousand dollars per day or four thousand on a good day. But here, I'm down in the hole five thousand. I'm trying to get even. I see the market break and I go up on three very volatile stocks. Given the volatility of the market that's like trying to make twelve thousand to fourteen thousand dollars. I'm trying to get this market to break and I'm going to be there for one and a half to two points on each of these stocks."

Mickey recounted his emotional trading: "I looked up and picked three market stocks. I didn't have to enter all three trades. I was just selling stocks to sell stocks. I sold too much of them. There was nothing behind the trades. I sold so much I panicked. In retrospect I was buying the top, after I got whipped. The first time, it was like the hell with it, I lost so much money; no way they're going to break them without me. So I sold them all out again. If the market had broken I'd've made fifteen thousand dollars. I was out of control. I felt, now I am going to sell them, the hell with the risk."

There are other forms of self-sabotage. Some traders show up five minutes before the market opens. They drink the night before. They blow up after getting hot. They think of success as luck, rather than as a result of skills they've practiced.

All this denial and rationalization, this unwillingness to face the truth and readjust, are psychological defenses of a trader who repeats yesterday's errors with yesterday's strategy. Traders like this can make several million dollars a year, but they can't get to be super-traders, nor do they get as much satisfaction and fulfillment out of trading as is possible.

Why Traders Hate Losses

Traders hate to take losses because it implies admitting error. Loss aversion combined with ego leads to gambling—clinging to errors in the hope that the market will reverse. We all know this, but what is interesting is that many traders believe, at least unconsciously, that loss is less painful when it is an addition to a larger loss than when it is a freestanding loss. It seems easier for a trader to resign emotionally from playing the game, to give up and allow himself to be wiped out so he can start fresh the next day, than to keep fighting to cut losses.

There is less sense of responsibility for losing big than there is for taking a smaller loss and owning the loss. This pattern was described graphically and dramatically by Mort, a 27-year-old second-year trader with a lot of guts.

"When I traded smaller increments I would get out at a quarter or a half point down. If I wanted to make a half, I had to get out at a quarter. Now I'm trading bigger and I don't sell something until it's not acting right and breaks the support level. I bought Stride Rite at thirteen. It came off when the market came off. Someone sold one million shares at twelve. I bought more at twelve. Sold it at twelve and a quarter. I should have been selling. It went down to twelve. I held on because I didn't think it was going to be as bad as it could be. I lost one and a half points on thirty thousand to fifty thousand shares. I was buying it, trading it, selling it. I didn't lock in the profit. I was trading for a bigger move. I needed to cut losses and was hoping someone would push me to sell it."

Mort continues the story:

"As it goes down, it doesn't look like I can get out of fifty thousand shares. I figure I might as well hold on to it because it is unlikely to hurt me where it is, and I am sure I am going to take it to the bottom. At the time, I am paralyzed. I'm too optimistic and listening to too many stories. By the time I sell, I have to sell and have no choice. I keep figuring if I can get rid of this situation my profits will soar. I believe it will move. I find it hard to make the sale; I don't want to lock in the loss. When it runs, I have my position on. What's wrong is the perception that I can't sell it because there is no buyer, and I am going to have to be the one who knocks it down."

Commenting on his trading, Sandy noted: "If you are aware of this mental shift, you need not resign yourself to being stuck with losers. You can learn to notice your thoughts and then act in terms of your discipline or the discipline imposed by the risk manager, who ideally can limit your position until you restore discipline. The objective

might be to make ten thousand dollars to twenty thousand dollars per
day versus making one hundred thousand dollars in stocks like Stride
Rite. To do this, you might need only five-thousand- to ten-thousand-
share positions in six names preferably in your group, maybe twelve
thousand to fifteen thousand shares intraday and seventy-five hundred
overnight. Perhaps you might get bigger in one. With a trading strategy compatible with your level of performance you will reduce your
volatility and risk."

Then, too, you may want to consider when to get out of a trade.
Here there are several general rules to follow: when there is a profit,
when there is no more profit, when the market is turning and it is a
market-sensitive stock, when the market has turned and dropped one-
half or three-eighths of a point.

It matters to some traders what stocks they make money on. If they
win with strange stocks overseas they may not be credited with as much
ability as those who do well in domestic issues. Conversely, traders who
lose in conventional stocks feel they are likely to incur less group deri-
sion than the ridicule they may get if they lose in unconventional ones.
The joy of winning in a special stock is less than the pain of losing in
such stocks. There is less possibility of being faulted for trading blue-
chip stocks even though the profitability is not as great as with the less
liquid and higher-risk tech stocks on NASDAQ.

Obviously, master traders have learned to insulate themselves from
concerns about the opinions of others. They have the emotional flexibility to trade what they want to trade without concern for the crowd's
opinion. While the crowd's opinion is a limiting factor for many traders,
consciousness of it can help free them from such constraints and therefore increase the flexibility of their trading.

What to Do about Losses

Without conscious attention to the process, it is easy for traders to get
caught up in losing trades. They may even report that they know what
they are doing, but cannot move effectively because of their emotional
response. Under stress, they may bypass their discipline and go for the
sucker pitch or take the path of least resistance. Others typically get into

a spiral of loss when they back off and become lax while doing well. They are emotionally paralyzed, and are afraid to risk trading bigger and perhaps winning bigger. Still others may get fatigued, press too hard, and/or stay at the table too long.

Not all traders believe in selling their losing positions. Ric, the experienced head trader I mentioned earlier, says, "I don't like losses, and I always preach, 'Watch your losses.' I regularly trade eighty stocks, but I look at only the ten or twenty that are moving and active, and particularly the ones that are causing problems. Why would I pay attention to a stock that keeps going up or a short that's going down or something that's not hurting? I'm only concerned with the ones that are actively hurting me. I am trying to get rid of them, or I'm reevaluating what put me in them in the first place." In reevaluating, Ric remains flexible. A decline could create another opportunity to add to a position. Or, the stock might be pulling back temporarily, then move higher.

At the same time, Ric adheres to his vision, one that helped him triple his profitability in a single year. He has a strategy for each stock. "If my stock is down a quarter or three-eighths, I'm out unless I'm there for two points. I'm not going to lose a half-point when I was only there to make a half at best. But usually I will not add to a losing position, either. The bottom line is if this stock is down three-quarters or a dollar, I'm going to take time and revisit my idea. If I believe in it, I may add to it. I'm not just going to sell it out because the market is down. I'm not going to get out of it simply because it goes down."

He also is always on the lookout for more information that can buttress a choice. For example, Ric bought some thin secondary and tertiary retailing stocks over a period of months, retailers that were not followed much. "If I get a chance to buy them cheaper, I'm going to buy them even cheaper because I like them. I think they're going to get recognized over the near term, over the next month or so," he says.

Ric realizes he could be wrong. If one of these retailing stocks drops too much, "I'll probably liquidate it at a larger loss than what I might have had." However, "if I made the selection right, I don't get to buy what I want at the cheaper price."

As a super-trader, Ric confronts his losses, recognizing that losing is part of the game. He does not get explosive when he loses. He knows that a shift in his perception is critical to tolerating losing maneuvers and turning around his trading. When he sees any of his stocks tanking, he gets rid of them.

If you're moaning, how much is that emotion influencing the rest of your trading? What trades do you make when you're experiencing pain? Do you try to get your profit from other trades to make up for it? Do you end up buying faster to balance out your loss?

The critical question is: Does holding on to losses contribute positively to the profit and loss (P&L) by turning profitable later on, or is the notion of getting out and cutting your losses a better way to raise your P&L?

It's my view that at the end of the day, the P&L looks okay because that transaction is buried within the P&L, so you don't see it. You win some, you lose some. Here, too, you want to avoid pairing up a second trade with a bad trade in order to defend your first position. But some traders like Ric argue:

"When you have five other positions working for you, and you're net flat on the day, you find yourself thinking, 'Well, if it's not going to come back, I'm going to make the sale on the things that are working to compensate for the loss.' "

According to Sandy, "Your strategy better be in place before the loss. Once the loss occurs, human nature makes it very hard to separate the loss that's hurting you from the quick profit. You just want to get rid of the pain. Therefore, when you start to see the loss, you've got to get out. That's how you do it. You may not want to exit what seems like a possibly profitable trade. To what extent is that feeling interfering with your awareness of everything else? You may buy something to offset it, or you may sell something too soon to offset it to make yourself more comfortable. The problem is that when you're really out, it's not comfortable."

Can you devise strategies that allow you to be in these uncomfortable places? A trader like Ric often can. If you can stay with your original discipline, you make sales at an earlier level. Then, while you still have a loss, or the position would be questionable, you'd have the option of either buying back what you had sold at better prices, or selling some more, because now you're averaging down the average cost of what you have sold. But if you don't make the sale at the time you said you were going to make the sale, you won't have that option.

Here's one of Ric's mistakes: "I'm losing twenty-five grand on a trade, but I've got three other trades that are making me five or six grand each," he says. "So on the day I'm down an odd lot, down five or six grand, but I can live with that. I'm going to wait for the turn to come so my loss comes back, and I'm going to lock up the profit on two or three of my other ones because I know they would eventually give up that profit, and I don't want that to happen. And then, one of those stocks that has a five-thousand-dollar profit is the one that pops for a two-point trade that I don't have that day, which might have made for a solidly up day."

Ric should have looked at the one that was losing money in the first place and dealt with that. He could have sold a third of it, or done something else—maybe covered a short. If he had, he wouldn't have made a premature sale on one of his stocks that was working. If as a trader you reach a level where you have to sell, you should sell, but sell based on what the stock's doing, not because you want to make sure you have $18,000 worth of gains to offset a $25,000 loss.

The point is to pay attention to the losers, not the winners. "You're aware that it's up but you don't want to be tempted to sell it just because it's up, when you think it's going significantly higher over a period of time," Ric concludes.

When a stock starts to go down and there are three different sellers, the master trader doesn't just stand there and say, "Well, I think I'm getting good information." You need to go with the flow. You need to keep selling. Sometimes you wait too long, but you've always got to sell. You don't know why you're selling, but you just know that it feels like the right thing to do.

How P&L Influences Decisions to Take a Loss

Some traders look at their profit and loss and think, "I'm having a good P&L day. I'll go through the sheets and get rid of some of these trades that are acting poorly." They take the loss because they don't think they'll feel it in their P&L on a good day. On the other hand, if it was a day when they were already losing money, they would probably not kick the trades out—even if the trades had been hurting them or doing nothing. They wouldn't want to add the loss to what they'd already taken.

Explaining how his P&L influenced his decision to take a loss, Ric notes: "I got pressured about a year or so ago to close off a third of my bank book program, a longtime bank stock program. I had sixty or seventy names, and took twenty percent of them off. I took off the ones that traded the least, had the least P&L, were the least liquid, and weren't producing. Of the names I took off, one stock traded sixteen dollars higher three days later. It was the worst thing I ever did. I never want to look at another one like that again. It takes a long time, sometimes, to accumulate these names. I don't believe in taking them off irrationally for no reason."

Ric points out that his group aims "to sell our weakest names because we probably shouldn't be in them at that point in time. But there's no hard-and-fast rule that works in every situation.

"We may be losing an opportunity while we're generating an increasing loss over time," he adds. "It's not really a rule. It's seeing how the need to feel like you're doing well fools you into doing things that aren't necessarily profitable."

Ric concludes, "The worst thing you can do when you're struggling is to try to make a profit to balance your loss. When it's two o'clock in the afternoon, you're down that day, and you start putting things on just for the sake of putting things on, that's not smart."

Winning as a Phenomenon over Time

In gambling, where each event is independent of previous events, it is possible to predict the probability of an event occurring. In the stock market, however, where present events are linked to many other events and probability theory doesn't apply, it's necessary to find that information edge, and to learn market mastery by mastering yourself. This is the essence of the "Trading to Win" approach—to master your automatic defensive responses to the uncertainty of the market in order to find ways to improve your decision making. The purpose is to increase your power over factors that affect your trading, and to maximize your creative strategies. This is especially important in light of the stressful nature of the market.

Winning traders view the results over a longer time. They have faith that if they do the right thing, over time they will profit. They don't focus on each trade in terms of the profit and loss. They can take some enjoyment out of the fact that they got out of a trade and it continued to go down.

Barry compares it to golf. "Let's say it's an eighteen-hole round of golf, and you have one bad hole or bogey. Do you keep focusing on the bad shot? No, you take one shot at a time. If you adopt a bad attitude and become defensive, it will only ruin the rest of your game."

Of course, it takes awareness, experience, and a long time to apply these ideas experientially to your trading. What does the super-trader do? According to Sandy, "You look at particular sectors and see which are outperforming. The market could be up 140, and drug stocks are down. Why are they down? Is the market taking cyclicals or growth stocks? Usually the flow of the money is not directed at the entire market. Even on good days, certain stocks are getting hurt. So, you can play both sides of the market and do well."

Sandy adds, "You need to weigh the strength of the market against the sectors. If it is a strong day, and you see a weak sector, you may not want to short it because it's a strong market. If it's a weak market where the AD [number of advances/number of declines] is lousy while the Dow is up, the S&P stocks are underperforming, and the NASDAQ is down, these are signs of deterioration in the market. You may want to start moving toward weak sectors.

"You should short stocks that are down and buy stocks that are up, because that's where the money is going and you want to follow the money. You will see it when all of a sudden a stock starts to trade down because of some weakness in a group. It depends on your time frame. If you are a short-term trader it's all well and good to know that drug stocks are cheap, but if they are selling them off today, how does that help you? You have to align your trading technique with your viewpoint. If you are a day trader, you can't have a long-term perspective."

Sandy continues, "You can get shorts off; wait until the market starts to turn. There is enough time to catch the next wave. You don't have to be there at the bottom. Fifty percent of the time you can be wrong and still make money, depending on how you manage your losses. If you keep your losses small and let your profits run, you can really make money."

Fourteen Ways to Be a Super-Trader

1. Look for best idea. Wait until a stock turns or buy it up three-eighths or sell it down, but wait for the tape action.
2. Be careful to watch the downside, and don't fight things.
3. Chill out. Make your daily number. Avoid getting frustrated.
4. Be in control of your competitive streak and don't overpress when you are long.
5. When you are losing, go back to basics.
6. Stay focused on what you need to do to produce your results.
7. Have the discipline to stick to your goals. Don't get too big and lose money and then chase after bigger amounts of money with an uncontrolled and undeveloped strategy. Set yourself up to make money and don't take an unlimited risk of the market failing and your positions crushing you.
8. Do self-monitoring. Have an awareness of mistakes and a willingness to admit mistakes and face the associated pain.
9. When your ideas don't work, don't be too quick to get out of them. Take a step back and evaluate your position. If you're down an eighth or a quarter, don't get scared and shaken out. Wait and see what happens. The stock may reverse and move upward and you won't have to chase your tail to get a profit. If you sell too soon, it may go back and you may have to pay up from where you sold it.
10. If you're trading strongly, stick with those names. Keep playing them as long as you are right. At the end of the day, stay with the stuff that you are willing to double up on. Avoid stocks that hardly move at all.
11. Develop patience and don't panic when you lose money. Don't try to get a loss back right away by trading foolishly or trying to hit home runs with high-risk ideas.
12. When you miss an opportunity, go through your list to make sure that you don't miss another opportunity. Look harder and closer so that you can take advantage of what you see, especially what you just missed. Keep reviewing what you missed.

13. Pay attention to research and try to get confirmation from the information you review.
14. Keep in mind that humility is helpful, too, especially in a market that is changing and where you have to admit that what you knew before and what you did before might not work today. Remember that you don't have a lock on the market.

Chapter Eight

Managing Risk and Other Advanced Trading Principles

"Can trading results be quantified to provide further insight into profitable trading strategies?" I recently asked Burt, a brilliant economist and risk manager at a large and successful hedge fund.

"They most certainly can," he replied. "In general, in most trading firms, the bulk of the profitability comes from a very small percentage of the trades. I call this the eighty-twenty rule, where eighty percent of the profit comes from twenty percent of the trades, although the figures are even more dramatic than that."

Burt continued, "The objective data points to definite patterns of repetitive behavior, which can be identified and then modified as you are doing in your seminars. It underscores the importance of placing big bets in those situations where you have an edge based on in-depth research and timing. This approach encourages the idea of getting more aggressive with winners and testing a lot of stocks in relationship to earnings, catalysts, and conferences, but getting out of high-risk ideas where you lack an edge."

Trading is about risk taking, not in the sense of blind gambling, but in the sense of utilizing available information, mastering the stress response and then taking action in the face of undetermined odds and unpredictable events, and staying with one's hypotheses in a way that produces consistently positive results. To do this, to dare to act in confident ways, takes knowledge, self-mastery, and the ability to sustain self-mastery in the face of high stress and emotional response. Ultimately the degree of risk involves choice and is not simply something that is determined independent of the trader. The master trader tries to reduce risk by understanding patterns in the market, the company, the market movement, his or her own distortions of perspective based on the nature of the market, past experience, and one's own stress response system. (The latter often protects traders too well from reading their own bodily cues to a situation that can help them to appreciate that situation.)

Statistical analysis of trading performance is a necessity for any first-class trader. Statistics enable you to examine a large sample of experience so you can determine any recurring underlying patterns that may be useful to improve trading. Those behaviors that are less successful and that can be modified or eliminated, and those activities that are profitable, can be consciously pursued in slower times.

Success can be enhanced by modifying behavior at the margins or the tails of the distribution. The greatest success is to be found in the outliers at the extreme tails of the distribution. This relates to the observation that the critical steps toward success generally occur in the last percentage of time, the extra effort put in, the extra mile, the last minutes of the game, or near the goal. The best traders recognize that small changes make all the difference, and they are able to hang in there to the end and wait for the miracles to happen, knowing that they happen in the outlying moments of events.

The successful trader sees marginal opportunities, and is a little bit more efficient on the best trades than the ordinary trader and less sloppy on most trades. This trader has learned that a small percent makes the biggest difference. This is why the most successful traders can have a fifty percent stock selection success and yet do wondrous things in managing their trades once the opportunities for maximizing performance begin to appear.

The difference between the master trader and the ordinary trader is in the differential between their winning and losing trades. The master trader earns more on winning trades than is lost on losing trades. In effect, the right bets are larger than the losing bets. The master trader's skill is in management of selections, not so much in selection of the right stocks. This trader is skillful in getting in and out and managing portfolio size relative to belief in the probability of success. The right bets become bigger than the losing bets after there is evidence that the stock is working. Profitability clusters in a small number of trades where the best traders hold on longer, trade bigger, and have more definable objectives in their winning trades as compared to their losing trades than do average or below-average traders.

Moreover, the bigger the trade, the more profitable it is likely to be. Master traders maximize their best trade picks by getting bigger. Profitability is also positively correlated with the number of trades, average trade size, and average position size, indicating an ability to correctly identify the best opportunities. By contrast, less successful traders are negatively correlated with these measures. The bigger they get, the less money they make; most likely they are unable to manage their best opportunities.

Successful trading is therefore based on the right combination of being able to measure probability and seize the opportunity. The key is information flow—assessing fundamentals, studying pricing patterns, analyzing balance sheets, and determining the relative value of a given sector relative to the group as a whole. Master traders are continually determining what factors move the market so as to change their fifty-fifty selection to sixty-forty. They are able to differentiate trades and make strategic allocations of risk capital on the basis of information flow. They are able to identify opportunities that allow them to maximize their trading. They know when to get bigger and do this on the basis of short-term fundamental analysis.

Looking at the trading profile of Sandy, the master trader, it is clear that his profitable trades are considerably more profitable than his losing trades are losses. He has twice as many winning days as losing days. When he has set targets for himself, he is likely to be on pace or ahead of pace. Most of his money is made in a handful of trades. Five percent of his profitable trades account for over 100 percent of his profitability.

Sandy recognizes that profitability is correlated to the size of the position. His objective is to get bigger and stay longer, and maintain good control over his losses so that he doesn't increase his losses as he increases the size of his bets. In effect, on a risk-adjusted basis he doesn't increase his risk as he gets bigger. He is always monitoring the downside risk by measuring how many trades he makes in a day, how much money he is making on trades, how many are profitable, and how much slippage there is.

He tries to gear his risk to low-probability events. He is always asking, "What will it cost if I am wrong? What is the upside of a trade? How is the measure of risk of each trade related to the volatility of stock, its correlation to the S&P 500, and the size of the position?" Contrast Sandy's performance to Benny, another big trader whose profit per share for winning trades is less than his loss per share for losing trades. In other words, the average size of his losses is greater than the average size of his gains, suggesting that he isn't taking sufficient profits on gains and/or that he's taking too much pain on his losses and staying in too long.

Contrast this with another trader, Sean, whose machismo and ability to tolerate great pain lead him to trade too big and to put too much capital at risk without sufficient knowledge of the group of stocks, without confirmation by price action, and without fundamental analysis. A trader such as Sean needs capital limits and more training in how best to get bigger in his trading.

Since three-quarters of trades are not based on commitment and conviction, Sean and many other traders need to do their homework and trade on information flows. When he is wrong, his liquidations can be ugly. He needs to talk more to others, and become less inflexible. His great strength—his capacity to trade in larger sizes—is a problem for most traders, but not for him. He has the potential to be a great trader, but he needs to develop caution, focus his aggressiveness, follow a plan, superimpose control, and trade more names that have stories. He needs to learn the difference between what he knows and what he doesn't know. He needs to learn direction and be able to see undervalued and overvalued situations. He needs to think out opportunities and correlate them with the size of their positions.

Still other traders tend to overtrade and spend more on commissions than they earn in their P&L. Too many positions can be catastrophic. Walt doesn't seem to measure the upside profitability against the downside risk and doesn't have specific events to help choose exits. For traders like Walt, there ought to be a minimum transaction size to reduce excessive trades with the expectation that with larger numbers of shares at risk he will be more cautious and will do more research and will not simply get bigger to get bigger. He needs to learn to trade less, hold on longer, and have specified objectives.

The task here is to back up what you do with facts and analytical work and increase the profitability per share and per trade, rather than simply trade to trade. The best trades are conceptually based, and reflect going with the trend and determining whether the fundamentals are deteriorating or improving along with tape movement. It is also useful to measure the risk-adjusted return on capital, to determine how much a trader is making relative to the risk being run. This approach enables you to determine what behavior needs to be changed to increase profitability, in terms of increasing the size of positions and increase the number of names. It enables you to compare profits to losses and determine the differential between the two.

A basic assumption of this book is that the uncertainty of the markets and the stress of trading both contribute to increased defensive and automatic thoughts, which color trading activity and contribute to swings in the market itself. These fixed patterns of decision making, while appearing to be rational, are governed by survival needs and automatic defense patterns. That behavior must be recognized and mastered if the trader is to be free to act in a difficult marketplace.

To control uncertainty, traders develop certain patterns of trading that allow them to impose order on the uncertainty and uncontrollability of the marketplace. Such patterns of thought motivated in part by survival needs actually conform to rational trading models, which might be developed by mathematicians and other objective observers of the marketplace. Make certain you are aware of these patterns in managing risk in the marketplace, since they relate to how you manage uncertainty. The master traders recognize the negative impact on their trading of losing and therefore manage risk psychologically by consciously keeping their losses down. In fact, for the super-trader control of loss is the most critical variable in the risk management profile of behaviors.

Super-traders put much emphasis on risk management, relying on such measures as the Sharpe ratio, a risk-adjusted measure of profitability that is calculated by dividing your returns above the risk-free range by the standard deviation of the return. These traders are motivated by the need to keep their risks down to avoid major disasters. They have a high Sharpe ratio; that is, they control risk even when they are increasing the size of their profit. For the same amount of risk they get a better return. According to Max, a risk-averse trader I know, "If, for example, you are trading stocks with a very high beta and you're in a very volatile market, you'd better be earning $200,000 a month based on the level of risk that you're taking, not $100,000 a month."

Super-traders do not get caught in the gambling fever mentality of some traders who keep doubling up to replace losses until they're tapped out. Super-traders respect the market and don't try to live by hope. They live by seeking out the good information, by following a strategy, and by practicing vigilance. The super-trader is also aware of the value of diversification to protect against the risk of volatility, and knows that time extended reduces the uncertainty and reduced prices of volatile stocks. The super-trader is fundamentally risk-averse and is always looking for low-risk situations.

Even super-traders can become complacent when they are doing well, and stop watching their risk management principles. Here's one example:

On Friday, May 3, 1996, Sandy sold Zenith short, violating his own rule against being short on a Friday on a stock that might go up on Monday. Knowing Monday would likely be an up day, he should have started covering the stock on Friday. However, the stock had been elusive. It had traded up, and at the end of the day had come down a dollar, as if exhausted, then run up again.

Sandy got caught shorting an upward-moving stock—which kept gapping up each day for a week—because he didn't think it could happen. His analysis was extensive but incomplete; he thought there were sixty-five million shares outstanding, and that sixty percent of Zenith was owned by a Korean company. He believed it was a liquid name. While he looked at the shares outstanding on the Internet, he didn't look at the corporate summary, which would have showed that it was not liquid and that there were far fewer shares available.

Fortunately, as it moved up, he wisely did not keep averaging up on it, but held firm expecting that in the long run it would turn around. He took paper losses but waited until the stock dropped to cover it. In the end, instead of losing $5 million, he lost only $800,000.

Sandy learned a lot from this trade, specifically that when you are about to enter such a trade, you have to weigh the upside of the trade against the risk and the opportunity cost of being involved in it, and consider what else you could be doing with the money. It is important to ask yourself how much time you will be taking from other trades if you get involved in such a situation. Understanding how the marketplace works may help you answer that question.

In retrospect Sandy noted:

"It's smart to get in the habit of putting in a forced cover if a short sale is going against you. Instead of averaging up and jeopardizing your capital base, you are better off when you are forced to cover at the end of the day at an absolute number of points. A dollar or percentage rule, or both, is a good idea. When you are trading gaps in hot stocks, and stocks are trading through their expected range, stops automatically get elected. When there is a bad short, someone must go over to the trader and establish a price against that level and where the trader will have to cover. That didn't happen.

"If a stock closed strong, the correct thing would be to keep covering like the specialists were doing. Then when it dropped in price, you could recover your loss from the short sales. However, there is a tendency for some big traders when they do go against a major trend to drag their feet. If it is a busted stock, they get in too soon and drag their feet, and if it is busting out, they are reluctant to take their losses."

Sometimes the magnitude of a trade stymies traders. At other times, it is simply that the event is so anomalous that they don't believe what they are seeing and don't follow their own rules. The only way to explain the vulnerability of the super-trader is that, according to Sharpe, increases in wealth give people a stronger cushion for absorbing losses and strengthen the appetite for risk. After a loss the appetite for risk has been whetted.

Dynamics of the Marketplace

The marketplace is an ever-changing environment, where the rules change as circumstances change. But too often there are *no* rules in the trader's mind. Often traders rationalize, "It's a good day," or "That's just the market." They may say, "Well, I lost money yesterday. But the market was flat. I wasn't trying to do too much. The market was tight at the end of the day." They try to justify their actions. In doing so, they fail to examine what fleeting thoughts occurred to them that led them to hesitate to get out of stocks before the market turned downward—a move that cost them dearly.

There are certain nuances in timing that every trader must learn, such as knowing when to hold on to a long position, when to sell a long position, and when to sell short. Traders must learn also to read the direction of the market and to assess the quality of information available.

Lots of traders don't measure the risk/reward ratio of their trades. If you can risk and lose $80,000 versus making $80,000, the stakes are not as good as making $30,000 while risking only $10,000. Many traders get dogmatic when they should start moving out of a position that isn't working. It is important to be patient and centered.

Trading is about getting something down, writing down an order, being very concrete, specific, and focused. Rely on your intuition. Trust your memory, your experience, and your ability to read the tape. Tune into your inner voice, and you will find the creative resources you need to trade.

The more you risk, the more you will discover that you can expand your limits. The main step to mastering risk management is to keep looking for new risks that you can take in your trading each day.

You also have to be aware that there are fewer ideas than recommendations. The analysts are not going to stick their necks out. In a volatile market being wrong is going to be more costly than in the past. Because of this your ideas have to be better. You've got to make more money out of the ideas to offset what doesn't work.

What constitutes a good idea? An idea should be good enough for you to say, "You know, I'm probably going to do it." What level of conviction do you need to back it up? Sometimes, you can pick up information if you've done all your homework from, say, 7 A.M. to 8 A.M., and get going with some ideas. But between 8 A.M. and 9 A.M., you might pick up some other ideas from other traders. So jot them down. Merge the two and get some information flowing with better ideas.

Getting More Aggressive

Traders must examine their trades to understand how their own habitual thoughts have kept them from following their trading strategy, and how awareness of these subliminal thoughts can give them greater flexibility and trading mastery, especially in highly volatile and unpredictable markets. Let's look at some examples.

In volatile markets when stocks are up, unless there is a reversal in the entire market, stocks usually don't go down the day that they are up. If you want to short them, wait until the end of the day. Although shorting a stock in the middle of the day was successful ten years ago, the market has adjusted. Today, buyers space out their orders, especially the first day off the bottom. Thus there are three or four days before you can start selling the stocks.

According to super-traders, it is a cardinal error to sell a stock the first day after it reaches a low point, since there's no upside to the trade. But they also say that the minute you think your upside is limited, you should get out. Pat is one trader who learned these concepts the hard way—he shorted IBM all day long on a day when IBM went up seven points. "I sold because it was up," he said, not realizing that he should have observed the trend sooner.

Firms are rated on their execution of orders. There are services that rank firms in terms of how they execute orders. Each firm tries to beat the average weighted price (volume weighted average price—VWAP) for the day, depending on how much volume it trades. So, if a stock trades a million shares at 64, and a firm buys a million at 64 and trades a million at $64\frac{1}{2}$, the VWAP is $64\frac{1}{4}$ and they have beaten the VWAP. This gives firms an incentive to run the stock at the end of the day and execute it at a lower price.

There are real reasons why stocks do what they do. For instance, why don't the prices of stocks drop down or "come in" all at once? Because the big firms space their orders out throughout the day—there is continuous buying. The stocks don't come in while they are still being bought. These big firms don't like to fill an order at 10 A.M., and then watch the stock go down. Those who are shorting get caught.

So, you have a tendency built into the market. A trader who has a million shares to buy and wants to beat the average, but it isn't coming in, should wait until 3:30 before starting to buy. The only time to average down is when you are in a stock that is following some trading theme that you have been with for a long time.

It is more difficult to play bigger when you are behind or have no money in the bank. When you have a lot of money or you're up, playing big is certainly easier. But this is not a reason to take a loss, or to stay in a losing stock because you don't want to face the loss. Playing big should be an incentive for averting losses, building up a stake, and getting into a position where you are confident about not losing. Then, you can begin to trade bigger because you have a cushion.

When should you get out of a stock? A super-trader's answer is: "Let it run as long as you can. If you want to sell at 3:30 and it's not happening at three o'clock, then start getting out. You want to see buyers underneath, not offers to sell all the time. Sell twenty-five thousand shares at a time, not your entire position all at once. Get in motion. Offer to sell another fifty. Keep scaling out.

"Keep talking to yourself," the super-trader advises. "Tell yourself to hang in there even though your impulse is to sell. Three-quarters to one is the magic number. Then, you have a winner. A half a point is a nice scalp, but three-quarters of a point is a winner."

All of this activity is about consciously controlling the impulse to take a profit so as to get the full value of the stock's momentum. If your entry point is good there will often be profit along the way. The key here is to get in when you think about getting in rather than waiting for more confirmation—and losing the edge in the process. Many traders aren't aggressive enough. They stare at the computer screen and don't get in very fast. "The best traders may be earning seventy times what others are earning on the *same trade* because they are aggressive, not because they are that much better," says the super-trader.

It is important to note that decisions regarding profits and decisions regarding losses are not made in the same way. Losses have far more enduring emotional significance than profits. When the choices pertain to losing, traders tend to tolerate more. They are generally willing to take the bigger risk of holding on longer to losing stocks to avoid the loss than to stay longer in a stock that is rising. They are more loss-averse than risk-averse and are more troubled by losing than they are by uncertainty. Losing trades produce more losses for this reason than any other.

One trader I know, Anthony, would always get out too early. As he noted, "By the time I was right, I was already out. I would go through the battle, but not the rout. Finally, I was exhausted. I found it hard to be there to seize the opportunity. You have to be in a position to maximize your shot."

Anthony recalled watching a stock like Micron go down seven points in a day. "I try it when it's down three, maybe kick it out. Then, if it is real, I'll hold it when it's ready to turn. I'm encumbered with all these bad habits from the past. I'm learning that instead of staring at stocks I can always take a shot, but I have to be positioned to maximize the shot."

The key for Anthony is not about getting bigger, but sharpening his focus. He has to find concrete ways to leverage what he is doing. He needs better habits. He has to trade the same amounts but get more out of those trades, get a bigger P&L, and have more money to trade. He should whittle his action down to eight stocks, and focus on getting good positions and getting bigger in ones he feels good about.

Anthony also trades a lot of three-thousand-share positions. "If he wants to join the big boys, he has got to play ten-thousand-share positions," a colleague declared. "He has to give up micromanagement. He needs to concentrate on his winners and a small enough number of stocks to give him maximum capacity to focus on his better trades. He might give someone else his bad trades to get rid of them, so that he doesn't have to watch everything. To run more money he has to be efficient." By contrast, the master trader puts much emphasis on cutting losses, above all, and in being counterintuitive—going beyond the natural inclination to be risk-averse.

Know More Before You Trade More

The edge you need to be able to win comes from information flow. Master traders are always trying to reduce risk by increasing their knowledge of factors and events pertaining to the stocks they are trading. The more information they have about what is moving the stock, the more control they maintain over their actions and the more they can maximize results. The problem is in obtaining good information that is needed and relevant and being able to assess the quality of the information. This is not as easy, especially because with today's technologies, information is disseminated much faster and to more people than in the past, making the moves more compressed than before. For example, something can happen, such as an announcement of first-quarter profits, and almost immediately a stock can be down twenty points.

These almost instantaneous results make it even more important to improve your access to information.

You can develop a system for research and for analysis of statistics that can help you determine new directions. You should also have a plan that takes into consideration your competition. To expand your horizons, extend your information network. Get ideas, but not necessarily recommendations. It also pays to surround yourself with people who can supplement your knowledge.

Let's examine how information can be beneficial to a trade. You may normally short 25,000 shares of a stock. With additional information that the stock is bad or that a sister stock in the same sector is bad, you might try shorting 50,000 or 75,000 shares. In one day you can make a considerable profit if you understand the significance of catalytic news events.

Much information can be gained from listening. However, most people are not inclined to listen to others, even though what others say can offer intrinsic value in terms of confirmation, creativity, and support. Naturally, you need to be sure that any opinions you get about a stock are based on solid research and investigation.

There is even value in sharing. It will strengthen your overall ability to communicate, to think more clearly, and to learn from others.

You don't have to wait for an incentive to talk with people who are good sources of news. Nor do you have to be trading all the time. To get an edge in a slow market, you have to take the initiative in gathering better information. Call upstairs traders and ask them what they're working on and if there is anything of which you should be aware. Push yourself to ask more questions rather than wait. Let the research analysts work for you in response to your ideas. Keep calling; keep pressing them. Develop a full list of research in the morning on a piece of paper and then spend time filling it in.

The Need to Be Alert and Take Profit

According to Ralph, a founder of a small but successful hedge fund: "Normally I would sell most stocks whenever they get to any sort of strength. I allowed one oil service stock to run up a bit, but we didn't take a profit, and now we're only breaking even. We started buying it around three and a half. It got as high as six and three-quarters a week ago, and now it's down between four and an eighth and four and a quarter. We doubled the position at about five and a quarter. We would have made a fortune if we'd gotten out at six. We had six hundred thousand shares.

"We wanted to take a portion of the position off when the news came out a week ago that the pipeline development agreement would be done. I did not sell it at that news; it came out very quickly. We thought the stock would run up and hold at that level, and we'd discussed a price of seven, seven and a half, maybe even as high as eight. And that was the time it traded at six and three-quarters.

"The announcement that all the money was finally committed and all the contracts were signed caused the run-up. However, we thought the stock would get a little higher, and that it would sustain that price move for a while, and we would sell it over a period of days on that price move. Instead, it didn't sustain it for more than twenty minutes. When it started coming down, it came down like a rock.

"It went from six and three-quarters back to five and one-half. Then the next day it went to five. We sold fifty thousand shares between five and five and one-half, so we went from six hundred thousand shares down to 550,000. At four and three-quarters, and five, I sold another one hundred thousand shares. Right now we're down to roughly three hundred thousand. I've sold as much as forty percent of the position in the range between four and three-eighths and five and one-quarter. So now all I'm doing is turning something that might have had a nice profit into a break-even trade.

"The way I trade, if I put up something and I have three hundred thousand shares, I'll still predict for you a hundred grand every quarter, on half a point, depending on what I think it's going to move in three-quarters. So in this oil service stock, every time it kept trying to push its way over the six dollar mark, I was there at six bucks. Even though I was willing to pay five and a half even for it. Three hundred thousand shares. I know that as soon as it got to six and an eighth, six and a quarter, it would get back to five and three-eighths, a half, and if I wanted to buy it back I would. And that worked well. So, the day of the news it began to move up before the news hit the tape, and I made a few small sales. Now when the news hit, I pulled all the offers out. We were having a data breakdown that day. We had no news services on the desk.

The quote services were broken. But we knew the news was coming out, and we were getting it from Bloomberg and from another source. While it was hard to assemble all the news, we knew that what we had been waiting for was coming. It was a Friday afternoon, and I got caught up in it and figured—well, you know, we thought it would get to seven and a half—'Let's give it a chance to get there—seven, wherever it's going.' So, at six and three-quarters I did nothing.

"Within about a half hour it was back below six, and that continued. I stood there and said the hell with it. In fact, I replaced the stock that I sold. I didn't try to get rid of it. I figured, well, it's a Friday afternoon, we're having trouble collecting the news, maybe other people on the Street are having trouble—because it was just not us. TrakData was down streetwide. I figured, you know, that as the news gets better after people read it on the weekend, the stock will begin to pick back up again, as it's the news we've been looking for. It didn't do that. It began to deteriorate further Monday. And again, when it began to deteriorate, while I was concerned about it, my friend Erwin said, 'Well, let's sell something.' So, we sold."

Reviewing Your Game Films

Perhaps this sounds obvious, but you should get in the habit of reviewing each day's trades, in the same way football coaches review films of each week's game. You should also try to maximize your edge by increasing your information flow. It is useful to try to figure out which of many factors and events were critical in determining the movement of stocks on a given day so as to be alert to them in the future, recognizing of course that the past is only one of the forces that impinge on stock prices.

Try to base your plan for the next day on your positions, on what's acting best—for example, what's been up three days and is going to sell off. However, you are likely to be most successful when you take the information that's given to you at the moment. You'll have your biggest days when all of a sudden it hits you that this is something good, that you have to do it. You wouldn't have been able to tell that trade was going to happen an hour before it happened or the day before.

Notice if you are inclined to rationalize your trading. If you are locked into a preconceived notion, you will not be able to make certain trades. Trades become available because you are in the now. You can't really know what you are going to do or what's going to happen in advance, but you have to be ready to buy a stock because it's acting great. If you don't want to be long on the market it is hard to buy long on a moment's notice, but that's what being in the present is all about.

When you're really on the edge and really tuned in you can't protect yourself with your preconceptions or with your defenses. It's scary to play out of commitment and do the thing that's new. But this is what being in the present at every moment is all about. It's volatile. You've got to take that risk.

Looking at one young trader is revealing. On a typical day, his profit and loss revealed that he had twelve trades—five winners, five losers, and two unchanged. That's not a good ratio. He was overtrading by fifty percent. He had five trades there that he probably shouldn't have done. The boss said to him, "I know you want to play, but that's not what we're in the game to do. We're in the game to win, and these probabilities are not good."

This trader is too indecisive. He's always on both sides of the fence. He's probably trading on hot coals because he doesn't want to lose. He's paranoid, and that pressure adds to indecision. This is typical when someone is trading poorly. He wants to see everything line up right before he gets into it, and by that time things have already changed. He keeps waiting for all these confirmations in order buy a stock right at the top. It's a sign of inexperience.

This young trader is playing an emotional game. It's not a road to profitability. He needs to know his entry and exit points.

Do you tend to think that if you lose in one trade, you may gain it back in another, rather than try to figure out how you could have maximized each position?

Here's an example. If a stock opened weakly because there was a seller in the stock, you might have been in a position to buy more stock and average down your costs. If the stock continued down, however, you might have gotten out, and taken as much profit as you could. At the very least, you wanted to get out before you lost money, and not tried to save money by averaging down. So you sold, took your loss, and waited until you saw the direction the stock was moving, before deciding whether to get back into it or to sell short. Perhaps you did not want to sell a stock that was dropping, if the group it is in was doing well. Or, you wanted to short a stock in a group that was faring poorly.

In your review of each day, see if you followed the trend, or you fought it. Consider whether you get stubborn in certain stocks and don't do what your own logic suggests you do. Are there moments when you could have shifted your trading decisions? Was there something else you could have done? And if it could be done, what kept you from doing it?

If the market is fluctuating wildly, there is a risk of falling back on old unsuccessful habits. Adding to positions as the stock price drops is dangerous to do. The only time to average down is when you are in a theme stock that you've been in for a long time.

You may be inclined to get rid of a position if it is down and then trade up, but this may be more of the same. What are the probabilities here? What will happen eight out of ten times unless you have information that changes your thinking?

If you are trading, it shouldn't make a difference if it's selling at seventy and you're at fifteen and adding twenty or adding ten. You are wrong. Why add to a position you are wrong in unless you have a concrete reason, other than "It's down, so I'm going to buy it"? You have a universe of over three thousand stocks to trade, and some of them must be a better choice than that. Why not buy something that is trading better?

You may have experienced pain when you were losing money, but didn't think the stock would get hit so hard. Did you see that the price was down but hope that it would trade up in your effort to get bigger?

When you trade breakouts, you should see buyers and not sellers. If you see sellers, then you should lighten up since the breakout was a false breakout. When the stock goes down, you should get out.

What was your initial entry point? Was it a good one?

In your review, see whether you're really managing your positions. You need to get out while a stock is dropping and be willing to get back in if necessary, especially if it goes up. You may be afraid that you won't be able to get back the same-sized position and you may be reluctant to sell it with the idea of buying back, because you don't want to pay up for the stock. Perhaps you shouldn't be afraid to pay up for a position to get it going if the stock is moving up and you expect to help out your buy position.

Meanwhile, a dropping position uses up much energy and can distract you from other opportunities. If you are playing bigger and your stocks drop, you are going to be down a larger number and may be reluctant to take the loss and free yourself up for the future trades in this stock or in another stock.

Habits versus Cues

Some of what you do is because you are successful. Some of it is simply habitual behavior. With practice, you can begin to learn how your automatic thinking leads you to ignore subtle cues. By doing this, you will become aware of thoughts that influence your trading. Control those cues, and you multiply your chances in a changing market.

Notice the tendency to trade safer stocks with little profit potential, as opposed to trading higher-risk stocks with more possibility of profit. In the face of fatigue, confusion, and high volatility, many traders shift toward safety—and less profitability.

There is also a tendency to play bigger with the wrong stocks, instead of getting bigger in better stocks where the slippage is less likely, because you usually pay more for better stocks. To save money, most traders opt for the weaker stocks in the process of getting bigger. In other words, most traders prefer to get into the smaller stock with a bigger bid/offer spread, which is easier and cheaper to do, instead of buying smaller amounts of stronger stocks. If you are not exact in little stocks, it can cost $50,000 a month. It is a bad habit, which keeps you from seeing the market. You stop thinking and instead make moves that look safe.

When the market is scary and volatile, it's tempting to take the quick way out, instead of steadily building up. Take your time. Don't take on lower-profit stocks unless there is a reason. Being in Occidental or other boring stocks may reflect overtrading. You can't make a lot of money trading these stocks and you can't lose a lot of money. You are better off with twenty thousand shares of Texas Instruments or twenty thousand LSI Products, both of which are likely to move. When you have twelve stocks on your sheet, then you can move to semithick stocks.

You may have bought the right stocks, but perhaps you didn't hold them long enough. Maybe you felt compelled to keep moving. Consider your costs on a stock. Why sell a stock and take profits if your costs will not be covered and there is no reason to think the stock will drop? Why sell it just to stay in motion? The only reason to sell quickly is when something you've bought goes bad immediately, and you have to keep trading to get away from the loss.

Macho Trading

Macho trading is equivalent to not facing reality. The ego-centered trader wants to fight the war instead of adapt. If you can stand the heat, buy bigger from the start.

Macho traders don't trade based on their own experience. They operate not in terms of what they know, but in terms of what they feel. Are you among them?

If so, you're being seduced by old beliefs about going against the market or assuming that the market is wrong and not following its direction. Or you may think, "Well, you win some, and you lose some," instead of looking for patterns in your mistakes. You can't simply hide behind a cliché, which keeps you from searching for changes you can make to improve performance.

Operating on rationalizations doesn't lead to change. You need to identify your trading patterns, understand the old habits behind them, and change the beliefs so you can become more flexible and able to trade any tape.

A useful pattern, according to master traders, is to manage risk by cutting down on long positions, especially when you expect the market to be bad. It is more profitable to sell stocks and buy them back after they drop, when they are starting to rise again.

This is difficult to do if you think that standing firm in the face of adversity is admirable, and that to cut and run is cowardly. That was General Custer's mentality, and look where it got him! It's also difficult if you think that strengthening your physical and mental ability may enable you to gird your loins and take more pain. You're better off when you try to limit your pain to one or one and a half days, rather than three days.

When the market is dropping, you also can go short on futures, anticipating the following day's trading. Futures are a hedge against declines in the market. They can also be an independent source of profitability.

Perfectionism and Risk Management

Personality plays a major role in how traders deal with their losses. Those who are perfectionists are always looking for ways to improve. They usually think they must work harder and get in better physical shape to take on more tasks, rather than figuring out how to work smarter or empower others to help them. At the same time, they are stopped by their high standards and are reluctant to get bigger unless they have more precise information. This standard often keeps them from succeeding.

Max is a perfectionist trader, one who often gets lost in the details of what he is doing. He spends his whole day rationalizing his decision to stick to one position instead of assessing the position and making a decision. He distorts the meaning of time. Instead of trading freely and observing his trades for errors that can become insights, he becomes mired in the fine points of specific trades, overthinking and overintellectualizing his every move. He becomes excessively focused on how he will look and what others will think of him. He constantly criticizes himself for making the trade and finds no joy or satisfaction in what he is doing. He is constantly thinking about what he did wrong, hoping the trade will turn around and thus eliminate the error. Arrogance and pride fuel his need for the perfect trade.

Perfectionist traders are willing to play only to the point where they are assured of winning. This keeps them from getting as big as they can. They restrict their winnings and do not watch their costs or their losing positions, which multiply rapidly.

To be creative, a trader must take risks. It is unavoidable. To grow, a trader needs to learn how to take risks by measuring the risk/reward ratio. The goal is to trade when there is a favorable risk.

To become a successful trader, a perfectionist must let go of self-imposed limitations, which prohibit even appropriate risk taking, and must also relinquish the ingrained, and often unconscious, beliefs that one is a failure. This means acting even when the results aren't guaranteed.

For such traders, it is useful to look at lost opportunities. How much money was lost by holding on to the stock or a portion of it as it dropped, even though it eventually came back and moved up? Here it is useful to factor in commissions and slippage and determine the volume necessary to make this worthwhile.

"Help! My Stocks Are Falling and I Can't Get Up!"

Reluctance to sell a long that is going down—hoping for a reversal—is a variation of averaging shorts as they go up instead of getting out. What goes on in the mind of a trader who does this? According to Neal, another short seller, "I got lax. I was just thinking I would break even. I let it ride, waiting until it comes in." Neal tried to reassure himself, saying, "I've got some money. I can withstand pain." So he gave the position a little more time, until he saw that he would have been happy to get out of the day even. His conclusion: "I was out of sync."

The next time, Neal must be willing to say, "If it goes down, get rid of it." But that's hard to do, especially when the stock is extending and you think it's going to collapse and you won't be there. The psychology behind such trading is that the trader always wants to be there. There may not be a plus tick. Still, traders want to have something in their pocket so they can say they were right. Let's assume the stock is down $1.50. If asked, "Are you short?" Neal can say yes, even if it is only twenty-five hundred. He is trying to be right and look good in the face of a loss, instead of confronting the loss. His behavior is based on protecting his self-image.

A super-trader would advise Neal, "If you are on your game, you get out. If you are not on your game, you get lax."

Neal replies, "I was hoping it would get better and I reverted back."

It's human nature to hold on to a losing position, hoping it will turn around. As a trader, you need to identify the tendency to hold on, and learn to make the decision to do the right thing in terms of your strategy, no matter how you feel. If you get out right away on a downturn, you won't lose your opportunity to buy back the stock. You have to build an intolerance for doing anything stupid and be willing to correct yourself even when your gut is telling you not to worry. You have to keep thinking, "If this isn't working, let me get out of it."

If you are serious about becoming a master trader, don't return to falling stocks unless conditions are changed. Be patient. Then wait until the risk/reward ratio is right. Bottom picking is good only if there is a story. But it is hard to pick bottoms. You are better off waiting until a stock goes up three-eighths to a half point. Stop looking for the low tick.

The best traders feed off the fact that everyone gets in too early. They listen for the pain of the other traders, and then they go in for the kill. A percentage of the bottom line of the best traders comes from "reading the room"—interpreting the psychology of the traders in their midst so as to extrapolate to what other traders elsewhere may be doing.

Managing Risk in Volatile Stocks

To look for the maximum play for your buck, while still managing your risks, you cannot get involved with every volatile name possible. Some experienced traders prefer to trade no more than one NASDAQ stock at a time. "Be careful about wanting to shoot the whole wad," says one. "If you get caught in one of these volatile stocks that jump rapidly, you're dead. You shouldn't be in them. You are better off sticking to Microsoft or Compaq markets for two points' profit. There's nothing better than liquidity. Buy two hundred thousand and make two hundred thousand dollars. Stay patient and get your trade.

"You also want to take advantage of what you know about a stock's trading range. For example, let's say you know that Teledyne is trading between twenty and twenty-five, and you start buying at twenty-two and a half. When it pushes up to twenty-five, make the sale and wait until it drops down again before you buy some more."

Don't Fight the Tape

Regardless of whether you're experiencing a good day or feeling that you are fighting the tape, you have to discipline yourself to act—to stay in stocks that are moving positively and get out of stocks that are weak.

Assuming that things are going to happen that are inherently unpredictable, you improve your odds by finding and playing good stories or shorting bad stories, and rely less on trying to be right on the market. Things may turn out to be more in your favor if you do this, as opposed to acting without an edge. Essentially, you want to be in the right place when the market turns, or when the story comes out.

If a stock is working, play the percentages by giving it time. The odds favor this tactic to work, unless something changes dramatically or there's a stock-specific problem. You have to keep practicing holding on, because of the inclination to fight the tape and overreact to every tick. Keep asking yourself, "How much longer can I stay and what can I do to make a difference?" Staying in a position from 9:30 A.M. to 4:00 P.M., instead of getting out by 11:00 A.M., ultimately may be very rewarding.

A trader named Alan is terrific at holding on. When a stock is up seven points, he'll say, "I think it could be up another two tomorrow on the opening." Alan acts rationally, while another trader might fret about how much the stock had cost and decide to lock in the profit. If your stocks are closing strong and you're on top of a situation, it's a stretch for traders to hold their position to make additional profit.

Trading to Get a Feeling of the Market

Marshall often trades to get a feel for the market. As he noted, "When I make a sale, I like to sell hard at the market. If I have a stock that's rising rapidly, I might pick a price. Say I think the stock's going to six, so let's offer it at five and three-quarters, five and seven-eighths, and if it gets to six, great. But if I have a stock that's struggling, up three-eighths, then a half, and I'm not sure it's going to make it . . . if I go to the market, and, say, sell three thousand or five thousand or whatever at the market, and I knock the bid out plus the guy gives me fifteen hundred at three-eighths, and the thirty-five hundred is done at a quarter, and the new quote is an eighth, that's the sign of a weak stock. But if there are two working buyers there, maybe you sell fifteen hundred at three-eighths, it goes a quarter, three-eighths, and a moment later you get taken at three-eighths, and it goes right back to three-eighths, a half. Now I know I've sold into a strong stock. So, I get a feel for the market also. In the same way, selling or covering shorts gives me an awful lot of information. If you don't do that, you can't tell for sure which way things are moving. More importantly, I think you might tie your hands too much in case you get a reversal.

"You know, it's nice to think that everything you do is always the right thing, but the reality is that a lot of times stocks go up a little and then start to come back down on you, or they move to a slightly higher price level. What do you do the next day when a stock moves to a lower level? If you haven't taken advantage of the higher price, are you really that free to add to the position? And is that the right thing to do?"

Take Risks and Grow

What does it take to go from trading a half point, which you regularly do automatically, to trading for a full point, especially when you've never made such a move? This is the essence of change, which usually means doing something new. It also means taking the risk of falling on your face and feeling stupid. This is the *dis*comfort zone, and all the pressure is on you *not* to do it. It's like picking up a new stroke in tennis—learning a two-handed backhand when you're accustomed to a one-handed backhand. What you do regularly is what stops you from risking a new swing and growing.

Many managers believe that inexperienced traders should be encouraged to scalp or take a half-point profit and only later learn to stay for a longer time to make two points. Viewed like skiing, scalping is like learning to snowplow rather than immediately skiing downhill doing parallel turns. Like the snowplow, it's fine to learn scalping initially so a trader knows how to put on the brakes to maintain control. The danger is to get locked into snowplowing, so that one is reluctant to shift out of the comfort zone to trade bigger.

Eighteen Risk Management Ideas from Advanced Traders

1. *Plan before you trade.* "Have an idea about the stocks you will trade. Know your entry and exit points on each. Know where to sell on the upside and the downside. Decide not to lose a dollar."

2. *Control emotion.* "The more you can trade without your emotions, the more effective you are."

3. *Take action.* "Channel your emotions into motivation. When I'm hot and doing well, it just pushes me harder. I want to be right, and I take more risks. When I'm wrong, I want to be just as quick to recognize it."

4. *Be decisive.* "When you want to be involved in something, don't bid it; take it. Be aggressive."

5. *Use the rules as guidelines but remain adaptable in response to changing circumstances.* "If you bought a stock at twenty-two, you're going to have a whole different feeling when you see three sellers out there and it trades at twenty-one and seven-eighths, twenty-one and three-quarters, twenty-one and five-eighths, twenty-one and three-quarters, twenty-one and five-eighths, twenty-one and a half. If there are three sellers, and an institution is selling a big print, my guess is that the three sellers are there because of the institution. You have to make a decision."

6. *Determine the amount of capital you are willing to risk on a trade.* Most books recommend no more than five percent.

7. *Be flexible.* Don't set a specific level on a stock when you get into it. In one trader's words, "If I short something and it picks up a quarter or three-eighths because the futures are running, but I feel that it's not going to perform at the market, then I'll leave it on. If it's crazy, I have to do something—but I won't say I'll buy it back right away if it ticks a quarter."

8. *Track your decisions.* "Follow up on the results of your decisions in order to evaluate your approach. Don't rely solely on your memory. The mind plays tricks and may give you a different result than what has actually occurred."

9. *Get into the zone.* "Create the zone. Learn to put yourself into the right frame of mind so you can play in a more successful way. Train yourself to create the mental state of being in the zone by learning to bypass negative thoughts and focusing on positive experiences."

10. *Prepare for recovery.* "If you lose your confidence, go back to the basics, start to trade, and make some money. Build your confidence by getting into a centered state and playing smaller. Build a track record. Hit a single before trying to hit a home run."

11. *Take time off if necessary.* "If you stick to your discipline and lose money five days in a row, it may be necessary to take time off to break up the losing patterns."

12. *Ask for help.* "Instead of taking yourself out of the game, let someone know that you need help. Ask a buddy to help you stay a little longer or get out sooner."

13. *Don't fret.* "Reviewing your trades is not about fretting over past decisions. It's about preparing for the next day and seeing patterns that have dropped out. Remember, too many opinions can be confusing. If you trade too much on other people's ideas you won't grow as much. There's nothing worse than losing money on somebody else's idea."

14. *Take your profits early.* "If you are losing too much, you have to stop the bleeding. So if you're down and a stock goes up a quarter, you may want to take the quarter. It's especially true if the group is weakening. You might even want to short the stock. Then if it goes down, you can cover it for a profit."

15. *Model the experiences of others.* "It's long been said that experience is the best teacher. Once you get to know your stocks, you'll know how to trade them both when they are thin and when they are trading heavy volume. It's also possible to model the experiences of others, so you can incorporate their best moves into your strategy."

16. *Select a goal.* "Set a yearly goal; then decide how much you have to make in a given day or month, so you have an idea of how many trades you have to make and how long you have to

Eighteen Risk Management Ideas (Continued)

be in them in order to reach the target number. This doesn't mean that if you lose X dollars today you have to double up on day two. But hit your daily marker on a regular basis and you'll soon hit that number twice or three times in a given day."

17. *Trade out of commitment to your results.* "This is like swearing an oath to produce a specific result and then doing what it takes. Commitment is like someone holding a gun to your head."

18. *Write your goal down.* "Your head is full of traps. Your mind plays games, convincing you that you're okay when you're not okay. But trading success has nothing to do with illusions. It's based on reality. Having your number in writing keeps reminding you of your commitment and helps you get past denials and other psychological defenses."

Chapter Nine

Teamwork

My weekly seminars focus principally on trading events and trading behavior. But every so often, there is an opportunity to expand into important issues of leadership, morale, and team efforts, which I believe are also very relevant in maximizing performance. This happened recently at one large hedge fund. A senior trader who had guided many of the younger traders took early retirement. Everyone was somewhat concerned about the future of the fund he left behind. What follows are some of the comments made by Sandy, the managing partner, to the remaining traders at this turning point.

"I am telling you straight out, it's going to be an experience for all of us," Sandy began. "Maybe we were successful because of Marty and will be very surprised to find out how we do now that he is gone. But my guess is that you guys don't know how good you are. If I don't make this place different from a normal trading house, then you aren't going to want to be here. The pressure is on me to make this place special—to make this place work *for* you—more than *on* you. Why do you think I do what I do? I want you people to be happy. I do not want to sit here by myself. If I am sitting at a screen by myself, I can do it, but I prefer to have you with me.

"I'm concerned about a show of support. It means a lot to me that you guys support me. If it was just Marty, we will find out that we weren't that great. That would be disturbing to all of us. It's a challenge. It's exciting.

"I look around the room and see an extraordinary amount of talent. I am not sure you people felt you were in a position where you could have that confidence. You are getting paid. You want to feel like you are not stagnating. All those things are available. I need your help. I can't do it by myself. I want to think that you can't leave this place," Sandy concluded.

Notice how open Sandy is in sharing his feelings, and how he turned what might be a demoralizing moment into a transformational experience, setting the sights of the firm even higher. Sandy is not only a great trader; he is a leader.

As you succeed it becomes essential to focus attention on the people trading with you so as to encourage them to follow your guidelines to ensure new levels of success. The leadership task is to become aware of the characteristics that make for maximum performance and then try to find ways of instilling this confidence and ability in other traders.

The shrewd leader is aware of the impact of his or her own feelings on the behavior of others as well as the irrational power and skill and expectations imposed on the leader by others who bring powerful images from the past into the trading arena. The more the leader understands these powerful dimensions, the more he or she can understand factors that lead people to stretch themselves beyond the comfort zone.

As a leader, you must help your traders feel in control. By teaching them principles of self-reliance and other concepts outlined in this book, you empower your traders. With a sense of their own power, they develop clarity of thought and will be able to work through any confusion they may feel. How do you show them they are in control? Simply by giving them control. Show them how to get a handle on the levers of their work, and they'll work more proactively and profitably.

The leader is responsible for the team's results and ought to apply discipline to make sure that their results are what is wanted, especially in down periods when traders may be doing things that are impractical or high-risk. The team leader has to notice any inclination to avoid this because of wanting "to give them a chance to grow," "to let them learn on their own," and "not to stifle creativity and independence."

The thirteen critical characteristics of leadership demonstrated by Sandy, the super-trader, include:

1. A vision of the future which provides a framework of purpose and motivation to the daily efforts of the team.
2. A single-minded focus on realizing the vision, no matter the time, the risk, or the odds against him.
3. A willingness to allow others to help him to realize the vision.
4. Preparation, preparation, and more preparation.
5. Patience—the ability to wait for things to develop.
6. High tolerance for original and idiosyncratic thought and behavior, allowing people to be different.
7. A zealous regard for telling the truth and facing reality of risks and obstacles.
8. Listening ability—the capacity to hear the truth, in the course of which people are likely to discover that they are not who they thought they were, making possible the discovery of hidden potential in oneself and others.
9. Humor—the ability to keep things light in moments of despair.
10. Discipline—adherence to one's strategies and rules.
11. Trust—have confidence in each other for creating the vision.
12. Commitment—a willingness to keep playing the game even when there is a pull towards retreat and withdrawal.
13. A willingness to set an example and to relinquish ego for the good of the team and the vision.

Some traders cover up their power because of a need to please and to look good. John, for instance, holds back in his trading because he is afraid of failing. How can you help him and thus help the firm become more successful as a whole? By offering him a way to equip himself with some of the tools I have talked about in earlier chapters, including centering, visual imagery, and concentration. Teach him not to ask other people what to buy. Teach him to mine his previously untapped potential.

The whole "Trading to Win" approach is designed to minimize the feelings of being out of control that so often occur when the market turns unexpectedly and the trader doesn't have a game plan for handling it. This program also teaches traders how to deal with discomfort so that they can interpret out of control feelings simply as further manifestations of stress. They also need to learn specific approaches to solving such problems as assessing whether the market and sector is moving upward, and, if so, whether to trade bigger.

Your strategy can help traders to double and triple their profitability. You do this by teaching controlled risk taking. By sharing your own vulnerability and use of the system, you demonstrate the actions needed to enhance the performance of younger traders. By working with them, you reveal how they can learn what to do to overcome obstacles.

Show your team what to do in terms of their own trading. Help them understand how their own thinking impinges on their trading or enhances it. Get traders to share themselves and, by so doing, illustrate your points.

Get them to take action that deepens their commitment. Make them write down a statement of their objectives and their plan. Train them in terms of their abilities and their approaches and help them reach their objectives by overcoming their own natural resistance.

One of the major obstacles to growth is the fact that as traders succeed they are less motivated to stretch themselves and expose themselves to greater risk. This accords with the observation that the utility of additional stock is inversely related to the quantity of goods already possessed.

Success puts greater satisfaction on retaining what has been earned than on acquiring additional money. Traders become more concerned with loss than with gain, and are more motivated to trade not to lose than to trade to win.

I have observed this phenomenon over and over again in traders who stop stretching when they have made sufficient money to satisfy their inner need. To motivate them to put themselves at risk for a greater gain when the utility of subsequent profits is less than the utility of earlier profits require a rethinking and reframing of their approach to trading. This is provided by weekly seminars that put value on stretching and expanding and playing in terms of their potential and their vision and not in terms of their comfort zone. There is sufficient negative value put on holding back and avoiding risk that traders are motivated to overcome their reluctance to trade or their preference for resting on their laurels.

In effect, the desire to be rich is tempered by how rich you already are. Presumably the richer you are the less you desire to be rich. The value of weekly seminars and a team approach to trading is that they help to override the natural instinct to hold back from trading when the marginal utility of subsequent trades is less than the original utility of previous accumulations.

Communicating as a Team

Good communication in the trading room is vital to the team's success and growth. Sandy, the master trader, has an uncanny ability and willingness to pay attention to the individual needs of the traders on his team. He understands the inherent conflict between individuality and being part of the team. To support this apparent paradox, we have spent much time thinking about the importance of these six requirements:

1. Being clear about the game plan in the light of the yearly objective, the daily review of the market direction, and survey of relevant catalytic events and other research information about the activity of various stocks and bonds and the markets in general. As much as possible, Sandy tries to develop a strategy for every trading day with the help and perspective of the entire team.
2. Acknowledging ideas shared by traders and encouraging them to discuss openly their thought processes and formulation of ideas.
3. Defining a concept of a team and rules for being on the team to reduce ambiguity and conflict. Sandy is sensitive to the traders' tendency to give up their drive to trade their own way as they seek to become part of the team, and notices also the tendency of some traders to drift toward dependency and the comfort zone.
4. Recognizing Sandy's impact on the team and trying to be clear about what he wants in order to reduce misperceptions that team members may have about his objectives and his attitudes toward them. This is a critical aspect of leadership and requires considerable maturity or perspective on the part of the leader to recognize and accept that members of the team are likely to endow the leader with extraordinary powers and concerns that somehow ignore his own capacities and sensitivities as an individual with feelings and concerns of his own.
5. Appraising honestly errors and breakdowns that are often hidden in the profit and loss statement of the day.

6. Being willing to hold traders to their commitment. The leader's task is to ask people to promise a result and then to help them to do what it takes to get to that result. This usually means getting them to stretch beyond what they are accustomed to doing and being accountable for it.

Unfortunately, it is not always as simple as it should be. There are certain characteristics of group behavior that must be identified and handled. There are also specific dynamics in any trading room. If traders think they are being unjustly treated, the dynamics will be affected. People pull their weight differently. What's more, traders often perceive themselves as moneymakers and forget that they still need to pay attention to people skills.

Communication is especially important at the start of a new project. How can new technical procedures be introduced with reduced resistance? Some traders may be vague about objectives. Vaughan, for example, lacks authority. He makes vague, soft requests and never demands that his needs be met. Without effective communication, you cannot resist resistance, adequately communicate objectives, or delegate proper human engineering at the outset of a project. One way to maximize communication efforts is to develop group leaders to implement projects. You can determine these leaders by knowing the informal structure of leadership already in the room. Who influences whom?

Communication is a big part of maximizing your trading. The first element to consider is whether you are trading the number of share lots that you are capable of trading. You can increase that number by bouncing ideas off other people and getting information from the room you are trading in. You may want to talk to the best traders and find out what they think about things in which you are interested. If you have enough conviction they might trade with you on a particular position. Others may help you to get into the game in a bigger way or reinforce your conviction to help you to trade bigger.

The Art of Pairing Traders

Teaming up traders helps provide mutual support. An outstanding stock picker who is reluctant to pull the trigger may do well to work with an active trader who needs more trading concepts. They may even want to consider pooling their accounts to maximize the potential synergy that is generated when two people form a team.

Dick is a case in point. He's fearless about executing trades, and he is able to make huge profits in highly volatile technology stocks. But this same fearless nature manifests itself in a lack of discipline when the market moves against him. There, he often acts in a contrary fashion by averaging up short positions, rather than closing them out when they move up. Try as he might, he could not break the habit. However, he began to get some measure of control when he teamed up with a more cautious trader, Milt, who has no tolerance of holding on to losing positions.

To maximize their profitability, Milt had to be willing to ride herd on Dick's bad choices. On one occasion, Dick shorted Pharmacia/Upjohn at $42\frac{1}{8}$ when all the drug stocks were strong. Milt pointed this out, and when the market was down, reverse and plus on the day, they covered it, and the stock went higher. Without Milt's help, Dick probably would have shorted more of the stock, even though it was against him.

Working together with another trader is one way to correct for one unprofitable trader's tendencies. Ideally, you want to combine two people who work well together and whose disparate skills complement each other. Dick and Milt created a team synergy. They complemented each other, and, working together, were able to make sizable profits.

What Makes Partnering Work?

Sometimes people combine as teams but do not really work out the parameters of working together so they are at cross-purposes and therefore allow their resistance to being managed or coached interfere with the process. Teamwork requires a willingness to let go of negative self-characterizations and old mind-sets, to tune in to the needs of others, and to allow mutual support. Members of a team must also be really committed to work toward greater self-enhancement and stretching.

Lou asks Don a question, and Don is sarcastic and in a negative mind-set. "Yeah, tell me about it. I'm already getting killed. I don't know what I'm doing. The trade is almost over." Don doesn't want to be late into a stock and is bad-mouthing himself. By complaining, he is tuning Lou out. Lou, being a nice guy, doesn't want to offend Don and backs off, discouraged.

There is no teamwork here. Lou is a family man with an outgoing personality, who always wears the same green sweater and who sneaks out for a cigarette throughout the day. A long-standing member of Alcoholics Anonymous, he brings much of the spiritual value of AA to meetings, and he understands what it means to change behavior. Don, usually an easygoing fellow, is a classic tape trader who has trouble adjusting to the new style of trading, which is based more on concepts and research.

Perhaps because they do not combine profit and loss statements, there is less incentive for Lou and Don to work well together. However, that factor alone wouldn't overcome Don's resistance to teamwork and Lou's helplessness.

Partnering requires:

- A recognition of vulnerability and bad habits.
- A willingness to identify those habits and ask for help at the moment you are about to crash and burn; for instance, Lou could ask someone else for help when turned down by Don.
- An openness among team members that promotes communication and teamwork.

Tracking a Partnership

When your partner gets off his or her strategy or discipline, it is incumbent on you to ask what is not being done that was being done before. What needs to be reinstituted? Research? Monitoring of each other? Mutual pushing? Defining goals and strategies? Sticking to an agreed-upon plan?

The best teams tolerate each other's mistakes. At the same time the partners are willing to speak the truth, pointing out what is missing from their trading that was previously there. Teamwork has value when you can accept your partner's observations about your trading so as to improve your results.

Profit and loss is a good thing to track, albeit many traders think they are freer if they do not. Your P&L can tell you about the market. If the market is up 30 points and you are up only 10 points, you need to consider whether you are missing some bids that are flying in the door underneath the whole portfolio. Does the discrepancy merely represent one stock? If the market is down and bounces and your portfolio erodes, you'd better get out of your positions.

Some traders have difficulty working as partners. Liking each other is not enough if the trader is motivated by the need to be liked rather than to succeed.

Here are some examples of those difficulties:

Kurt prefers to go short on rallies, while Stuart can't tolerate any losses. Stuart is often negative about stocks he just bought, and constantly thinks he has been sucked into buying them. Kurt can't define his exit points and often gets in trouble. He would be better off if he waited until they were fully into a top. Then he can sell into it and pick his point. It's the same with the bottom. As long as he has a game plan, he can manage it. But he is stubborn—he'll take the whole loss of a stock rather than trade out of it. He needs someone he respects to make that happen.

Kurt may benefit from a strong partner who can track and control the downside aspect of his trading. The benefits of giving him leeway so he feels independent do not outweigh the negative effect on P&L and the negative effect on his confidence if he keeps losing. If he can make more money because someone took the trade away and sold the stock, he will feel better and begin to rely on the help and appreciate it, and perhaps eventually learn to do it himself.

Waiting for him to learn to do it himself doesn't benefit anyone. He knows what to do but doesn't exercise his judgment. To narrow the scope of his trading, he can use a partner who will manage the risk by narrowing his trades. He can't do this on his own. If the trader is unable to change, the manager must superimpose structure in the form of a partner with risk management responsibility.

Prodding Others to Change

After you have defined your goals and have set your trading in motion, you need to establish a structure of support to ensure that the strategy is implemented and that the lines of communication are open with others.

Your plan of action must involve the commitment of the rest of your team. Create agreement around your goals by helping others to find value in your objectives and by encouraging them to participate. You must learn to empower others to assist you in accomplishing your strategies, which can help them to discover their own capabilities. By asking for their help, you assist others to get beyond their own thinking and their own limitations by doing something for someone else or for a larger cause.

Most of us stop somewhere in our efforts to establish a strategy for the future. We are reluctant to commit to our visions and reluctant to enlist the support of others in the face of resistance. We withdraw from the negative responses of others instead of enrolling them in our activities. In this regard, it is important to share the objective with others and get others to agree to participate or to help you by making requests of them in relation to your objectives.

At the outset, assess how much time, space, and/or additional personnel are needed, or assign someone to take responsibility for making the project work. Establish channels of communication with those involved so as to make sure that there is a structure for handling events. It is also useful to establish a time line for the pursuit and completion of the project.

The typical problem develops from the fact that once you are committed to your objectives you are likely not to establish the necessary structure for monitoring the project to ensure that it stays on target. Too many strategies fall by the wayside because of the failure to demand accountability. Part of your role is to make sure that people don't fall into inadequate ways of functioning and begin to operate out of the belief that it is not possible to make things happen. To establish accountability, you yourself must overcome your anxiety about making demands of your team.

Persevering with Your Team

When other people are working with you, you need to communicate your objectives to them and get them to sign on to the results. It is not always easy to clarify designated duties on trading projects, and the team leader often fails to ascertain the willingness of others to participate.

It is essential to establish the trust of others and to ensure that they understand what it is that you want them to do. This holds true even if the people who are helping you are experts. You have to specify what you want. It is also important to put in place a system for checking on what is done, so that you can be certain people are cooperating with your plan. Here, too, there is often a tendency to assume that everything is okay, or to accept excuses when people fail to do what they promised. Here, it is necessary to correct the tasks and realign the targets in line with what you want to be accomplished.

Projects often fail because leaders, as well as team members, don't remain committed to their objectives. You have to stick to your original intention and move forward in the face of fear and frustration. The more you do, the more likely it is that your team members will meet their assignments.

In the early stages of a project, try to be as economical as possible. Narrow your focus on what is absolutely necessary. Don't get carried away going in too many different directions. Be ready to stay in touch with the people around you by demanding performance from them beyond what they may be willing to do, or beyond what they think they are capable of doing.

Being clear and demanding performance from others may be difficult for you if you are too concerned about what they think of you. This could be the biggest factor in keeping you from achieving what you set out to do. Perhaps you are wary of appearing in an unsatisfactory light. That's why it is crucial, at the outset, to be as lucid as possible about your goals, so that others can support them.

The early stages of a project usually involve more effort and fewer results. Recognize this, and realize you'll put an initial effort in without seeing too many results immediately. Remind yourself that down the line there will be greater results. This is a matter of faith. Too many people give up in the early stages when they don't see results, without realizing that it takes considerable effort to create the structure necessary for ensuring positive outcomes.

When you act in your trading as if you make a difference, you appear more powerful. You will speak to and listen to others with new authority. To have an impact on others you have to support them out of a sense that you indeed do make a difference, rather than out of an attitude that you are being taken advantage of or exploited by them.

People do care, but they are run by their own self-limiting beliefs and self-doubts, which interfere with their productivity. To become a leader you have to relate to others in a supportive way, helping them accomplish what it is that you want so they too can become powerful individuals.

Managing Your Team Players

Asked about his concept of a team, Sandy, the super-trader, noted:

"If you look at the composition of most teams, people are doing different things, just in a natural sense. The beauty of a team is that people will tend to gravitate to different areas anyway, so that they can play from their strength.

"In effect, this means giving up your sense of being an outsider for whatever reason. To be on the team you give up this sense, even though it is part of your sense of yourself, so that you can play in terms of a larger objective. Ideally a team gives you the space to play beyond your limiting self-concepts. Ideally, you have to trust the team and its belief in you and acceptance of you and stop worrying about looking foolish. To play maximally on the team means to play in terms of being totally honest."

Of course, there is a certain amount of tension associated with this. For some traders like Lou, it is difficult to be independent and be a team player. The pressure to conform to group expectations may clash with independent thinking. Even advanced traders have to watch their tendency to look for approval. "If you look for approval you are going to compromise yourself unconsciously to fit what you think the boss wants, and that will get you off your game. Play your own game, but be willing to use the team to enlarge your perspective—especially if you are blind to a situation," Sandy advised.

"You should step up to doing stuff that you want to do," he continued, "and let the head trader be the arbiter of whether the group has too big a position. You're not going to get anyone angry if you trade on information. Just relax and let it run. And if you start feeling some angst, just turn around and say, 'I've got a winner here.' It's not that hard. You just have to keep forcing yourself to do it.

"The value is in sharing different opinions, not in the agreement. This is tough. It's not about getting pats on your back. It's about being

Twenty Tips for Managing Your Team

1. Each day, have a good reason to be in a stock. Do not simply trade the movement of the tape.
2. Consider how to manage your risk and how to increase profitability by better control through risk management or partnering.
3. Remember that partners work better when they share P&L.
4. See that problems with partnering are worked out.
5. Work with a partner if you can create a synergy together.
6. Look for structural changes that will enhance performance and correct for habitual error patterns.
7. Work with someone who will comment on and be vocal about what you are doing.
8. Be in the flow of information in the room. Be able to decipher which research you like during the day.
9. Don't let partners get irritable and preoccupied. Don't permit them to put each other down for trying to ask questions of them.
10. Don't delay in changing your seat. How people will react to your finding a better situation for yourself is not a reason to avoid moving your seat.
11. Ask yourself what it is that you want. Then, figure out the logistics.
12. Don't reject an idea of what you want because you don't see how the logistics will work.
13. Notice your hesitation to take action because of your concern about upsetting other people and being responsible for movement in the room of people in seats.
14. Develop a buddy system where you give someone your positions to assess and help you stay in or get out.
15. Get as much information as you can and learn to do your own research. Learn to share and exchange information in order to increase the flow of information exponentially.

> ### Twenty Tips for Managing Your Team (Continued)
>
> 16. Change the group you follow. Find one with action in it and one that you like. Get on your game and trade big stocks. Trade ones that are moving. Subscribe to a research service like "First Call" as a source of new ideas.
> 17. Compartmentalize your time. Use your time in the car on the way to and from work. Call your colleagues and analysts over the weekend or on the car phone.
> 18. Don't fight windmills.
> 19. Find people who have access to the companies you trade and try to get information on trends and so forth. Get to know the chief financial officers (CFOs)—these people know where their companies are going. Many of them like to talk. They know what will happen before it shows up on the tape and, over time, you can learn to read the nuances in their voice.
> 20. Watch the stock. Watch if the sector gets weak, if a product is coming out, or if the company people are buying the stock. Don't wait for the research from salespeople.

able to play in a game with people who yell and scream and feel rejected and so forth.

"The trade is made when it's on, not getting out. The position is on and someone's watching it. Or maybe the next day the guy pares back twenty-five. It's a flowing situation. We're not going to hold hands together. We're all going to go dancing around a circle," Sandy says.

Looking closely at Kurt's trading, Sandy noted: "I don't think Kurt is in any position with a reason. He's trading because he thinks a stock is acting badly. That's not a good way to trade. He's in Gillette 'because it looked lousy yesterday.' That also is not a good reason. How can he have conviction based on that kind of information? This is evidenced by his P&L. There's no reason why he's in half the things he's in."

When managing traders, you need a set of guidelines to implement and reinforce. Refer to the accompanying checklist of twenty tips that can help you keep your traders on track.

Model Successful Traders

If someone's style is compatible with your personality, you can learn to trade the same way. Figure out what makes you comfortable, what will lead to greater productivity. You can learn to do new things by adapting another person's actions without slavishly cloning every aspect of that style.

Build your own individuality, but also copy from others each day. Keep expanding your abilities each day. Find a trader you want to imitate and learn new behavior by trading with that person. While you will develop over time, you can expedite the process by deciding now what to do and deciding to play at another level. Maximum performance teaches you to become conscious of what is possible and what is more useful. It teaches you to practice and gives you the access to try it. Your game will expand only so far by itself. To keep it expanding, you have to commit to expanding it.

Charlie is an example of a young momentum trader who relies solely on chart analysis. A man short in stature but brilliant in intellect, Allan was an economics major in college, and his good study habits have stayed with him. Each night he reviews close to a thousand charts, and he reviews every one of his stocks each weekend. Admiring Allan's performance, Vinnie, an up-and-coming trader, listed eleven characteristics of that he would like to imitate:

1. He buys stocks that look good and are trading well.
2. He shorts stocks that are going down.
3. He is not distracted by anything.
4. He looks at changes, goes through a lot of names and criteria, and is familiar with an enormous number of stocks, while following more than twenty of them.
5. He watches the tape.
6. He uses a real-time system—he looks at his P&L. If he's in the

right stocks and the market comes in and his P&L doesn't change, he keeps buying them on the decline. If the market turns, he has all the right names and he's going to explode.

7. He uses his P&L as an indicator.

8. He watches the momentum; he identifies the momentum early, and follows it. Very often, he reviews more charts.

9. He isn't afraid to get into a stock up a dollar and a half. Many traders are reluctant to initiate a position that is up because they feel they are giving up an edge. He is trading so many stocks that it doesn't matter. He sees a stock being up a buck and a half as a good sign to buy it.

10. When the momentum ends, he gets out. He is not emotional about stocks.

11. In down days, he is short. (He may have accepted pain up to that point. Until he is convinced of the direction, he may stick with his positions and get hurt.)

By copying actions of someone whose style fits yours, you create your own style—one that works for you—and then you refine it.

Watch Younger Traders

"New traders must be watched so that they don't buy too much to start, get in too late, or get out too soon," says Tom, the head trader at another large hedge fund. "Let's say your position size is ten thousand shares. If the stock doesn't immediately spring out and move higher, you have too big a position. Most young traders are too new to the business to take a ten-thousand-dollar hit on any one day.

"Let's look at somebody who's producing five thousand dollars a day rather consistently," says Tom. "If that person, with a fifteen- or twenty-thousand-share position limit, immediately takes a ten-thousand-share position and that stock drops, the trader can actually lose the five grand that you thought he would make. So now he has to make ten grand just to get back to his daily goal.

"One guy recently took a bank stock," Tom continues. "Granted, bank stocks had been depressed. Then they started acting better, and all the rest of the banks were rallying. But this one was not. I don't know why there was a seller sitting on this particular stock, and I have no understanding of what the seller was hoping to accomplish by sitting on it for so long, but I do know it was underperforming the group. It continued to underperform, and at the end of the day, as the group came off slightly, this one outperformed to the downside."

Tom concludes, "I asked the young trader, 'Why start strong in that name?' Sometimes what we believe is that the selling will abate in the laggard, and it will have catch-up to do. And that does work occasionally, but I think it works more when stocks are in an early part of an upward move."

Managing Time

Sometimes a trader's responsibilities may seem to be more than one person can handle. When each trader learns to manage time effectively and delegate duties responsibly, the team will become even more successful.

The first step to time management is to give up micromanagement. Do not try to control something you cannot. Concentrating on your winners and a smaller number of stocks will give you maximum capacity to focus on your better trades. To run more money you have to be efficient.

Why be in three-thousand-share positions? Ask yourself, "Is it distracting me, or is it making money?" If you want to play big you have got to play ten-thousand-share positions.

Do what super-traders do—give someone else your bad trades. You may have an assistant dispose of them.

Assistants can be a big help to traders. Perhaps two traders on your team may share one. A leader should be responsive to needs such as this and should have the attitude that anything that will make the team more productive is worth the extra cost. By using the process of delegation, traders can free themselves to concentrate on making more money. After all, it is difficult to enter trades, watch the phone, and trade the tape all at the same time.

Another aspect of time management involves knowing what your day is like in order to determine what time allotments are best for which activities. Ask yourself questions like, "Do I get many calls during the day? Am I busy in the morning? More specifically, how busy am I at 11:30 A.M.?"

Nobody Is an Outsider

Everybody's got some sense of being an outsider. Being on a team means giving up your sense of being an outsider, even if you've held on to that concept from childhood. Ideally, a team gives you the space to play outside of your self-concept.

"My goal is to keep the risk manager away from me the whole year and make a lot of money," says Jennifer. "To do this, I have to give up my old attitude that I have to be different. Every day is the day. That means my saying, 'I'm going to play to make this amount of money,' and maybe the tortoise wins the game. You can come away with two million dollars by making nine million and losing seven million. Or you can come away with four million dollars by making five and losing one. I'm working on when to play, and having that patience. I just have to mature more, I think. My goal for the year is to be good at getting out of things, because I know I can let things ride and make money. Another goal is not to have down days. My problem is that I can't trade by joint committee."

Jennifer has to allow herself to be coached and not be so egotistical that she thinks she can and must trade alone.

Teamwork Is Sharing Ideas

Team members should encourage as much feedback as possible on positions, rather than ridicule each other. Individualists ought not to have to acquiesce to the team, but they should use the team in a situation where they may be blind to a situation or they've got to be able to defend their positions.

When people tell you something, listen to it very closely. Don't ever disregard it. If someone has something important to say, listen very closely, especially to people who are willing to put themselves on the line. If someone thinks you're doing something that you shouldn't be doing, or that you should do it differently, listen carefully. And, don't be reluctant to share your views with others. Don't be afraid of being wrong, or being shot down. At the same time, you have to do your own thinking. The other guy may not be seeing things correctly. So you have to come back and say, "Well, that's wonderful—that's a great answer, but I don't agree with you, anyway." Teamwork is sharing ideas, but it is not a group trading situation where you need absolute consensus to make a trade.

Planning Your Expansion

With the right team players, your organization can grow to be as large as you want it to be. Here is a set of questions you can use as you plan your expansion.

- What are underutilized or intangible assets in the firm?
- What are special assets of other traders that can become added sources of strength? What do they do well that they are not now doing?
- What are other sources of profitability in the organization?
- What other assets can be leveraged toward an infinite upside with a minimum downside? In effect, how can you use the same underutilized cost structure to become a source of profitability? How can you enlist other available capital to expand income with the same infrastructure?
- Where can you increase transactions and increase profits?
- How can you quantify the results in all profit centers?
- What is the baseline measure of each business process, the variance?
- How can you expand the number of profit centers?
- What are feasible profit centers that fit the mix and orientation of the existing structure? Should you expand profit centers or develop them from existing personnel?
- Who are your customers? Are they investors? What can you do to increase the number of customers? What can you do to increase the cost of the unit of sale?
- How can you increase alliances through joint ventures that are compatible with your mix?
- Is there a customer base that is not being reached, something to market, a market to market to, a potential salesperson, a referral network of investors, possible deals and/or joint ventures?
- Where is there room for internal development—underdeveloped areas of the company that can be sources of increased profit?

- What vision, plans, or structural features need work?
- What is the gap that you are willing to create for profitability?

Leadership Can Create Momentum

The more you help others to stretch the more you will stretch. One of the best ways to grow is by developing a team. A team approach to trading, whether it is a firm's trading desk or a partnership between two traders in a larger firm, can produce exponential results far greater than what one would expect from the addition of talents.

To the extent that you help your staff make money, you'll help yourself. They can learn faster if you point the way, and you'll get to the next level if your ego is out of the way. Everybody here can help you to get bigger. The more you help them, the more they're going to help you. It has to do with being more communicative and exchanging more information.

PART THREE

Mastering the Trading Game

Chapter Ten

Dealing with Stress

"I was losing and got scared. If the stock went down an eighth, I would sell; if it went up a quarter, I would sell. I couldn't do anything. I believed there was nothing I could do. It was a spiraling downfall."

Maryann, a marathoner and one of the many young women learning to trade on the Street, was at a seminar of mine, describing one of her bad days. "I was afraid of losing, whatever I did," she declared.

Listening carefully, Jack, her boss commented, "I think you have a misperception. If anything you were overdisciplined. Sure, you lost a thousand dollars in six different stocks in the course of the day. But your discipline protected you. You didn't knock yourself out of the box. This is good work, not bad work, but the stress is distorting your perception of your performance."

Stress has been defined as the body's response to stressful events. It is characterized by the "fight or flight" response, where an increased flow of adrenaline increases alertness to stimuli and enhances performance. The stress response prepares you physically and psychologically to deal with stressful events by increasing blood flow to the brain, sharpening your capacity for memory retrieval, and expanding your ability to handle complex tasks.

Some people actually find exhilaration in stressful experiences, and often gravitate to careers that take advantage of their ability to manage stress. This can certainly be said for many traders. Others are attached to systems analysis, which puts an emotional distance between the trader and the trading.

The stress response isn't necessarily negative. In fact, an optimum stress response can help you get ready to trade, and it can also help you juggle complicated situations in which stocks are moving in unpredictable patterns. The optimum stress response may also help you concentrate when you could otherwise be distracted by events or by your own thoughts. It can help you gaze at the tape, think about your own internal trading signals, and maintain your own pace and trading strategy in the face of conflicting signals.

The stress response can help you maintain the pace necessary in the trading business. Emotional arousal is also important to keep you from getting bored if things are getting slow, from being scattered if things are getting too hectic, or from being paralyzed in confusion if things are turning against you.

Beyond the optimum level, however, stress responses become negative. At the very least, you retreat to a comfort zone and defensive trading. Additional stress translates into anxiety and is associated with declining performance. Fears intensify the reaction to stress, which in turn may lead to mistakes. Stress-induced anxiety may awaken negative memories from the past, leading to fear of failure or criticism, misinterpretation of data, as well as misunderstanding of your own responses. In turn, you feel further anxiety and indecision.

Stress-induced anxiety is also anticipatory. It can produce worry about how you will trade next time. Before you realize it, your anxious anticipation of repeated failure throws off your performance.

How do you know you're under too much stress? Typical symptoms include palpitations, difficulty in breathing, distractibility, muscle tension and cramps, noise sensitivity, severe hand trembling, and loss of appetite. These symptoms usually recede as trading begins. Indeed, performance anxiety seems to occur mostly before and after the trading day, not so much during it. The better you get as a trader, the more you can tune these negative thoughts out and fine-tune excessive stress responses so that you can channel your adrenaline into your work.

Efforts to reduce anxiety, paradoxically, may create a new set of programmed responses, which can undermine trading flexibility. These can be temporary or permanent handicaps to good performance. They can

---

Seven Common Stress Triggers for Traders

1. Pressure to make money
2. Pressure not to lose money
3. Indecision about an uncertain and fluctuating market
4. Uncertainty about the most desirable entry and exit points
5. Difficulty in controlling one's emotional reactivity to the uncertainty of market fluctuations
6. Pressure to process a massive amount of information coming through in high-speed fashion
7. Pressure to look good and maintain concentration and focus in the midst of pressure to perform

---

stop you from growing and improving as a trader. These behaviors may seem to be adaptive temporarily, but once they become fixed patterns they have a rigidity of their own. You thus limit yourself from adapting further and modifying old habits.

Attempts to lessen anxiety also may lead to a misinterpretation of events. Your misinterpretation is based on experiencing the emotions of trading in terms of the life principle previously mentioned, which is built into people—the little voice from childhood that often insists you are insufficient and are missing something, which you must hide from yourself and others. In fact, what you see in the marketplace is a reflection of your automatic thinking or life principle. Your own thinking creates stress for you and makes it difficult for you to trade purposefully.

Your reactions to trading events, and your reactions to your own reactions, create the stress in your life. How often do you automatically assign meaning to events because of your emotional response to them? And when you do, how often does this lead to decisions that reinforce the same life principle? I suspect your answer is, "Very often." Time and again, you respond to present events in the same way you did to events in the past.

The basic mechanism and physiology of stress is identical from person to person. However, what triggers the stress reaction will vary from job to job, as well as from person to person. A lot depends on your ability to detach yourself from the stressful situation by distinguishing the automatic stress responses from the stress trigger.

Self-Fulfilling Prophecies

Individuals differ in their capacity to distinguish the automatic responses to stress from the interpretation of the stress. When you make a decision in a stressful moment, you may be automatically responding to a situation from your past. This reaction sets in motion self-fulfilling prophecies; you already are predisposed to respond to stressful events in a particular way. Thus, your response creates the very events in the environment that you are trying to avoid. What a vicious circle!

Traders caught in this web cannot escape from it until they change their basic underlying assumptions of the world. To get to this place is extremely difficult. First, it requires you to stand outside the events long enough to see the sequencing of them. Next, you must develop habits of mind and behavior that help break the cycle at any step along the way. As I have said before, you need to notice your physical and emotional responses, but *not* react emotionally to them. Instead, you need to recognize that your interpretation of events is just that—an interpretation—and not necessarily an accurate depiction of the events. Finally, you have to recognize that any decision made in the moment of reactivity is likely to be a stereotyped response such as withdrawal, denial, rationalization, or quitting.

The secret is to separate events from their interpretations and from the emotions that go along with them. Only then can you can change repetitive trading behavior that locks you into performance plateaus year after year.

It takes a lot of time and effort for traders, however motivated, to learn to get beyond their natural resistance to self-examination. I know, from years of observing traders, that it takes a major effort for them to become conscious of their own decision making processes and habitual actions. However, once you make this psychological breakthrough, you can catch yourself the next time you are trading compulsively. Accomplish that breakthrough, and you can change your behavior to be more consistent with your trading objectives.

Stress and Your Comfort Zone

As stress-induced anxiety mounts, you may become nervous, uncertain, or depressed. Perhaps you begin to feel convinced you are destined to fail. These reactions are especially likely in the face of either significant profits or losses. This is generally the point at which traders become paralyzed and unable to make appropriate decisions to hold on to winning positions or get out of losing positions.

To keep stress responses within reasonable limits, most traders simply begin to function within a range that is comfortable for them, although possibly not the most profitable. Numerous fears come into play when trading beyond the psychological comfort zone. These fears occur independently of the market performance of any stocks you may hold in your portfolio.

What are these fears about? They include concern about losing and disappointing others, the fear of shame and embarrassment for not succeeding, and the fear of making errors and looking bad. For some, fears of going broke or trading beyond the comfort zone are triggers related to earlier-learned anxiety about attaining positive results and competing with others. These traders may want to outperform parental figures who failed in their own trading experiences, and/or may worry about inadvertently duplicating those failures.

These traders may be afraid of recreating some earlier traumatic experiences from which they have never fully recovered, the memories of which are activated every time they approach the same level of performance, positive or negative. One trader I know admitted that he was afraid he would be "chastised" by his family if he succeeded. "If I don't make too much," he said, " I can maintain my relationship with my parents, who tend to put more emphasis on spirituality than financial gain. If I succeed I will really be out of the family."

When these traders approach a new, higher level of performance success, they squeeze a stress trigger. At that point, they tend to sell and take their profits on the basis of what is comfortable rather than holding onto or increasing their position in a rising stock to maximize profits. Similarly, these same traders may not cut their losses when their positions reverse. They may engage in elaborate, self-induced ruses to avoid acknowledging their losses and then end up losing far more than they should have.

Different Situations, Different Challenges

Different situations present different challenges and trigger different stress reactions that must be mastered if the trader is to succeed. Some traders have trouble dealing with success. Feeling significant anxiety as their profits rise, they unintentionally sabotage themselves. Indeed, most traders lose more often when they are worried about losing. In such cases they are on a losing streak or have had a significant loss, and are trying to recover their profits in the same stocks or are reluctant to sell out and cut their losses. Their anxiety narrows and freezes their focus of attention so that they can neither respond effectively to incoming data nor rely on their internal models to reproduce past successful patterns. Any increase in anxiety further distracts them, and leads to a fixation on internal physical reactions, further intensifying anxiety.

Anxiety depletes energy and causes fatigue. As tension grows, your ability to maintain a broad attention focus on stock activity diminishes, and your preoccupation with your own anxiety increases. To make matters worse, anxiety interferes with your reasoning powers, producing more mental errors.

Here is some background about where anxiety originates, and some suggestions to help you manage stress to your advantage, the way master traders do.

The Power of the Past

You are never anxious for the reasons that you think. You may have an explanation for being frightened or depressed, angry, or jealous. You may attribute your upset to something that just happened, or something someone has said. In fact, it is more likely that you were already receptive to being distressed before the event occurred. The present experience may have reactivated an old experience, which in turn also represented a reactivation of a prior experience.

You are dominated by the past—the source of the concepts that color your perceptions of the market, of your own thoughts, and of the thoughts of others. These concepts, what I've referred to as your "life principle," serve as the central focus of your personal story. Your life principle is the core emotional position, the source of all your self-fulfilling prophecies.

Let me state this another way. You bring to all situations a set of lenses or perspectives comprised of life principles formed in the past. These perspectives slant your reactions to all trading situations. You often misperceive the tape action and see only what you saw before and what you expect to see.

This was true for George, an experienced trader, who, in the middle of the prolonged bull market of the 1990s, said:

"I hesitate to buy stocks that are moving up because I don't believe they will keep on going up. I have a great fear of heights now that the Dow has reached six thousand, and I don't know where it is going. I have a great fear of being long on everything and walking in and having everything go down two hundred points."

George preferred to buy weak stocks and sell strong stocks. "I try to sell the strong ones after they've made a new high. Sometimes I'm shorting them already when they are making a new high," he said.

In fact, George was trading the tape as if it were a zigzag tape from the past. His problem was not just lack of information; it was as if he had a mental image of the tape and how to play it that was contrary to the way the tape really was.

Have you been stuck in the same situation? If so, you are not as alert as you can be, nor are you tapping as much of your potential as you can, because you are not functioning in the present. Rather, you are trading in terms of your own internal system, which was developed in the past. No matter where you go, you carry this internal map with you. This makes for predictability and even comfort, but it keeps you from producing the best results possible.

The same belief applies to concepts about yourself and others, which are colored by past experiences and which limit how you function in the world.

This is a profound and no doubt upsetting thought, and I can understand how you may not want to accept it as true. That's all right. I am not asking you to believe it, only to look at the world as if this perspective were true—so that with this new perspective you become aware of the impact of your thinking mechanism on your trading.

Try a little experiment used in the Japanese system of Morita psychotherapy. Ask a friend or relative to close their eyes and describe the

room you are both in, to demonstrate how little people see of their sur-
roundings and how absorbed they are with their own mental preoccu-
pations, which prevent them from apprehending the here and now. Try
reversing roles in another room to see how much this applies to you.

Overcoming Performance Anxiety

All of this is important to you as a trader, if you wish to break out of the
habits that prevent you from trading in the here and now, and begin to
trade in a proactive way.

When you learn to observe your own frightening thoughts, you will
be able to reduce their intensity, using methods mentioned in Chapter
5, from progressive relaxation to yoga, to visual imagery rehearsal, to
breathing exercises. I realize this may sound suspiciously New Age, but
these techniques will stop you from being afraid, curtail your worries
about external events, and help you reach a centered state.

Just by deliberately breathing slowly and deeply, you can calm yourself. Each deep breath you take in the here and now helps you to modify your automatic physiological reactions to stress. The more you can
practice this, the more you can fine-tune excessive stress.

Once you learn to observe events objectively, rather than in terms
of your own automatic, fearful interpretations, you will understand that
they are not the cause of your anxiety. Once you become aware that
your explanations are not accurate, and that you need not overreact, the
situation takes on a more neutral meaning and becomes less distressing.

Moreover, you will be able to trade in a more purposeful way so as
to fulfill your creative potential. You'll be free to choose new principles
for your trading without being afraid to go past your previous habitual
limits.

Ideally, by scrutinizing the data needed to follow your trading strategy, not the emotion-laden issues of winning or losing, you can focus
on the trading issues themselves without becoming too anxious or overwhelmed. This is particularly true during a trading day, when you
should be able to concentrate only on doing what is necessary for your
strategy rather than thinking overly much about your goals or the consequences of trading.

Having mastered certain principles of anxiety reduction, you can extend your trading boundaries beyond the comfort zone and begin to raise your level of performance. Personal stretching of this kind can take many forms. Among them is the ability to overcome an inclination to ignore proper risk management on the downside, to avoid marking your losses to the market at the end of the day, and not to free up capital for profit-making opportunities elsewhere. This is particularly relevant for contrarians, who prefer to trade against market trends and who may have experienced great success in the past when they have come from behind.

Stress and Staff Management

Another source of stress relates to the management of staff. Right now you may be tolerating insufficient or inadequate performance rather than speaking truthfully about how people are doing because of an unwillingness to hurt their feelings or a mistaken belief about your dependence on them. However, the frustration and stress involved in withholding your opinion will accumulate and cause chronic psychological problems.

Don't be afraid to dispense with your sympathy for others. It is draining and not directly related to productivity. Some managers will keep supporting staff who are no longer contributing at the same level or whose performances have not kept up with those of the rest of the trading organization. These managers actually do a disservice to unsatisfactory staff members if they don't present new standards of performance and don't try to empower people to play at a higher level. Although these managers may be afraid of harming staff members' self-esteem by speaking truthfully about what needs to be corrected or modified, in the end, withholding constructive observations reinforces a sense of inadequacy and self-pity in staffers. In addition, these managers allow the pressure to build within themselves and distract them from their own goals. Some master traders even hold themselves back by having less talented people around them and then accommodating to their demands or resistance.

Under stress, many traders such as George can't distinguish what is really going on and have difficulty adapting to new situations. They may be willing to change their behavior, but do not know how. Or, they would rather make excuses than do what it takes to change their assumptions.

Of course, some staffers are more prone to seek adventure and have a greater tolerance for experiencing the physiological manifestation of anxiety. They still need encouragement from their managers.

With training, you and your staff may still get anxious about the same things but you can notice this and then move on. The underlying pattern may not change, but you can learn to function independently of it. Becoming a master trader means, in part, maintaining a level of consciousness despite stress, which permits you to keep adapting to new circumstances.

Chapter Eleven

Overcoming
Common Mistakes

It happens to everyone sooner or later: Disaster strikes. When the market goes against you, stress responses may manifest themselves in misinterpretation and overreaction to the marketplace. The end result: overtrading or unplanned withdrawal from trading—and substantial monetary losses or minuscule gains. Such a pattern is likely to persist until you can develop a more proactive and disciplined trading response to adverse events. However unsatisfactory this behavior may be, it is familiar to all traders.

"What's keeping you from increasing the size of the positions you take?" I asked Jack, a hedge fund manager whose daily target was $100,000.

"Swings bother me," he answered. "When I make a lot of money it is because I don't have big losses. So, when I lose money, I am afraid it's ruining my month and I start getting paralyzed even though I am basically up for the year and the losses are only a small percentage of my overall performance. When this happens, I start expecting the worst and start trading poorly, and I can't seem to break the cycle."

As your fear in the face of stress intensifies, you start recalling every bad trade you made in the past; and then you waste time worrying about how bad future events might become. In this state of mind, no trader can analyze the market rationally or plan a strategy with confidence.

Stopping Points

This split-second sequence of reactions, interpretations, and decisions made in the moment of reaction to adverse market developments, this series of negative ideas that keep you from being fully engaged in trading opportunities, constitutes what I call a "stopping point." In baseball, it's a slump; in marathon running, it's hitting the wall. It's the opposite of being "in the zone."

A stopping point can even be the absence of a trading objective. It rationalizes your position as satisfactory when, in fact, it may be covering up your unwillingness to take a larger, necessary risk. It probably reflects a long-standing life principle to trade in a habitual way, governed by such clichés as "look good," "tough it out," "never ask for help," or "never admit defeat."

Trapped by anxiety, the stopped trader is unable to follow the market trend, cut losses, or let profits run. Most importantly, such traders are unable to follow their own rules. An overly cautious trader becomes afraid to use his or her own market assessments. A stubborn trader won't buy a stock if others are in it, not wanting to be thought of as "a follower" or as someone who is "late to the party." A reluctant trader may refuse to risk more capital on an advancing stock. An impatient trader may book a profit by selling too soon. An egotistical trader may refuse to insert stop losses or try to outguess the market by clinging to a self-image as a "home run hitter."

Some traders are addicted to the ups and downs of winning and losing. Their actions reinforce their penchant for gambling or for taking risks when they are inappropriate. These players are not trading to win, but trading to experience the emotional roller-coaster effects associated with a roll of the dice.

To be able to trade proactively, you must know when you have reached your stopping point and are trading on automatic pilot. As you read the following scenarios, ask yourself honestly how many you yourself have participated in, at some point in your career.

The Home Run Hitter

Ted is a trader who is always trying to pick a stock's high. He bought America Online one day and was up $8000. Then the stock started filling in, but he refused to sell it and take a profit. "I wanted to sell it at the high," was his explanation. He held on to a belief that he must make his goal of $10,000 in one trade. He has to learn to log in portions of his goal in reasonable increments.

"I didn't think we wanted to make half a point," he said when questioned about his patterns. "When I have an opportunity to make some money, I feel I have to stay with it. When I'm up five thousand dollars, I think I'm up nothing."

Adding incrementally to his profit for the day by selling stocks that are starting to drop is just as good a way to realize his goal of $10,000. To do this, he needs to let go of any fixed notion he has about making his daily target on only one move of a stock. This requires awareness of his underlying thought processes, so that he can change his thinking. If he can identify this pattern, he can stop it.

Part of his problem is that he would like to be a home run hitter. "I'm trying to reach higher goals by pressing it up," he explained. In doing this, he has given up his patience, discipline, and well thought-out entry points. He has to start with a bigger position, and not hang in when the stock starts to drop. But deep down he believes he has to make it on the first try. This pattern is related to his tennis game, too, where he doesn't have a second serve and so feels he has to serve up aces all the time.

He is also making market calls without specific reasons. "I knew when it started filling in that I should have gotten out. There were some buyers coming in, and I thought I'd better get out. Then I thought I'd better hold, that the S&Ps would rally back and that I would be making a bad sale if I got out. I thought it was going higher, and I started getting angry when it didn't. I held on, hoping it would turn around. There was really no evidence that the S&Ps were going up, no evidence that the market was going up. I just thought they were going to sell off and then hold," he said.

"I bought some more down lower. The market was weak, and technology stocks were lower." In sum, Ted panics and misses the entry and exit points, and then chases the stock.

Possible solutions for him? He must establish a goal, and play stocks he is researching. If a stock goes down, he must learn to get out and take his profit, rather than trying to hit home runs. He needs to be more rational about making a bigger profit.

Holding On to Losers

Another trader, Seth, is inclined to hold on to a stock too long. He held on to Glassworks because the stock was down only one-eighth when the rest of the market was getting killed, and there always seemed to be a bid around. All of a sudden, the bid disappeared, and the stock was down a half dollar in a matter of minutes. Additionally, he held on to it because the stock was a half dollar from its high at the opening, and he was mad that he hadn't already sold it and was hoping that it would be back to where it was.

Seth must learn to follow a stock, rather than kick himself for not getting out. He has to abandon his desire to get to the top, as well as fear of letting go of the stock. He worries about missing the chance to ride it back up, when in reality he can always buy it back after it drops, and then stay with it as it moves up. As he noted, "I'm taking the stock too personally. I thought I was right and that the stock shouldn't go down, and it did, and then I thought it would go back up." He's getting too reactive and wedded to his picks.

In another instance, Seth came in long on Storage Technology. The stock reversed and went through the previous day's low, which was his stop point. The specialist let the stock trade so quickly on such light volume that as soon as it hit Seth's stop point, it was already trading three-eighths below it. He was hesitant to sell it there because it traded down on such low volume. He waited a little bit, and it went down another eighth. He then decided to get out. It went down another three-fourths in the next hour. The message here? Stay with your discipline. Seth didn't believe what he was seeing, so he should have stayed with his strategy and sold as close to his stop as he could.

What can you learn from Ted's and Seth's mistakes? They—and perhaps you—need to step back a bit from the stocks. You need more communication in a proactive way with someone in the room who is willing to listen and with whom you can share information. You need more discipline about exit points and should not hold stocks when they drop. And you must notice when you are getting angry that your trading is about to be thrown off, so you can control your impulses. The key is to keep correcting for the misperception, or for the lack of information. The more information, the more you reduce your risk.

Shorting Stocks That Are Rising

One trader, Ed, got into trouble when the market turned in May 1996. "I went back to all my old habits of shorting when stocks were rising, because that was comfortable. Now the market has changed directions again, and I'm still locked into shorting things," he said. "I don't sell Citibank or Chase anymore if they are up two points, but I might not buy them. I guess the next step is to buy these stocks.

"I call the analysts all the time. But when I call, I get too much information and don't know what to do. If I'm uncertain and get too much information, I become paralyzed and revert back to my old ways of trading. I have to be careful about certain bullish calls. There are factors out there that are more important than just the analyst's call if he is trying to sell a stock," Ed concluded.

Awareness of a personal habit, which in this case is manifested in a particular defensive style, is a first step in gaining control over the automatic reaction to stress. The lesson here is, don't be inflexible, locked into a specific strategy to the point that you are unable to recognize downward reversals.

The ability to short stocks requires an appreciation of the value of trading with a negative expectation about the direction of a stock or the market, which may be compatible with your general level of optimism or contrary to it. There are characteristics of stocks that also ought to be considered as well in making a decision to short a stock. So it is more complicated than merely having an intuition about the direction of markets.

What are the characteristics of good shorts? A first consideration is whether the stock is overvalued or something is wrong with the company. This requires some understanding of the fundamentals of the stock. Additionally, it is useful to consider the way in which the stock has been trading. Did they run the stocks up artificially at the end of the day? Is there relative weakness? Is there a pronounced downtrend? If a stock is oversold in a bull market it is likely to do poorly in a bear market. Has the stock been going down and is it now up in a down tape? The best shorts hold up the worst in a down market. Be careful here of the beginner's error of mistakenly looking for the top tick in a good stock when the market is going down. These stocks may go down only marginally in the short term and then go back to their prior levels.

Additionally, it is wise to notice any inclination you have to always look for things that will work, and start looking for things that aren't working. This might include a stock that went up for no good reason or one that deteriorated in a strong tape with lower highs and lower lows. Or it may be a stock in a group that is deteriorating in the setting of a negative catalyst event suggesting that people may be shying away from it because of a broken deal. Here you may find an identifiable resistance level that will tell you that you are wrong. Pay attention to stocks that are losing price or momentum, or are in industries with problems. Most of all, trade stocks that are down on the day, not ones that are up four points but you think they will reverse.

Plateauing

Max, whom I introduced earlier, mentioned that he had lost $40,000 on the last day of the month for the past two months. His interpretation? "Half of the loss was due to being lax. Half of it was not listening to myself. I'm usually up three hundred thousand dollars for the first two weeks of every month, but I can't get past that number. I sit there. I can't make five hundred thousand dollars. To make the three, I focus on a situation and get big enough in it where I feel good about it and make a couple of points.

"When I get bigger, I have fewer positions to concentrate on. But I sell the good ones because they are not down. I hold the worst stocks, and my P&L drops instead of getting rid of those poor stocks at the outset. I had eleven stocks. The seven that were good, I got out of. The four I should have been selling, I couldn't get out of."

When Max gets to $300,000, he reverts to old habits. He is governed by his reactions, and not by events or previously planned strategies.

"When I started out flatter, when things were harder and I had to be more selective, I had more risk control. Once there was money in the till, I got less strict," he acknowledged. "The moment I get lax and take it less seriously, I start thinking I can do anything. I stop having respect for the market."

Max has come up with his own personal solution to this common error. "I need to have a list of my own rules next to the Quotron." This, he thinks, might prevent him from becoming reckless. "The final rule is to follow the rules under all circumstances," he says.

Seasonal Stopping Points

Max had another stopping point. He was convinced that he didn't do well in April, May, and June, and on through the summer, so he entered these months with less energy and less consciousness, and with the expectation of not doing well. It was a self-fulfilling prophecy.

"These are slow months. I have fewer positions," he said. "We're in a tight little range. It is hard to make ten thousand dollars to twenty-five thousand dollars. I am not trading during the day as much. I try to get positions for the day and feel comfortable."

Max noted that he usually struggles after the first quarter. Then, September through February, he does very well. He rationalized his ho-hum months by attributing them to the summer doldrums. However, he knew that he had to "get out of the drama, let go of the old programming."

Then one year he came through July and August with a profit. His explanation: "I toned down what I was trying to do. I wasn't trying to turn it into one of my more productive periods. I had to settle down. And in settling down, I eliminated losses. I didn't add so much on the gain side. So the net result was I personally had a better season." By the end of August he was up $1.2 million for the year, "and then that gave me a little more comfort to play bigger in September." September turned into a million-dollar month, which he had never had before.

What changed? "I saw what I had to do, and I saw an opportunity, and I traded aggressively enough to capture that opportunity. It was great. There were one or two very significant large trades where I did a one-hundred-thousand-dollar P&L in one trade or more. That was something different." By noticing his pattern of a long summer yawn and then deliberately trading bigger and bolder in September, he turned his previous stopping point into a victory.

What Are Your Own Stopping Points?

All of the situations just described illustrate different stopping points—that point in time where your fears and beliefs keep you from entering fully into the next moment and instead keep you trading in repetitive and possibly destructive patterns. To overcome these stopping points, you must begin to view market events as neutral and handle them in terms of your conscious objectives, not in terms of old beliefs, such as your fear of the unknown.

Recognizing your own stopping points is a big step en route to managing fear, stress, and trading discipline. Traders may find it difficult to relinquish old habits because doing so means acting contrary to their underlying negative self-concepts. All of this is really the fear of change. These traders are afraid to commit to a larger objective.

Ask yourself these questions about whether you are functioning in terms of your potential, or being tripped up by a stopping point:

- Are you willing to let go of aspects of your life principle that keep you from learning new trading techniques?
- Are you willing to define a larger trading objective and a trading strategy consistent with that objective and then commit to trading in terms of your strategy?
- Are you willing to record entry and exit points as well as a stop point for the trades you wish to make?
- Are you willing to mark your profits and losses to the market so you know where you are at the end of the day?
- Are you willing to analyze your trades to see what strategic elements are missing from your unsuccessful trades?
- Are you willing to develop parameters of measuring your performance so you know what you need to do?
- Are you willing to recognize that to get past your stopping points you must develop the willingness to take risks?

Repeating Habitual Errors

Some traders repeatedly make certain trading errors because habit and temperament, more than trading strategy, dictate their behavior. If you are aware of your predilections, you can be better prepared for them when the same errors rear their ugly heads.

Like most of us, you have probably been conditioned since an early age to avoid mistakes, to minimize them, or to cover them up. Trading is an occupation that offers its players many ways to hide their mistakes, rationalize them, or blame them on others. Even if you make all these errors, you can still make a living. However, by recognizing them as potential learning experiences, you can use them as tools for growth.

As you read the following descriptions, which are based on interviews with a group of traders, once again ask yourself if these are among the mistakes you are inclined to make. Then ask, "What can I do to change this habitual response?"

Inability to Take a Loss

It is a market axiom that most traders are likely to be wrong at least fifty percent of the time, if not more often. Rarely will you be right more than sixty percent of the time. Whatever your percentage of success, you have to be able to take a loss and keep on going. This means you must be able to define and acknowledge your loss and then make the next move to reduce it. Why is it so difficult to take a loss early on, thereby minimizing the ultimate size of a loss that may occur if you hold on too long?

Losing traders may be focused on their losses. If they have a bad day and don't want to take the loss, they start compounding it, hoping a stock will come back and watching as it keeps going down. By focusing on a bad situation, as opposed to focusing on new things, they lose opportunities.

This was true for Eric, who kept shorting Compaq late in June 1997. "I tried to trade in terms of my twenty-five-thousand-dollar daily goal, but I didn't stick to the goal. I got beat from the beginning. I was down twenty-five thousand dollars, wanted to make it back and then make another twenty-five thousand dollars. I traded in terms of fifty thousand dollars and didn't follow my strategy. I was beaten in this stock and should have covered and moved away from the stock," he explained.

"If you lose twice in a stock, you shouldn't go back to it. I kept covering and going back trying to get it right. I wouldn't admit my idea was wrong. I believe in my convictions even though I have been proven wrong so far. I can't admit I am wrong. I know there's going to be a big trade in that, and I don't want to miss it. So, rather than miss it by getting out of the stock, I stay in and take the pain and the loss, and hope it will eventually turn around. I don't want to wait until it is two points for me. I get in ahead of time, and it keeps going up against me. I keep paying more for the stock when I cover."

Reluctance to Get Out of Losing Positions

While it may seem natural to hope that losing positions will turn around, they often don't, and smart traders avoid getting stubborn and staying in stocks that are dropping. You can always sell short, or buy them back if they reverse and start to move up. Only if there is a good reason to believe that you may not be able to get back in should you hold on to the stock as it goes down.

Some of the toughest decisions involve watching stocks you believe in go down. Pat, for instance, is a trader who suffers with his favorites. In one case, Pat was long for four million dollars, and in five minutes managed to shave his position to two million dollars. Still, in the last two hours of the trading day, he lost about thirty thousand dollars in those two million dollars' worth of longs. He didn't want to let go of a stock he loved and was afraid of selling it lest it went back up. He is a prime example of a trader who needs to truly absorb the idea that he can always get back in. What Pat forgets is that he is a trader, not an investor. On his best days, a trader can have the most buy/sell motion possible.

Another trader uses the example of REITs—real estate investment trusts. "The REITs have really been the hidden secret of the market," this trader said in February 1997. "They're up about thirty percent this year. And they just don't stop. There will be days where they'll be up two dollars. They're thinner, and they're a little more difficult to trade because of the liquidity problem. There's not a lot of stock up on the bid or the ask. The spreads might be wide. And so you have to be more nimble in that group.

"If you're carrying a good profit, you may want to go ahead and hit a bid if there's a bid that's growing or if you just don't like the stock anymore and you want to get out. And when the buyers come, they all come at once. They really take them. If I think a REIT is going to go down, I get out. I've held some a pretty long time and felt a lot of pain. Where it hits a certain point, that's it. I'm out no matter what. If you're learning to get out of losing positions, you can keep on getting bigger and bigger, hold it a little longer, move the stop up. But the critical thing is being able to manage that downside. It gives you a lot of confidence," this trader affirms.

In sum, super-traders say, "Get out, period," if you find yourself in a bad situation. Keep looking for positions that work. Don't return to bad ones unless conditions are demonstrably different. You can avoid some of these losing positions by testing all associations before spending money and time on them.

Trading from Your Emotions

Most traders rely on instinct to trade, and much of their trading, especially when it is stressful, is built on efforts to keep emotion under control. They have more difficulty in developing the discipline, patience, and a plan to win. They make their decisions based on hunches, instead of investigating what the best way is or what else needs to be done to reach their goal.

How do emotions negatively affect your trading? Some traders may become complacent after winning because they are feeling "lucky." Or they become complacent after losing because they are feeling unable to change their "destiny." Super-traders don't grow complacent, but keep aiming to upgrade their game. They center on the process, not just the result.

Overcoming the propensity to play emotionally requires a conscious commitment to specific trading objectives. This entails choosing a target, developing a strategy, and finding a method for adhering to it. A goal enables you to keep a relatively even keel through good and bad periods, to sustain momentum, and to keep from becoming bored.

There are several concrete things you can do to grasp what part your emotions play in your trading success or failure. For instance, keep a journal of your feelings so that you can track your emotions and more easily see your progress or setbacks. By having this detailed written information, you can visually follow your progress, and your notes will help you more readily find solutions to your problems.

Another way to help manage your emotions is to share your feelings with others. By discussing your feelings about trading, you can hear, out loud, what you are really thinking and how it impinges upon or enhances your trading. Listening to others may bring to light similar underlying beliefs you may be fostering.

Overattachment to Stocks

If you are committed to succeed, you can't afford the luxury of trading what you like on an emotional basis. An attachment to gold stocks is not uncommon and should be considered when deciding what stocks to include in your strategy. Gary is one trader who loves gold stocks. He plays them and generally loses. He rationalizes his failures and reasons for continuing to trade them, even though he has been successful only once in three years with this strategy.

Gary trades gold stocks emotionally, without knowing a lot about them, instead of trading something more rational, thicker, with greater predictability and a better track record. With gold stocks, there is no one to call, other than some analyst who likes them on a technical basis. It is not like buying a company with earnings or a good story.

Some traders may argue that you shouldn't stop trading a stock because you are losing money on it if "the fundamentals are still right." One master trader's retort: "If the statistics show you aren't making money, you should consider getting out. If you have a concept about making X amount of dollars and you have to design a strategy consistent with that goal, would you include a stock that hasn't succeeded? Probably not. Build a strategy not around what you like, but around what really works."

Even if you would love the profit in gold more than the same profit in another stock, smart traders advise looking for actively traded or thick stocks, like the oils or Micron. Trading out of attachment to a stock or sector is a bad habit. Take responsibility for your results. Do you dramatize your trading losses? This often has a repetitive ring and suggests a trader is reinforcing one's own sense of losing while trying to be likable.

You may believe gold goes up after the presidential elections. "That's like saying stocks will go up after an NFL team's Super Bowl victory," one master trader responds. It is impossible to accept a statement like that at face value and assume that because it happened before, it will happen again.

The same principles apply to other emotional elements that you need to deal with in changing your strategy. Keep examining how you lose money. "When you feel you got it right one time out of five, you are playing out of emotional memory," the master trader says, "very much as if you were gambling."

Emotions also may be part of any tendency you have to fight the market by picking tough stocks. Emotions may be involved as well when you tend to sell a stock that is just starting to work with just a one-half or seven-eighths gain. Master traders don't sell just to take a profit. "Take a walk to get away from the impulse to sell too soon," counsels one successful trader.

Old beliefs and old attachments keep you from getting bigger. Benny, a trader you have heard about earlier, refuses to get into momentum stocks that are moving up. He believes they are going to "get killed." Sure they will—but they are going up first and there will be a profit to be made.

By the same token, master traders suggest that you be cognizant of when you ought to take yourself out of a stock. Even if you do get out too soon, you can fix the scenario right away, and get back the next day. Experience doesn't necessarily mean maturity in the trading game. Players trading for twenty years are still likely to make mistakes because of old habits.

Selling Too Soon

"It is difficult to know when to take a profit," said Jack, a hedge fund manager, the week after the Hong Kong debacle on October 27, 1997. "In a lot of situations it is difficult to know if you can make more. It's tough to know if a stock is going higher. Stocks don't go straight up necessarily."

Many traders too quickly get out of a stock that is moving in a profitable direction to lock in profit before the stock turns, or to make up for losses elsewhere. However, super-traders argue that every time a stock makes a new level, you have to realign your thinking and see the new level as the new floor. "You need to hold on," says one. "Don't worry about the winners, even if you have no idea where they are going. A strong stock often closes near its high, or at least is likely to be higher at 3:30 than at noon. The reason for this is that many buyers are stretching out their orders during the day in order to beat the mean price." Therefore, a lot of forces are creating that strong momentum in the last hour.

The stretch is to stay with the strong stocks. The odds are that seventy percent of them will close higher than they were sold at. Master traders who are in a strong situation and have a sector behind them see no reason to be uncomfortable. On the contrary, says one, "Every time you take a profit for the sake of taking a profit, you will wish you didn't. That momentum buy can go a lot further than you can imagine."

Most traders get out of stocks because they want to take a profit before they lose it. Unfortunately, they don't play for the bigger gain even if their information supports that. Some even rationalize this by saying, "You make a sale and hope it's wrong." Playing momentum means leveraging what you are doing. Let the profits run, say the super-traders. Forget about micromanaging your positions.

A key point, which bears repeating here, is to have a good reason to sell a stock. If you don't know where it's going, hold it. By selling, according to the momentum experts, "You give up control of the situation—you are like a ship floating down the river without someone steering." It's better to stay at the helm and stay with a stock.

Furthermore, you may not want to sell a stock that is dropping because the whole group is doing well. You may want to short a stock in a group that's not doing that well. Follow the trend.

One trader who suffers from premature selling fever is Benny. He had a stock just starting to work, and he wanted to get out once it was up seven-eighths. His colleagues objected. "Why come in long in a stock, sell it, buy it back, sell it up, and then buy another one in the group instead of keeping the best one in the group?" reasoned one of them.

Even when master traders take themselves out of the game, they jump back in the next day. As one master trader noted, "If it wasn't getting better and more interesting, I wouldn't come back. I still haven't mastered the game. That's why I come in, even though at times I can't sleep." Super-traders keep assessing the changes they must make to elevate their game. There is no burnout in this setting. Burnout occurs when you are not stretching yourself and you get bored.

Averaging Up on a Short Position

Averaging up on a short position instead of getting out is another prevalent mistake. The up move may be a "dead cat bounce," which will rapidly drop since it is not really a rise in the value of the stock. You can lose a lot of money trying to short a stock that is moving up, anticipating that an upwardly moving stock will hit its top and turn around. That stock may keep going higher.

One trader got into a stock at the wrong time. He shorted it at $77\frac{1}{2}$, then averaged up—shorting more at a higher price—realized he was wrong, and then covered—bought it back at 79, thus increasing his loss.

This trader was going with the trend when the stock opened down. But once stocks are in motion for the day, it is better to wait until later in the day before you lay out shorts, unless you are expecting a big reversal. Let's assume you made a bad trade and a stock such as J. P. Morgan is up a dollar. Why get involved in a bad situation and compound it by selling more?

Traders have to work on positioning themselves. One super-trader argues, "Why not wait until later in the day if the stock is up? If the stock is up, it will often stay up for the day. So why not store it, and lay out your shorts in the afternoon? At $75\frac{1}{2}$ maybe you thought that it would open up and sell down. So, you sell more at $78\frac{1}{2}$, but you're shooting from the hip. Why not look for another stop? If it's a dead cat bounce, you can come back in and take a look.

"Often when you are averaging up, you make that move so that the first loss didn't cost you as much," he continues. "Many times you know you were wrong and are trying to make yourself feel better. Don't do it. You don't have unlimited capital. That's like playing roulette by doubling up—except that you lose all your money before you can win!"

Mel was losing. He lacked specific goals. He was in the habit of buying more when a stock was dropping, trying to avoid facing the loss and keeping it small. There was no reason to buy more of a bankrupt company. A review of how he had changed his strategy and what was missing from his trading that had been present when he was winning revealed that he was no longer trading the market and was increasingly relying on others for ideas. His real strength was in retailers and banks. When he started relying on others, he began to trade with too much risk. Taking a twenty-five-thousand-share position was far too much given his objective of $5000 per day. Having ten stocks was far too much when he could make his daily numbers with three stocks. When traders succeed they sometimes get away from what had been successful and start to take bigger but less rational risks. Then, when they lose they are reluctant to go back to the old way of trading with discipline, which got them to success in the first place.

Commenting on Mel's trading, Ric, his manager, noted: "You shouldn't be trading ten thousand shares of a thin stock like LPX. It is a big deal if you are not willing to whack it if it's not the right trade. Who cares if you lose a thousand dollars in LPX, but if you don't trade it aggressively and you lose twelve thousand dollars, that's a problem. That's more than two days' worth of work if your goal is five thousand dollars a day. You are trading as if you had a bigger target and were succeeding. When you go back to the old style, you will take pressure off yourself. You need to reduce your losses and gain some confidence by getting some winners and trusting your intuition in the areas you know."

Wasting Energy with Low-Profit Stocks

A rule stated by one master trader is: "Don't play for a quarter of a dollar." It's easy to see why. "That's not much of an upside and is a waste of time and energy. There are only so many stocks you can look at in a day, so you're better off looking for a situation to make two dollars or three dollars," he says. Another way of viewing this mistake is, don't simply buy comfortable stocks. "You can't make a lot of money, or lose a lot, trading Occidental or other boring stocks," he continues. "You are better off with twenty Texas Instruments or twenty LSIs, both of which are likely to move. Once you have twelve stocks on your sheet, then you can move to semithick, boring stocks."

Scaling in and out can also squander your energy and distract you from playing much bigger elsewhere. Some traders buy twenty-five hundred shares at a time in order to scale into a stock when, in fact, they can buy a bigger position to start with. They also scale out at twenty-five hundred shares at a time and use up time doing this, when they could scale out with much bigger positions and have more time to trade other stocks. "You need to tap into the fluidity of trading and manage your time more effectively. There is so much to do on each trade that it doesn't make sense to spend time thinking of eighths. To get back on track, you need to buy upgraded stocks, and larger numbers of them," the master trader advises.

Becoming Too Passive

A trader named Bob noticed that he was not being aggressive enough in a lot of trades. "I'd be down three-eighths on a stock and it wouldn't come in. I'd borrow from my position hoping everything would come back right. I tried to hang on to things, and in this environment it was not smart to hang on to anything too long."

One stock that he held long was Ford. "I bought it at 55¾," he says, "and it closed at 55¼. The next day it opened up and it came all the way down to 54⅞, almost a point from where I bought it. So I sold ahead of it. It traded down to 54¾, then came right back up a half from the day before. I got back in at my original buy price. But my reaction time was pathetic."

Bob knew that in order to trade to win, he had to move faster. "The first time I sold Ford, it was in a good spot. I waited for the market to turn and by the time I decided to get back in, it was three-quarters of a point higher than where I sold it, or more. I bought it back, and it didn't come in. So, I sold it again, and it went higher again. I was just chasing my tail."

If you have repetitive trades, it may not be the stock, but rather a predisposition to trade in a certain way. This is where you need to examine your patterns to see if you're reacting to outmoded ideas.

"I was getting hit small," Bob notes. "I was trying to protect my account. I wasn't being aggressive enough. I would have the idea to buy, but I would hesitate. I should have jumped in. I was waiting for too much confirmation.

"Sometimes I'll wait for the size to get a little stronger. Or I'll see if there is a large size that's kicking in, or if it'll be a new high for the day. I'm not wrong, but I'm not helping myself," he adds.

In analyzing his patterns, Bob also admits that he is especially passive when the market slows down in the middle of the day. "There's nothing going on from 11:30 A.M. to 2:30 P.M.," he says. "I have a tendency to do nothing during those times. If I stop buying stocks from eleven to twelve o'clock, I'll be watching, and they'll come in. I can really get faked out."

Listening to Bob, Benny says, "The entry point is very important. Bob's are late pricewise, but they're probably early timewise. A lot of younger traders have a lot of remorse at missing prices. You have to accept the fact that sometimes you're going to miss things. You have to have a little patience."

He uses U.S. Surgical as an object lesson. "A week and a half ago, I bought it and it ran up real fast to the point where there were a few people around trying to buy it. I tried to hang on to it for most of the day. It took out points from where I bought it. It started to come in, and the market would come in, so I'd sell it. Then it would start to run back again against the market. So, I'd buy it back. I made a dollar in U.S. Surgical and that was it. The next few days, it went up six more points." Benny's conclusion: As you get a little money in the bank, you can let your positions run a bit more.

Trading Not to Lose

Some traders mask their fear of losing by trading cautiously to protect their winnings. At one weekly session Seth reported, "I don't really have any concrete trades to talk about. Today I probably traded ten or eleven stocks and I probably made money on eight or nine of them. I think I've been ultraconservative for the past few days, and I don't think I should be. I feel I'm finally having a little bit of a breakout month and I just want to make sure I finish the month with that. I'm playing smaller—I'm making money and trying not to lose."

Sensing the rationalization behind his strategy, I asked him: "Is there a risk that when you start trying to conserve your position and protect yourself from not losing that you are putting yourself at greater risk?"

"You may be right," he replied. "I set myself back for the beginning of the next month. It may be hard to switch back to the old way of trading once the next month rolls around. I don't know if I will be able to do that after being conservative and cautious for two or three weeks."

In effect, after making some profit, Seth had begun to trade not to lose, an approach that reactivated certain kinds of fears and concerns that he didn't have when he was trading in a focused way. Fortunately, discussion of this enabled him to identify this trend and he was able to go back to a more provocative style at the start of the next month.

Motivated to Lose

As absurd as it sounds, some traders are more motivated to lose than to win. Why would someone want to lose? Most of the time it comes from an unconscious fear of success. Familiarity with losing keeps these traders doing things that are contrary to what the tape and current experience are telling them to do. They perform poorly, make excuses for their actions, and then keep doing the same thing. To change this pattern, they must change their underlying rationale.

Most of these traders believe that they want to win. But do they? If many of them examined their real thoughts, they would find that as long as they are a little bit ahead, they accept the attitude of, "I've got to take my losses with my wins."

Do you get into no-win positions too often? Do you know the difference between a good and bad trade? Do you know how bad your bad trades are? How good are you about getting out of bad trades? Do you compound your mistakes by holding on to losing positions? Why? Do you think things will reverse? Are you able to trade independently of your own prior experience?

Ask yourself these questions to see if you are among those caught in the motivated-to-lose bind. The purpose of these questions is to encourage you to identify your current, perhaps subliminal trading patterns so you can correct them.

Losing after Winning

Winning days are often followed by losing streaks. There are various reasons. Some traders feel guilty and believe that they don't deserve to win. They give back to redress the unfair balance. Others feel too good or euphoric and allow discipline and control over losses to lapse.

Why does this occur? Often because traders start to think they have some magical prowess or that Lady Luck is shining on them. They get careless and stop being conscious of the fact that the market is fickle, treacherous, and seductive.

This pattern is especially common after a string of successes. What does it take to expand right now and to start trading in terms of an expanded objective? This is not comfortable to consider or to do. Most people opt for doing it gradually, if at all.

What drops out after a high-water mark? Why does performance drop down or plateau? Why can't the trader repeat a stellar performance or easily move to a new level?

I asked a trader you've heard about earlier, Eric, how he could make $100,000 in a day but fail to match that performance in the months since. His ideas are good enough to make $1 million a month, but in discussing this issue, he confesses he is limiting himself by not utilizing all his skills. Maybe he is not getting involved in the game. Maybe he is getting afraid, not realizing how good he is.

After facing this problem repeatedly with both inexperienced and experienced traders, it has become increasingly clear to me that once you reach a new level and realize it wasn't that hard, you have to create a new expectation of another $100,000 day. Sure, you had great ideas and played them right yesterday. Today, you need to find bright

Six Questions about Losing after Winning

1. Do you relax too much and retreat to your comfort zone?
2. Does it becomes harder to keep stepping forward into the zone of uncertainty, and to sustain a new level of trading?
3. Do you stop making calls?
4. Do you stop making the extra calculation or whatever additional effort ensured your progress?
5. Do you stop consulting with the better traders for more information?
6. Do you seek such a high new level of confirmation or confidence that your perfectionism takes over?

new ideas and execute them. The concept of a larger goal should influence your play. You also have to get over the belief that it can't occur every day.

Eventually, after you keep seeing the pattern, you feel internally pressured to take the necessary action in terms of the concepts you have selected. In effect, the creative action reduces the internal tension between belief in the vision of the future and reality in the present.

If you find that you are having difficulty in duplicating or surpassing your successes, you will find some benefit in giving some thought to the accompanying questions.

Unfortunately, making more than $1 million a year at any age—particularly the middle to late twenties as occurs among so many traders with whom I have had the opportunity to work—introduces a note of cautiousness. This may be more than you ever expected. You would have settled for $100,000 a year four years ago. Therefore, you don't want to screw up. The effect of losing a million dollars is a lot more than that of making another $500,000. As I have noted in earlier sections, people always favor not losing to winning big.

For instance, Eric probably thought there was no way that Informix would trade at twenty-eight the day I spoke to him. He wanted to short it for a week. At least he didn't short it prematurely. But then the day came, the trade was there, Informix was up a dollar, and he started questioning himself.

Eric mistakenly believed he was wrong. In actuality, it was a great opportunity; it took a lot of effort not to lose. He allowed himself to be run by the moment as opposed to following his knowledge. He began the day on a confident note, yet once the market opened, he lost conviction. Once Informix started to fail, he should have acted. His thinking was correct but his execution wasn't.

In such cases, say the master traders, the only thing you need to examine is not that you missed a shot, buy why you missed it. Do you get caught in the last hour when you're short a lot of futures because you tend to move very fast? If so, you need to be very cautious during the last hour if the chart looks a certain way. Says one trader: "If Micron was thirty-seven and an eighth and now it's thirty-six and five-eighths coming off the high, maybe you're not sure about it running up again, so you need to examine your thinking. If you missed it because of technical reasons, you might not have been able to get it because of the way it traded, which forced you into an uncomfortable mode of operation."

Overtrading

On occasion, some traders will, in the words of Jed, "overtrade even though I don't really have a good idea, or I get in late. Or I'll trade just because I want to be involved. It doesn't hurt the P&L that much, but if you do it every day it can lose a lot of money. And I can't seem to stop doing it. I guess I just want to be involved as an active trader."

Mort describes the overtrading impulse this way: "You feel, I'm a trader and I should be trading. Here I'm sitting here, not trading. I'd better trade so I look like a trader."

Mort has learned to know when he is in this psychological state. "The question is, what compels you to do that? Is it uncomfortable to sit there and do nothing? What else could you be doing when you're sitting there doing nothing?"

Bob also has this problem on occasion. "What do you do at eleven o'clock in the morning and you're down a thousand dollars, and your goal is to make five grand a day? You're not going to make it sitting there watching. So you try to come up with ideas and you ask people around the room. That's what leads me to overtrading. Sometimes I get in and I get right out. All I do is I lose commissions."

Traders who find themselves in such straits need to ask, "What's in my thinking and in my behavior that leads me to lose one new idea after another?" Is it the execution, the habitual pattern, or the anxiety?

Now, says Bob, "My attitude is, if I have an idea and I like it, and it's reasonable and the tape isn't acting too crazy, I'm going with it. This approach is working more times than not."

Greedy Trading

One trader, listening to tales of traders who hesitated, says, "I have the exact opposite problem. I know I can always make money. I know that I can always generate a good idea or two.

"I was up a dollar in Allstate. I'd bought seventy-five hundred shares at about sixty-three and it was now about sixty-four. The first time the market dipped, my stock went up a quarter from where the market started to decline. So my stock was going up and the general market was coming down. The market went down the second leg, and my stock faded a little. Now I was trapped. I thought the general market was going to bounce, so instead of selling it at sixty-four where I could have definitely sold stock, I sold some stock at sixty-three and a half and then I didn't sell the last twenty-five hundred until about sixty-two and three-quarters. I had the best-acting stock of the day. I mean, there were a jillion buyers, one or two sellers, and it just went tick, tick, tick . . . and it didn't tick up. I had been up about ten or twelve grand, and I finished the day minus three hundred dollars."

Looking back, this trader reasons, "In the effort to make more money, I ended up not making any money. That's greed, and that's fear. And it's operating all the time. I'm saying, 'I want to get more.' I want to hold on to my winners. But I don't take enough profits."

Fear of Pulling the Trigger

It pays to heed what goes on in your own brain, says another trader. "If you already know that Allied is a trade, that should be a signal to you that you need to buy it. You have to get to the point where you act once that thought pops into your head.

"You need to monitor the internal conversation you're having. Listen to yourself every time you catch yourself with an idea. That's the whole point of looking at the screen. You've already made the decision. That's the trigger," this trader declares.

He warns, however, that you should not necessarily obey all thoughts. Notice, but don't pay attention to the inner voice that says: "I'm a new trader. I don't know enough yet. I'd better wait and watch this to get more confirmation."

Maybe you have all the confirmation you need the first time. Thus, you need to understand that your own self-doubt may delay taking action, and lead you to seek additional, yet unnecessary, information.

It is understandable to doubt yourself because you're new. But as you get more experience, you will have less self-doubt. The sooner you start noticing the self-doubt and stop paying too much attention to it, the faster you'll have gotten to that experienced point. You don't have to wait five years to begin to know that your first judgments were good. You have to trade with conviction today.

Mario is certain he is not trigger-shy. Instead, he attributes his hesitation to his youthful impatience. He knows that he has a problem sticking with his ideas, however. In one session, he was holding America Online when "it ticked down to thirty-nine and five-eighths and maybe thirty-nine and a quarter. I was out a quarter on three thousand shares. I sold it. I lost money, and then the stock ripped."

Talking about the stock later, he was disappointed in himself and realized that he needed to "figure out a way that takes advantage" of his good instincts. "At the very least, I should have taken a partial fill," he said.

"What are you willing to do in the future?" I asked him.

"From now on I am not going to sell my whole position unless I have to get out. I'll sell a little bit at a time and make my moves within a minute or two, or five minutes, or ten minutes, whatever time frame is appropriate for that trade. But I am going to keep a checkpoint all along the way." Mario knows his next step on the road to experience is learning when to listen to his gut reactions and how to tune out all other distracting static.

Whatever you think about yourself as an explanation for your trading—"I have this personality," or "I'm in this kind of mood," or "I'm new," or "I'm too old," or "I'm forgetful"—interferes with listening to your thoughts about the trade at hand. Emotion-laden or judgmental thoughts have to be noticed, but must be put on a back burner for consideration at some other time. None of these other thoughts has anything to do with trading. The principal difference between inexperienced traders and those with bigger P&Ls is that the successful traders trust their instincts and pay little mind to the noise.

How to Make the Most of Your Mistakes

When you start asking what you need to do to improve your trading, you will start making all kinds of moves that you don't ordinarily make. If you don't make calls, you will start trying or doing more research, narrowing the number of industries you follow, learning more about the industries, or measuring lost opportunities. You will recognize which routine patterns have become part of your trading style.

One objective? To reach the point of self-awareness where you notice your automatic thoughts and self-doubts. That's exactly the point where you can get past them. You notice when you are feeling uptight and starting to engage in old habits, and are therefore able to shift from such thoughts to your trading discipline. You can't control the markets or stock movement, but you can control yourself. To get this control, you have to learn to see how these unconscious thoughts influence your behavior.

Unfortunately, trading is like slipping on a ski slope a good part of the time, and the more you can learn how to control your slipping, rather than avoid slipping, the more you can master the game.

Learning to change your old patterns of behavior is at the center of trading to win. It also must be said that a little humility always helps in trading and in dealing with a market that is constantly changing. You have to admit that what you knew before and what you did before might not work today. And you have to accept that you don't have a lock on the market. The information is there, and you cannot wait for it to come to you.

It's not a simple process. Everybody must face one's demons—impatience, fear, negative thoughts—when facing a trade. In the day-trading business, you can make a fortune and you can lose your shirt. The better you are, the more you have mastered that internal anxiety that causes common mistakes.

Chapter Twelve

The Power to Change

At a recent weekly seminar, I asked Tim, the bright, hard-driving Asian market specialist whom we met in Chapter 3, what had changed since he began participating in our get-togethers six months before.

"I am listening more carefully for opportunities, and am beating myself less about yesterday's trades, especially when I haven't taken as big a position as I should have," was his prompt reply. "I haven't raised my P&L yet, but my level of satisfaction has improved considerably. I am still struggling to purge my portfolio. I hate to admit I was wrong to sell if something turns positive, but I can see now that I can overcome seller's remorse by buying back stocks that start running. I don't have to be attached to my earlier decisions."

"Anything else?" I asked.

"Yes," he replied. "I measured my ten worst drawdowns and found that they average two and a half days each, not months like I felt they had lasted. It's useful to know that there is an end to these drawdowns."

Tim's remarks illustrate the key point of this book: It *is* really possible to learn the principles of great traders. I believe that the true purpose of life is the unfolding of the undiscovered and undeveloped talents within you, and that trading provides an ideal arena in which to discover this. You can unearth a potentially rich vein of ability within yourself by taking on challenging projects, which go beyond the limiting myths of your own thinking. As you move toward your objectives you will tap creative and spiritual dimensions within yourself and will have fewer thoughts of failure, self-doubt, worry, and anxiety.

The more you are in touch with your hidden potential and are evolving into what you are destined to be, the more capable you will be of giving up fantasies of omnipotence and fears of impotence. The acceptance of reality will bring greater awareness of your genuine strengths and your weaknesses.

However, trading to win is not an intellectual exercise as much as it is an exercise in reframing your perspective. You need to interpret how your fundamental set of assumptions about life, the world, and trading influences both your trading style and the steps you must take to enter into the realm of mastery.

Reframing Your Viewpoint

You can change your perception of an experience so that negative feelings don't get anchored to a particular bad event. You do it by changing your way of framing the event so that you view it in a more neutral way. Reframing involves changing your perspective so you understand the basic structure of your thoughts and experiences and how they influence the way in which you trade. You can do the same thing by attaching positive feelings to negative events and learning the value of those experiences. By seeking out the advantage in adversity, you are in essence letting adversity become mother of invention. You can find a new method of dealing with your problems instead of being locked into a negative mind-set.

By switching gears and getting into a positive state of mind, you will begin to see trading possibilities differently so as to optimize your trading. First, though, you must change your mind-set. Start by tracking your failures and examining how your negative feelings color your perceptions. The pain is the lesson. Great successes will not give you pain, but painful failures are learning experiences.

When negative feelings begin to infiltrate your day and your trades, get back to those positive feelings. Why should you allow devastating feelings ruin your mood, when you can put a positive spin on them that will allow you to feel more comfortable about the trades you are making? Don't act from desperation. The day is governed by your state of mind. Go into your emotional databank and locate something positive. Find whatever will give you confidence and play out of that. Even if you feel lousy and are losing, you can still get revved up, provided you dismiss excuses such as, "I didn't think. . . ." or "I didn't know. . . ."

For instance, if you bought a stock on Friday, and it went down, then came back, you may have waited for one and a quarter points, and sold at one and a half. It felt great. There was no stress. Can you now feel that same smooth, easy, confident feeling of success? Can you remember the trade, review it, see the numbers, see the symbol? Tune into it. Put yourself in that same state of mind before you begin trading today. You can create your destiny by remembering how you have already been there.

As you begin this next phase of your career, your success will be immeasurably enhanced as you abandon neurotic or compulsive expectations from childhood—the internal controls that place a false limit on your horizons. With each control that you shrug off, you will become more and more capable of facing anxiety-ridden situations that you currently avoid because of fear.

Let's peer into that dark pool of fear for a moment.

The Fear of Success

In most of us, fear has more to do with succeeding than with failing. Your fear of success results in part from excessive concern with self-image and a reluctance to surrender to the next action. Many traders have been socialized in terms of such values as "doing your best," "looking good," and "not losing," rather than in terms of playing or trading to win. Few, if any, have been reared to do what it takes to produce results in line with specific goals. They prefer to stay in the comfort zone, to play not to lose.

Many traders have not identified the critical levers of their trading game and don't know what to focus on consistent with their objectives. They are content to rely on trends, staying with the herd and hoping for good results. They may overvalue the opinions of others while undervaluing their own judgments. This is what accounts for so much superstitious behavior among traders.

You saw examples earlier of how fear of change and fear of the unknown lead traders to blow up immediately after successful trading runs or to avoid success altogether. Attached to a grandiose sense of their own abilities, they may stubbornly hold on to a sell position long after it has turned around and should have been covered. Such traders are reluctant to face failure, declare a loss, and move beyond that losing position.

Taking responsibility means continuing to do what it takes to reproduce the successful results. Why are so many traders loath to do this? Even when successful, few people are able to sustain repeated successes. Few athletes have ever won gold medals in successive Olympic Games, and fewer football teams ever have won back-to-back Super Bowl games, in part because they are averse to committing to the tasks involved in achieving such a goal. It is easier the first time, when there is no pressure to repeat a winning past performance.

As I have said throughout this book, success requires a conscious promise to a future result without any certainty or guarantee about the outcome. This calls for a willingness to part with the comfort of past habits and beliefs, and a desire to enter into the uncertainty of the unknown, guided only by a larger inner vision.

Your life principle creates fear by creating a domain of "what if," a pit filled with the prospects of doom and disaster, loss of control, and panic if certain events don't take place or if they do take place. You generate fear by imagining a future loaded with frightening and negative ideas mined from that pit of negative assessments of your ability to do the impossible.

Preoccupation with the past and the necessity to cover it up saps your energy. This takes many forms. You may hold on to grievances toward those who injured you, and not allow in love and affection. You may intensify resentment toward others by being kind and helpful while masking your resentment. You may feel guilty about what you hide, and live out of the conviction of being inadequate and undeserving of better experiences. You may be reluctant to express your vision for fear that others will not support it.

The Cover-Up

It is a paradox, but the refusal to acknowledge fear, pain, tension, and other unpleasant feelings contributes a huge amount to perpetuating those feelings. Taking a leap beyond the pit of fear is difficult, since it means letting go of the image of being in control. To mix metaphors, success means jumping in the water. That's what we are all afraid of. We don't want to acknowledge how vulnerable we are. Our hearts beat fast. We can't swallow. We can't get enough air. Many traders pretend they never get afraid, envious, jealous, or angry. They try to control their emotions as if to be in control is the appropriate way to be.

There's no big deal about feeling anxiety or fear. Just allow yourself to feel your feelings and let them pass. Don't put a heavy interpretation on your feelings. Each one triggers emotions from the past, which trigger more meaning, which also doesn't mean anything. To be human is to feel discomfort and to want to hide from your feelings. We are all brought up that way. A lot of the energy of our lives is taken up in keeping feelings stuffed inside.

If you don't try to control feelings, you can allow yourself to be as powerful as you can be. You can use your energy to trade more successfully because you're not spending it on a big emotional cover-up.

It's handy to learn how long specific feelings last. It's also great to learn that you—the whole person—are not your feelings. Your feelings are merely the subjective correlates of adrenaline pumping through your blood.

The more you resist or deny feelings, the more persistent they become. When you act defensively to protect your ego or self-image, you keep the illusion of self in place and reinforce the notion that you have something to cover up. This defensive reaction prevents you from flowing with your trading and recognizing that market fluctuations are not personal. If you are open, if you simply allow events to unfold without responding in a reactive way, these feelings will dissipate. They won't build up a reservoir of negative reactions or expend your energy in masking your reaction.

Your success has to do with your competency, not with how you appear to be. But you create enormous stress for yourself if you are afraid someone will notice that you are afraid and you will thus lose your power. You are run by a need to appear competent. As soon as someone addresses an inadequacy, you are scared that your cover has been blown. So even when you succeed you aren't nurtured by it if there is no integration between your core sense of self and your performance.

When your success is linked to your image, you feel it is fraudulent and that you have to keep appearing a certain way lest you be found out. As you succeed without knowing who you are, the tension mounts. You've succeeded without feeling successful. You are unable to use what's left of your limited resources in pursuit of important and meaningful goals.

It's Okay to Blame Your Parents

The reason for fear is simple. First, the relinquishing of defenses produces fear. Second, the defense system enables you to trade in a predictable way. But while your defense system is stabilizing, it also constricts the chance for spontaneity, originality, and creativity to appear in your trading.

Your defense system is based on memory, including critical memories of your parents' responses to you as a child. It is also based on memories of all the people who ever sat in judgment about what was possible for you, what was desirable, what was good. Many of these negative memories are likely to come into play whenever you are about to embark on a new project. These memories appear as "conversations" in your thoughts, which caution you about the "dangers ahead" or the "inappropriateness" of what you are planning to do. They keep you inside the pit of fear, and perpetuate your predictable patterns from the past.

The most prominent reasons for not drawing on your hidden potential, therefore, are the lack of belief in your authentic self, and your reliance on the internal conversations or interpretations you have about yourself.

A trader I introduced earlier, Bob, is a case in point. Bob is afraid of success. He is reluctant to outdo his father, who was an unsuccessful part-time trader and who, over time, has come to rely on handouts from his son. Bob is convinced he is like his father and that he will never succeed. Even when he succeeds he has problems, because he is afraid his father will be jealous and angry at his success. So, he tends not to tell his father the truth about his successes. All this keeps him from being overwhelmingly successful when he has the chance to be so.

It's time to accept the idea that when you are unsuccessful, it's often because memory dominates your trading and manufactures a self-fulfilling prophecy. Your potential sits there ready to be tapped, but you are unaware of it because you trade in terms of an identity based on reactive memories. This outdated identity is holding you back. It is full of myths about success.

When you begin to feel overwhelmed, it is useful to ask yourself what you are responding to. In all likelihood, the answer is defensive or automatic responses, which make it all the more difficult for you to relax and respond appropriately. As a result you are unable to bring all of your resources to bear on present trades.

"Stuck in the Past"

Being "stuck in the past" often borders on panic. In that state of mind, your thoughts are likely to focus on past inadequacies and failures, which may magnify the obstacles before you. You may have an exaggerated fear of failure, may anticipate ridicule or rejections, and may begin to act as if failure is inevitable. In effect, negative expectations generated in the past set in motion a self-fulfilling prophecy that may bring about the feared result.

Perceiving the world through a fearful life principle can make you feel helpless, anxious, frightened, and inclined to exaggerate your weaknesses and inadequacies. That leads to additional problems. You can't rely on your own resources to work out the best strategy or game plan that you may have prepared. Fear can lead you to become less responsive and less adaptive. You may also freeze in high-pressure situations. Awareness of the helplessness associated with fear sometimes leads to an intensification of helplessness, a lack of energy, and an impulse to end the trade.

Trading in terms of past images makes it difficult to adapt to changing conditions. Because you are frozen in a fixed intellectual and emotional position, you are unable to adjust your course around obstacles. This in turn makes it hard to trade in terms of a long-range financial objective.

Governed by the concept of minimizing stress while looking competent, you may establish conflicting goals that are unrealistically high or unnecessarily low. Concerned with your image, you may take on too many goals at once, establish goals unsuited to your abilities or temperament, or let others set goals for you.

Sounds like a terrible set of circumstances, doesn't it? What's more, once you begin to take action toward your goal, your fears may go into high gear in sabotaging your efforts. An outmoded, defensive life principle governs the choice of goals as well as the approach to them. Often it prevents the realization of a goal and imprisons you in a model of self-defeat. When you get absorbed in fantasies of disaster, you can lose sight of your goals and become thoroughly confused. Alternatively, you may create too many solutions, thereby becoming paralyzed with plans and procedures. Or, you may focus too much attention on ultimate, distant goals and ignore what can be done in the present.

In short, fear is the most common, and most debilitating, effect of the life principle that unconsciously manipulates your emotional core. You can see the results all around you. The avoidance of failure at any cost is obvious among people who are preoccupied with results and believe that the results reflect who they are.

Denial and Fear of Success

Fear of being isolated and rejected by peers as a result of success can lead traders to do less than their best. If you are uncomfortable with success, you may unwittingly invite failure as you approach success. Or you may function at less than your capacity, avoiding the possibility of success or failure. Here, fear of failure and fear of success coalesce. The prospect of success intensifies fear of failing. That idea leads to a reduction in effort, increased distractibility, and the acceptance of a mental "ceiling" on your effort, which serves as the rationalization for not maximizing your potential.

Only by coming face to face with your own self-doubts can you free up the enormous energy that has been devoted to denial. You can accept your anxiety and begin to trade in terms of your commitment and vision, independently of the self-criticizing voices and fearful life principle.

Denial is not the same as the willingness to persevere or remain committed in the face of failure. The most creative people are willing to admit to their fears, acknowledge their failures, and keep going until they have achieved their objectives, never ceasing to give anything but maximum effort, despite the odds. The critical thing is to recognize and admit to failure and to keep going. A case in point is Thomas Edison, who did 2999 experiments before he invented the electric lightbulb. His insistence on all-out effort, even in what seemed to be a hopeless cause, reflected his ability to approach failures unflinchingly and to keep going even when the odds seemed insuperable.

This kind of focused effort in the face of intense stress is what makes for outstanding performance in all fields. Creative people are able to keep going no matter how insufficient the results. They tap great reserves of mental strength when they are faced with seemingly impossible odds. This is as true in business as it is in the creative arts.

A master trader does not deny the presence of uncertainty, anxiety, or fear, or waste energy covering up such responses or avoiding maximum effort in order to appear to be more relaxed. Rather, he or she accepts the distress as part and parcel of the experience, but soldiers on, engrossed in the task at hand.

Master traders have learned to distinguish conscious commitment to a financial goal from the natural inclination to be comfortable and to withdraw or retreat to the more familiar terrain of habits and attitudes conditioned earlier in life. They have learned to make this distinction and to keep living out of their vision.

Goal-Setting: The Beginning of Change

How do you set change in motion? One way is by considering what you are doing now that you really don't want to do. How much of each day do you spend on tasks that you are doing out of a sense of obligation or tradition, or to meet the expectations of others? Eliminate those tasks to free up time and brainpower for things that you do naturally and which you may have taken for granted until now. This is more difficult to do than it seems. You—like the rest of us—probably have been taught to think in terms of accomplishing goals or acquiring abilities that you do *not* have, rather than cultivating undeveloped abilities that you *do* have.

Use as much of your talent as possible on activities that are meaningful to you. If most of what you have accomplished already resulted from using only a portion of your abilities, think of how much more fulfilled you will feel once you begin to use all of your faculties.

Facing adversity in the form of crises is another good path toward change. Whenever you deal with obstacles and challenges, you discover new potential within yourself and may actually increase the gifts that you can bring to bear on nurturing new dimensions within yourself.

To begin to change, you must commit to a larger and more concrete financial goal. This will give you a standard about which trades to pursue and which to avoid.

A goal functions like a mantra. It gives you confidence and helps you to focus your efforts on what can be accomplished. It helps you to stop thinking about maintaining an image or recalling negative experiences. A goal fortifies you against indecision, procrastination, the demons from the past, and the expectations of others.

Your vision creates a context of possibility, very much as a canvas provides the artist with a context in which to paint. The canvas shapes the magnitude and parameters of the painting and sets the boundaries. So, select a feasible but challenging goal and then within the frame of the goal decide what you must do to trade at that level. The goal draws you into it and creates the moment-by-moment experiences of your trading. Once you choose a goal, you will notice a quickening of your senses and an enlivening of your sense of self.

Start immediately today. If you create a large enough goal you will immediately find yourself at risk, in the gap described in Chapter 1. It is at this moment of uncertainty that you have to decide to act consistently with your vision. Define the necessary steps to take to narrow the gap. When you are in this space, with all of its anxiety and uncertainty, it is useful to have support of others who understand the process and are willing to keep encouraging you.

Be willing to live daily in the gap between where you are now and where you wish to be. The simple decision to act will reduce any fear or self-doubt you may have and will activate motivational processes within you. From the decision to take action you set in motion a positive self-fulfilling prophecy. Each day, begin to do what is necessary to realize that goal.

As you succeed, raise the stakes. When you feel yourself retreating into your self-doubts and rationalizations, it is important to notice the patterns of withdrawal you employ to take yourself out of the action.

Don't assume things will be taken care of. You must produce the results. You must be clear with those who are assisting you about what you want and must review this with them. Don't assume things will go the way you want them to go unless you outline your regimens and establish a structure to ensure the outcome. Don't expect someone else will do it for you. There are no shortcuts or easy results. Commitment is about being fully engaged in your trading, not about getting the results. You play to win. But the game is not about winning. It is about playing wholeheartedly. Even if you produce the result you must be careful not to become enthralled with yourself or full of pride, which can lead you to lose it.

Dealing with Envy and Jealousy

Don't compare yourself to others, especially when the going gets rough and you are discouraged, even if it appears that others have reached their goals effortlessly or that they have what it is you want.

When you become envious, stop to see how engaged you are in your projects. The chances are that you are off-center and are not as engaged as you can be. Jealousy is a signal of your insufficient expression of talent and insight. It suggests a fear of taking the needed risks to attain your goals. It masks something you want to do but have been reluctant to do.

You are jealous only of those who are doing what you would like to do. Use jealousy then as a clue to determine what you want to do. If you are jealous of the master traders in your shop, it is because you really want to be as successful as they are. If you want to be part of a trading team, don't complain about what you deserve or talk about how you will perform if you are given the benefits the team members have. Instead, focus on what you can do to get more for yourself. Your jealousy keeps you from pursuing what it takes to get what you want.

Jealousy can be a good thing. It demonstrates what you are afraid to do. If you use jealousy to learn more about what you want and what your fears are, you can grow from it. If you allow it to consume you, you will be stopped dead in your tracks, and success will elude you.

Taking the First Small Steps

Choose a new financial goal, declare it, commit to it, and pursue it—and you will discover an enormous drive in yourself that will enable you to realize it. I am not talking about doing more about what you are already doing. I want you to break out of limited concepts of yourself and to trade courageously in terms of your commitment. I am talking about making a decision to act in the face of fear, to confront those obstacles which frighten you and stand in the way of your trading success. I am talking about training your sights on objectives on the other side of the fear, and acting in terms of that commitment.

When do you begin the process? Start now, even when you are uncertain, and allow the process to unfold. Let the idea incubate in darkness and in silence, and then take action and let it build up as you slowly confirm your hunch. As it begins to percolate, get more involved and give it full steam.

Throughout this book I have emphasized the importance of going with the flow, of not resisting your responses, of not covering them up. Your emotional reactions will be part of the experience of creating a context, but will not be the limiting factor.

By trading with a goal you yourself have created, you will be able to experience fear and anxiety without attaching meaning to them. The feelings are simply part of your life experiences.

Start small. Change can be brought about simply by becoming aware of what you are doing. This increase in consciousness will give you choice in controlling your automatic responses in your activities. This can have profound effects on how you trade. Small changes in your trading can provide proof that you can have an impact on your life. From this you will learn how to harness the power that is released in the process of change. Keep making small adjustments to keep aligned with your goal. Don't rush. Don't push too hard. You only need to concentrate on producing concrete results.

Focusing on strengths and not weaknesses, you will be able to maintain morale without becoming too involved in the possibility of error or the prospect of criticism from others. The less effort you make to keep up a public image and the more you pursue goals related to your own potential, the more you will be in touch with aspects of yourself that are most suitable for change.

Act Now

The longer you wait to act, the more likely you are to create problems and obstacles in your mind that will lead to more delay. If you put most of your energy into planning and preparation rather than actually trading, you will not work out the trade in the midst of the action. As a result you will tend more often to remain in place, rather than creating something. You may get good at preparation and planning but will not develop the kind of knowledge that comes only from engaging in the trades themselves. It is possible to learn to respond to events as they occur as though you were already the super-trader you wish to be, developing mastery by repeated contact and interaction with the experience itself.

Take action in the next moment. Having committed to a vision and operationalized the results, you need to act consistently with your goal. Listen for opportunities, which will appear before you in line with your commitment. Be willing to surrender to them.

Your commitment will enhance your capacity to see those opportunities and to empower yourself and others in pursuit of your goal. When you are in motion you can shift directions, change your pace, increase your intensity, and utilize all of your potential to realize your goal. As you do this you will begin to see how making small movements toward a goal, not the achievement of the goal, is what matters in helping you to become all that you can be.

There is a level of information that can be derived only from the experience itself. Moreover, there is a capacity to respond to such unpredictable events only by participating in the experience. Participation allows you to respond to the events themselves, not from your thoughts or interpretations about the events. A critical distinction exists between the preparatory and analytical thoughts you may have about events and the actual complex actions and responses that occur in reaction to events. To learn white-water rafting it is necessary to ride the rapids. You learn by doing it and experiencing the unpredictability and uncertainty of the ride, the sense of being at risk.

The value of action is that it enables you to see an aspect of reality quite distinct from your concepts of reality. Action breaks through your fixed way of seeing things and enables you to see the truth between the cracks. Essentially, you need action or change to see beneath the veneer or the facade of reality. By being engaged in action toward the goal, you are able to let go of the personal, and be fully present as a human being.

Reflections, Results, and Reviews

A goal is not just a directional device; it works as a source of inspiration and motivation. A realistic goal can be exhilarating. It empowers you to concentrate on genuine interests, and provides a sense of excitement.

However, while you may feel excited and fulfilled by achieving a goal, and while this may enhance your self-esteem, it is not an end in itself. Once you achieve a goal you must move on toward new goals if you are to maintain your vitality. Otherwise, the goal becomes part of your identity or concept of yourself, and once again you are subject to the stresses and strains that come from trading in terms of some fixed self-image.

Some people who believe in the positive outcome of their projects still cannot look objectively at the way they are approaching their activities. They are unwilling to view results as a measure of where they are. They deny the realities of their trades and are inclined to avoid looking systematically at how they are doing. They resist using objective criteria such as profits per trade, P&L, and duration of trade to assess their progress and refuse to see anything but success in their projects. They confuse involvement and investment in the outcome of the project with success. Traders in this category don't like to audit their efforts or stop to look at their work long enough to reformulate their objectives and establish workable guidelines. That's why traders must carefully examine their failed trades; these are clues to solving the mystery of what was missing.

Reduced Effort or Avoidance

Fear can manifest itself in avoidance or noncommitment to your vision. Trapped by the need to remain in the domain of the familiar, you hold back and give less than your best, because you believe that you can't succeed—or that success will prove problematic.

This pattern of avoidance is lodged somewhere in the nervous system. It appears to be organized to suppress negative emotions and to limit the extent of highs and lows. Such a neurological pattern may explain why the excitement of success often turns into a painful sense of withdrawal and disappointment. It's why many people resist success, believing that good feelings cannot be sustained or sensing that the only place to go after success is down.

In these cases, the life principle is based on the erroneous notion that it will hurt if you go all out or go beyond what is familiar to you. It supports the status quo and provides a rationalization for producing less than maximum results. How can you feel you have failed if you have not put in your best efforts?

In actual fact, failing after giving 100 percent effort will move you to a new space where ultimate satisfaction comes from striving, not from succeeding per se. You can be gratified by the feelings associated with expressing yourself and experiencing a sense of your own competence.

Rationalization and Fear of Success

Another limiting aspect of the life principle is characterized by rationalization, the effort to justify yourself and minimize your responsibility for not taking committed action.

In many instances, you can choose to be in a situation and not just be the victim of the circumstances. You can be more powerful and effective; look more precisely at how you get victimized beyond the simple act of caring for people, and find small ways in which you get victimized which you can change. You don't have to abandon people, but can change the way in which you provide support. You may begin to get some power back. If you are a caregiver and too gentle with your team members for fear of hurting their feelings, you need to learn to set up the ground rules and don't have to be run by them.

If you are doing things out of a sense of obligation, it is not usually a very genuine or authentic or supportive sentiment and tends to generate in you a lot of anger toward others. They pick up the resentment, leading you to have to be even nicer to show them that you care.

The "Winning" Dilemma

Are you excessively attached to your results? Some traders confuse their success with their identity. If you do this, you lose a great deal of your freedom to create. Driven by winning or succeeding at all costs, you may create so much pressure on yourself that you get little satisfaction from your efforts.

The former pro quarterback John Brodie formulated a sensible approach to winning that stands somewhere between Vince Lombardi's aphorism, "Winning isn't everything, it's the only thing," and Grantland Rice's famous line, "It's not whether you win or lose, it's how you play the game." In his autobiography, *Open Field* (San Francisco Series: Houghton Mifflin, 1974), Brodie wrote:

> You play to win. There's no doubt about that. But if winning is your first and only aim, you stand a good chance of losing. You have the greatest chance of winning when your first commitment is to a total and enthusiastic involvement in the game itself. Enthusiasm is what matters most. If I was enthusiastic about the game, enjoying it and doing my absolute best, then I had the best chance of winning it. But then I could also handle losing, because I had done my best. If you can't handle losing, you'll never be a big winner. It's never easy to lose. But if I knew I had performed at the top of my ability, with total involvement, that would take care of the winning or the losing.

John Brodie would have made a good day trader after his NFL days were over.

Getting to the Here and Now

As each trading day begins, consider how you can view developments without reacting defensively or relying on past actions. The more you do this, the more skilled you will be in bringing the here and now to trading events, including losses. You will immediately begin to operate in a new, innovative way, where you will not be so dominated by your habitual perspectives.

Does that sound a bit scary? It should. We're all afraid to see things in a new, creative light, rather than the old familiar, albeit inaccurate, light. A new approach won't be without fear and anxiety. But it will encourage a more powerful way of trading in the present.

I am not asking you to stop thinking. You can't block all thoughts. But you can learn to observe how your life principle leads to the avoidance rather than the acceptance of fear. You can train yourself to stand apart from those negative reactions. Indeed, once you realize that fear and anxiety don't mean anything about you, your decision, or your vision, you can begin to create a new life principle. Fear then becomes just one of a number of things you experience as you let go of the past and start trading more successfully.

Having created a new life principle and a greater financial objective, you need to take action every single working day. The fulfillment of the vision is not simply one of positive thinking or the repeated expression of positive affirmation, or even focusing on the goal like a meditative mantra. Trading in the here and now includes confronting your fears and inhibitions daily. You have to learn how to ride through this discomfort and pain associated with these confrontations.

To do this, recognize the fears that hold you back from your vision. Regard success as a series of developments including breakdowns as well as breakthroughs.

It's not as contradictory as it sounds. Breakdowns should be handled without putting personal meaning on them but seeing them as necessary challenges on the pathway to fulfillment. Otherwise, breakdowns or failures are experienced as reflective of your personal worth and can trigger enormous anxiety, embarrassment, and guilt. You need to tell yourself daily to push on beyond these feelings, and welcome them as an opportunity for breakthroughs.

Sometimes, it will seem easier to step down, to avoid commitment, than to accept the problems and breakdowns on the path to enlightenment. Yet when you backtrack, you are likely to be more anxious and more dissatisfied than when you are willing to risk yourself and trade on the cutting edge of your commitments.

Let's review some of the sequences that traders experience, including ones I covered in depth in earlier chapters, and see what new avenues there are for you to travel with them.

A Loss after a Win

The fear of losing is inextricably tied to the fear of winning; this was the case with Conrad, a trader who invariably overtraded and lost. Conrad had an unrealistic notion of his abilities based on past successful trades and was unwilling to integrate knowledge of his losses into his self-concept. He needed to learn to win small and to avoid the impulse to plunge heedlessly. He needed to monitor his trades better and not get carried away with the notion that his stock would go up simply because he felt it would.

Others suffer a loss after a win because they refuse to let go of their negative expectations. They trade for brief periods, fail to follow their own analyses, and rarely build confidence in their ability to master their craft. In effect, they are stopped by a need to look successful.

Are you this kind of trader? If so, you need to decide in advance to stay longer when the stock warrants it. Write down entry and exit points ahead of time, and stick to them. Put your daily target on your screen. This is promising a result, which becomes a creative object and creates tension in your mind to make that number. Facing the internal pressure, you learn to do things you can't ordinarily do. You learn to perform and stay focused on the goal under pressure. Here the result is built into the promise and you trade with the result in mind.

This contrarian style is sometimes rationalized as being appropriate for new traders. According to Ric, who manages five beginning traders: "The size of the bet is more important for being comfortable than staying for a longer term and risking your profit for a longer time. The less experienced the trader, the more I would encourage someone to take the half point and make the profit. You don't want to run the risk of staying longer, because you may lose your profit. Learning to scalp is the way to learn to trade. We don't teach people by pushing them off the top. You have to make the shift from the comfort zone. It takes a year to learn to hold them longer."

Jerry is one trader who is uncomfortable sitting with a position and waiting to trade for a point when he can get a half point and lock in a profit. The fluctuations are so great, he is trying to maximize profit. On a normal, average day, he can do the point. However, there is, of course, the risk if he scales out. He may be wrong and maybe he should wait for what he thinks is right. He has to learn to see his stock go down before getting out. He can protect himself from losing money by putting in a stop.

Fear of Failing

Nat, another trader, was beginning to learn to stretch. He increased his position in one stock to 150,000 shares—and then started to think of falling as though he were looking down while rock climbing. He panicked and got himself out of that position down to where he felt comfortable, but lost the opportunity to make a larger profit. To get back to playing as big as he wanted, he was encouraged to keep noticing the transiency of his fearful thoughts so that their reappearance would not throw him off course. He had to learn to ride out the panic, to notice the fearful thoughts and feelings but not to react from them.

Zack has been known to blow up after successful trades and lose all his month's profit. He always gets lax after succeeding. He does this because of a basic underlying fear of responsibility. He is more comfortable being a victim than being successful. Success means taking responsibility for his trading. Inside himself, he actually prefers carelessness because he can do what he learned early on. He can stay on automatic pilot, rather than remaining conscious of what moves to make.

Being Overcautious

Dirk's conservative trading style stood him in good stead for many years. He had been able to justify every cautious move he made to preserve his capital and cut his losses. But he was reluctant to look at new perspectives and see that his ability to get out of bad situations would not change if he were to take larger positions that could expand his profit potential.

Are you as cautious as Dirk is? Then you need to work on your negative thinking, just as he had to. See your self-doubt and self-criticism for what it is—a stopping point that keeps you from being receptive to events around you and able to adjust to them. Observe yourself the next time you have an impulse to sell long positions too soon, or not to cover your short positions soon enough. Observe, too, your tendency not to go back to a stock that lost you money, even if it is beginning to do well.

Welcome to the Abyss

Trading is like climbing the flat-faced rocks of the Grand Canyon. You need to focus on the next ledge to grasp as you move up the solid sheet of rock. You can't think for a second about falling, or you will lose your concentration. The same applies to trading. Pinpoint focusing will free you of fearful concerns, memories, images to convey to others, and preparation of your rationalizations for the day, all of which set you up for failure.

Perhaps the biggest obstacle to trading successfully is the reluctance to accept the need for change. To succeed requires not that you work harder but that you transform the way you currently function to a way that is consistent with your new level of performance. Transformation means not doing more or less of what you are doing, but actually focusing on changing your perception of the universe.

Did I hear you let out a long breath and say, "Wow! That's a tall order"? You're right; it is. But it's doable. Welcome to the abyss.

Facing success means taking responsibility for the outcome of your actions. It means more preparation and more self-examination to acquire the skills necessary to make things happen. It means facing the anxiety that appears when you are about to go beyond the customary. It means reacting to events not as personal threats but as opportunities. It means reviewing your trades after the markets close, recognizing the mistakes you made, and marching on past them. Most of all, it means continually asking analytical questions of yourself. What skills are you missing from your repertoire? How and when do you get off track?

You may not be asking the right questions—what your trading objectives require of you, for example. Can you commit to do everything that is necessary to make your trading work and stop worrying about negative results? Can you trade at the level of excellence you have set as a goal? Can you decide what must be done and then do it?

Since the result is ultimately built into the strategy you develop, you must consciously develop a strategy to realize your final objectives. You must learn to look only at the strategy and whether you veer from it, as well as how and what happened as a result. What was missing from your successful performances? What is still missing from your strategy?

Can you alter your life to fit your trading commitments and larger objectives? How much time do you spend doing obligatory family chores when you might be spending your time in preparation and study?

Successful trading requires discipline. Formulate a set of rules that you can apply without second-guessing yourself. Learn to distinguish between the right trade and the comfortable trade. (In fact, the right trade is often uncomfortable.) Your personal set of rules will provide the capacity to override your emotional fears. Trading is a profession in which each day you run a new race, play a new game, take new risks. The risk of losing is a constant. Ideally, you minimize losses by measuring the risk/reward ratio, but you cannot trade without uncertainty.

You have the power to change your trading style. But in order to change, you need confidence in your ability to ride out a variety of feelings from anxiety to fear to shame to guilt—all of which you may experience when you start to review your trades. This confidence will help you be secure enough to explore all facets of your current trading, examine your behavior, and modify it to meet new conditions. In order to change, you must deconstruct your own decision-making process and realize when you are inclined to act impulsively. Then, you can learn to catch yourself when you are trading that way and can begin to change your behavior at the moment it is happening.

You must decide what you want and then think through the changes you need to make in your work to achieve those goals. A successful trader is one who accepts the challenge of change.

Taking Responsibility

Once you accept responsibility for what happens to you by seeing how your response to events colors the flow of events, you will be able to start making decisions about the direction in which you want things to go. By doing this you will soon begin to influence the outcome. This simple change of perspective to trade in the realm of action, pur-

*Four **Questions** to Unmask the Hidden Perfectionist in You*

1. Are you self-critical?
2. Do you often view your own efforts as insignificant or insufficient?
3. Even when you are making progress, do you downgrade your own efforts and allow voices from the past and the anticipated criticisms of others to lead you off your mark?
4. Are you caught up with a range of time-consuming activities that absorb attention and distract you from taking responsibility for the full development of your interests?

pose, and self-determination will have an enormous effect on the way you trade.

When you see how your own perspective influences events and consciously accept responsibility for what happens in your trading, you will no longer feel like a victim. Nowhere is this willingness to take responsibility more important than if you are inclined to be a perfectionist. If you are self-critical, you may be unconsciously hiding the fact that you are frightened about risk and errors, and are more dependent on approval than on serving a larger vision. The self-centered nature of perfectionism is seen in an inclination to obsess about potential problems as well as the attitudes, responses, and anticipated criticism of others. See if the accompanying attributes apply to you.

Gaining Faith

Faith is letting go of control, and is an important part of becoming a successful trader. It is all too easy to sabotage your efforts by controlling too many minor, irrelevant details, or allowing them to throw off your focus.

Trust your intuition. Choose your own trading direction on both large and small scales. Get information from others, but don't ask others to make your decisions. Commit to your dreams and strive for them, and the world will mirror your own commitment and sense of certainty.

If you are ambivalent and uncertain, the world will seem the same way. The more you can trust your inner voice, the more you will be able to find the path that emanates from your own choices.

Trust your instinct to act in the face of fear, and the fear will disappear. As long as you keep your distance from your fear, it will cause you to maintain feelings of inhibition and resistance. Feel yourself enter into the fearful moment and embrace the fear, and you will discover that it disappears as you do it.

As you get closer to your expansion into the creative zone, you may see yourself pulling back slightly. Or, you may find yourself turning to someone who kills your dream on the basis of practicality, but who is in effect activating your own self-doubts. For example, the wife of one trader discouraged him from taking new trading opportunities and running a joint account. Because of that he began to hesitate. He was looking for too much certainty and was not strong enough to trust his instinct. He wanted guarantees.

To help prevent this type of anxiety, you must preserve your creative vision. Keep your dream to yourself, or gingerly share it with only those you can trust to nurture it. Don't dilute your goal by sharing it with the wrong people or seeking reassurance. Protect your vision, and don't share it with anyone who would discourage you, however well intentioned they are.

Hobbies are good activities to ground you, help you overcome anxiety, and give you a sense of expansion into new territory. You get humble by learning something new. Get into these activities by way of rejuvenating yourself and learning to take yourself in a lighter way. Then go back to trading with a renewed sense of yourself.

To advance past fear of change, you're going to have to alter a basic precept most of us share—that you must always succeed and that failure is bad. Withdrawals, breakdowns, or creative backsliding do happen. The key to surviving these breakdowns is to come back to play. You need to stay on target until losing and winning are not seen as anything other than opportunities for information.

When you backslide, and you will, forgive yourself. Creativity and great performance are scary because you don't know where they are coming from. But they are coming from increased consciousness about trading—holding positions longer, playing bigger, being more patient, getting out of losers faster and sooner.

Eight Steps to Help Move beyond Fear

1. Notice which obstacles frighten you most. Which trades stump you the most and throw you into panic?
2. Determine what advantages you are gaining from following your old routine of trading.
3. Admit your need for help. Don't focus on being so much of a lone wolf or an individualist.
4. Get coaching from someone who has been exposed to the same obstacle and recovered.
5. Set achievable goals that do not create fear.
6. Commit to trading to win, to enjoying what you are doing, and to doing things on your terms.
7. Decide what actions are needed to reach your objective and take those actions.
8. Visualize the future you expect once you have reached your goal.

Picturing Yourself as a Model of Success

In Chapter 2, I offered general ideas about what successful traders look like. Sandy is a real-life example.

Sandy took pains to become a self-starter pursuing his own concepts rather than a passive, reactive player who is controlled by the movements of the marketplace. He is not afraid to enter a stock's climb or rise after it has begun. He works on developing an internal visual image of his stock or an ideal trading model to follow. He has an exit strategy and is always proactive in his relationship to the market. Because he is focused on his trading, he is able to play bigger, be less emotional, and concentrate more on his trades.

Further, Sandy is confident about his decisions. He marks his losses to the market and curbs any tendency to rationalize his losses. He is able to keep expanding his activity as he succeeds and is able to avoid shutting down if he loses. He is willing to admit to and cut his losses. He is also able to lengthen the time he spends in a position so as to extend his time horizons and maximize the profitability of his trades.

Finally, Sandy pays attention to his state of mind as another critical trading variable. He can utilize relaxation and visual imagery techniques when necessary to restore his energy. A successful trader like Sandy knows himself. He understands and accepts his needs and self-concepts, but also knows what he must do in order to trade profitably. Most of all, he knows that success takes a conscious commitment to a future result—trading profitably—without being overwhelmed by doubts and fear.

Creating the Future

Your trading life is a blank canvas on which you can create your vision. Your future results are not predetermined. If you can trade in the here and now, without regard to the limiting thoughts you have about how things are supposed to be and without regard to what others expect, you can begin to trade in line with your financial objective.

You create the future by speaking it and then living in terms of what you have said. In effect, you create yourself not by acting automatically in terms of some unconsciously determined sense of yourself or even by pursuing a goal that seems as if it will complete you or fulfill you.

Rather, you create yourself by committing to a vision and then becoming the living embodiment of that vision. The goal is a statement about how things ought to be that gives you a place to come from, rather than a goal to achieve. It is a stand to take, a way of trading defined by the result.

In trading at the highest levels of effectiveness, satisfaction, and fulfillment, you allow events to unfold with a minimum of stress. Such awareness and the mastery of some of the principles outlined in this book help you to conquer fear, maximize performance, and dramatically improve your overall trading performance. You speak the future and begin to act in the present out of the future vision until gradually you become the vision itself. By doing what is necessary to bring about the result, you can transform yourself into a master of trading to win.

Index